Liberating Knowledge

Research, feminism and adult education

Liberating Knowledge

Research, feminism and adult education

Jean Barr

niace
promoting adult learning

To the memory of my beloved parents Muriel and Adam Cruickshank

Published by the National Institute of Adult Continuing Education
(England and Wales)
Renaissance House, 20 Princess Road West, Leicester LE1 6TP
Company registration no. 2603322
Charity registration no. 1002775
The NIACE website on the Internet is www.niace.org.uk

First published 1999
Reprinted 2003
© NIACE

CATALOGUE IN PUBLICATION DATA
A CIP record for this title is available from the British Library
ISBN 1 86201 046 3

Typeset by The Midlands Book Typesetting Co., Loughborough
Cover design by Boldface, London EC1
Printed in Great Britain by Antony Rowe Ltd

Acknowledgements

For various forms of encouragement, inspiration and practical help I wish to thank: Alison Sutton and John Benseman (without whose generosity, support and friendship during my sabbatical in New Zealand this book would have been stillborn), Eileen Aird, Colin Barr, Brian Barr, Ouainé Bain, Ann Berlak, Lynda Birke, Carol Craig, Lynda Haddock, Sue Innes, Annette Kuhn, Wendy McKaig, Rosemary Menzies, Alison Miller, Margaret Reid, Sheila Riddell, Sue Scott, Maria Slowey, Tom Steele, Lyn Tett, Jane Thompson, Centre for Continuing Education, University of Auckland. I am also indebted to all of those who took part in the research which figures in the book.

Contents

Preface: A Glasgow childhood

I was born in 1944, in Glasgow, the only daughter and younger child of a pharmacist father and, before she married, a shorthand-typist mother. My father was an employee of Cockburn's the Chemists and he managed their shop in the Gorbals, the one area of Glasgow which most people outside Scotland know of because of its notorious gangland reputation. He was the younger son of a prison warder father, himself the younger son of small crofting farmers in Aberdeenshire, who came to Glasgow to find work in the early 1900s. I was brought up near the Gorbals in a working class/lower middle class area close to Weirs Engineering works where several of my early friends' parents worked on the assembly lines. I lived there until I was 12 when we had to move to a bigger house – roughly one mile away – so that my grandmother could come to stay.

Although I have lived and worked away from Glasgow for a number of spells – in Florence for a year, Durham and Coventry for a year each, for example – I have always returned. And although there is much that I dislike about it – the weather for one thing – my roots, which are strong, are there ('there', because 'here', is a beach batch on the Coromandel coast where I am writing this – and it's raining). These roots are as much to do with my own political history and the relationships built up with groups and communities over many years, as they are to do with more personal relationships and places of employment.

Being born in 1944 I was one of the early beneficiaries of free State education provision, orange juice and school milk, and of a fairly widespread optimism and faith in education to transform lives and bring about individual, social and economic prosperity. (I sometimes wonder if my own commitment to adult education is due in part to my awareness that the educational opportunities I had could as well not have been had if I had been born twenty years sooner or later.) My parents, certainly, believed in education (my father perhaps more than my mother, who believed in the superiority of 'the school of life') and I was brought up to be an achiever, each prize won at primary school being celebrated as if I had brought home the sun on a plate (see Weiner, 1994).

Both my parents were Christian socialists, Labour voters, with a strong sense of social justice and a belief that 'There but for the grace of God . . .'. Despite gestures towards the distinctiveness of being Scottish – sometimes taking the form of sayings, such as, 'Wha's like us? Gae few an' they're a' deid' – my brother and I were brought up to believe in the essential sameness of all human beings. My father, especially, was immensely proud of the British Welfare State, seeing in it both potential for redressing inequalities of birth, and a reassuring safety net. I can still recall the affection and respect in his voice when he spoke of Beveridge.

My mother envied the choices education gave me. She left school at 15 and believed she would have been a social worker had she been born in my generation. Intelligent, sharp, a good friend to many, the go-between in numerous neighbourhood feuds, she was also very angry and frustrated much of the time. The daughter of a beautiful mother ('the belle of Rutherglen') who preferred men, she spent her life playing second fiddle to her younger, preferred brother. And the felt absence of her mother's love – despite looking after her, as a diabetic, unable to walk, for many years – was at the front of her mind when she herself died of cancer, in my presence, at the age of 75. In any case that experience no doubt contributed to her determination to treat my brother and myself just 'the same'. Both my parents were also firm believers in equal rights for women; I don't remember ever doubting that I was 'as good as' boys – in fact much of my childhood seemed spent proving my greater proficiency at climbing trees, playing football and getting high marks at school. I was certainly a tomboy. Puberty came as a shock. I think I really believed I'd escape breasts and periods and I hated the change from being wild and unconstrained – a real street kid – to being watched: puberty seemed to inaugurate a kind of generalised prohibition from then on which I had not been aware of before.

1 Introduction

You tell me it's self-defeating to talk about it instead of just up and doing it, but to acknowledge what I'm doing while I'm doing it is exactly the point.

(Ashmore, 1989, p 191)

The shaping assumptions on which influential knowledge – which is always knowledge-accepted-as-such by a particular group in a particular culture – continues to be based, are influential not despite but because of the fact that most people are unaware of them.

(Minnich, 1989, p 333)

This book offers a reflexive account of my research on women's adult education in various settings – and of doing research as a feminist – over a period of fifteen years. It also represents a journey of sorts, focusing on various stages in my development from academic philosopher/social scientist to seeing myself as an adult educator.

Training in philosophy produced in me the view that before speaking you should be absolutely sure what you are going to say and be able to justify it. Experience of the Women's Movement and of informal women's education in the Workers' Educational Association (WEA) taught me otherwise, that it is better to allow yourself to start speaking before being completely sure that you can justify what you say; otherwise you will never speak at all.

It is of course possible to be so open-minded and unfocused that your brains fall out. Christa Wolf speaks of 'brooding' – a way of 'thinking towards' that mulls rather than argues. Such open-ended thinking is suppressed in our education system by a built in preference for systematic, rational thought, a preference which can lead to the dismissal of more conversational, story-telling modes as the mere 'rhetoric of digestion' (Modjeska, 1990, p 151).

I begin from a particular propensity, the personal knowledge that: 'You can sit to your dying day, recollecting and taking notes, living and reflecting on the process. But that can become dangerous. One has to draw the line somewhere, before one reaches the end of one's rope' (Wolf, 1988, p 93). I suffer from what has been called the philosopher's disease. This is nicely captured in Borges' story, *The Aleph* (quoted in Malcolm, 1994, p 72). At the end of the story the narrator goes to the cellar of a house, where he has the experience of encountering everything that exists in the world and can see every place and everything from every angle: 'I saw tigers, pistons, bison, tides, and armies; I

saw all the ants on the planet . . . I saw the circulation of my own dark blood.'
In my experience, paralysis results from trying to enter that cellar; much better
to remain in the 'attic of partial expression', to say what springs to mind, and
to accept that it cannot be the whole truth and nothing but the truth. I very
much hope that through writing I can break certain habits of thought. By
approaching this piece of writing as itself a method of inquiry I am already
breaking the habit of a lifetime, that of not putting anything down until I have
thought it through *completely*.

The book seeks to question the abstractions and pretensions of much disciplinary knowledge but without being seduced by what has been called
'experientialism'. In appealing to personal experience as a source of knowledge
I do not claim it as the trump card of authenticity. Indeed, as the unfolding of
this book will show, my understanding of my own experience (specifically, my
experience of doing research) changes (see Griffiths, 1995). Personal experience
is not immune from reflection, re-interpretation and critique – an insight that
has been central to feminist pedagogical practice. In using this book as a way of
finding my voice – but not, I hope, in a narcissistic sense – I want to remain
critical *and* personal throughout.

In this Introduction I sketch in some of the main themes and aims of the
book and outline its structure.

Three case studies

The book's main focus is a re-appraisal of three research projects which I carried out at different points in time over a period of fifteen years, a period
described in the book as one of struggle over adult education's definitions,
purposes and very existence. In returning now to this historical research material, I re-view that research for what it masks as well as reveals, for its blindspots
as well as its illuminations. The three pieces of research were all, broadly, in
women's education.

They were:

1979–81 – an evaluation of a pre-school community education project in
Glasgow, as part of a national study of alternative forms of pre-school provision.

1989–90 – a research study on the influence of different forms of feminism on
New Opportunities for Women courses in the North of England, as part of a
Masters in Education (Guidance and Counselling).

1991–93 – a research project on Women's Perceptions of Science, undertaken
with Lynda Birke when I was Senior Research Fellow at Warwick University.

The strategy employed in the three case studies is to write myself back into the
text, in contrast with the original research texts and reports. Such a strategy of
putting myself in the frame is adopted for three reasons. First, because I believe
that the effacement of self which is the norm in most research reports is a kind
of cheat since it obscures from the reader (and, more often than not, the writer)

the inevitable locatedness of all research. Second, because I want to draw attention to the wider social context within which knowledge is produced and legitimated at any point in time: I seek to illustrate how what we do (as adult education researchers or practitioners) at any historical moment is implicated within various power relations and discourses which permeate and reach beyond these practices. Third, I want to maintain that what we do and how we conceive of what we do as adult educators and researchers matters; it can make a difference.

In the book the three research projects are reappraised in the light of subsequent theory and my own changed personal agendas. This reappraisal is the occasion for an exploration of a number of interlocking themes. These pivot on: the politics of feminism and adult education as played out in each of the case studies under scrutiny; changing fashions in feminist theory and research and in adult education (especially women's adult education) theory and practice; the relationship between autobiography and empirical research; and, finally, the relationship between the relative power of words and things, ideas and structures.

Uniting the three research projects and the project of this book is myself as a self-defined socialist and feminist and the changing meanings and implications of this for my current practice. I spell out these themes more fully below, beginning with the now familiar one of 'words and things'.

Words and things

My interest is in adult education and adult education research as 'sites of struggle', and, in relation to this, in the significance of a shift in ideas which has been underway for some time in social theory and philosophy. This has been summed up as the ambition to dispense with 'things' and to value 'words' more:

> What, in short, we wish to do is dispense with 'things', to substitute for the enigmatic treasure of 'things' anterior to discourse, the regular formation of objects that emerge only in discourse.
> (Michel Foucault, quoted in Barrett and Phillips, 1992, p 201)

Within academic feminism, this is being played out in a shift in balance of influential disciplines – away from the social sciences and their concern for causal, structural explanation and towards the arts, philosophy and the humanities and their concern for the understanding and creation of cultural meanings.

My own research over a period of 15 to 20 years could indeed be read as mirroring this wider shift in the relative status which I, and academic fashions, accord 'words' (women's discursive marginality in science and intellectual history, for example – final case study) and 'things' (low pay, wife-beating, lack of childcare, a gender-segmented labour market – first case study). This would be a mistaken interpretation. Nevertheless, the issue of the relative status of things and words is, in a sense, the 'problematic' of this book and, certainly, in terms of my own autobiography, it is an absolutely central strand: healing the breach of words and things, rather than substituting one for the other, is, though, how I prefer to see it.

Writing now, what strikes me as strange is that while I started my academic/professional life as a philosopher and shifted to social science – partly because of my feminism, which was grounded in concrete, practical struggles around childcare, welfare provision, abortion rights, employment, immigration (real 'things') – fashions in feminist theory seem to have worked in reverse. Nowadays, philosophy dominates much feminist theory – particularly the kind of philosophy which is preoccupied with questions of knowing rather then questions of being (1).

The fragmentation of feminism

The gulf which separates feminist theory of the 1970s from feminist theory of the 1990s is certainly becoming a major theme in feminist writing (see, for example, Barrett and Phillips, 1992; Weiner, 1994; see note 2) as is the fragmentation of feminism as a political movement. Gone it seems are the days when we confidently separated ourselves out neatly according to the political categories: liberal feminist, socialist feminist, radical feminist – each distinguished by its specification of the cause of women's inequality or oppression. Although we differed in our answers – liberal feminists specifying the absence of equality of opportunity between men and women; socialist feminists, capitalist economic relations of production; and radical feminists, patriarchal relations of reproduction – we were all agreed on the central question for feminism. The political categorisation of feminism reflected the nature of what was afoot.

Various commentaries have charted how this consensus in academic feminism concerning its central problematic has now broken down. They specify among the major reasons:

1 black women's and lesbians' critiques of the ethnocentrism and heterosexism of western feminism – the emphasis on 'difference' between women;
2 a growing interest in psychoanalytic analyses of sexual difference and identity and a growing celebration of the difference women could make to an alternative kind of society;
3 developments by feminists of poststructuralist and postmodernist insights and, in particular, the alleged Foucauldian emphasis on 'words' or discourses referred to above (see Barrett and Phillips, 1992).

Postmodernism and poststructuralism

The influence of these changes on my own work will become clear in the unfolding of this book. However, it may be worth indicating my own present position in broad outline here. Much recent debate within feminist theory is marked by a distinct squeamishness or lack of confidence in the category of 'woman' *per se*, paralleling (or part of) the poststructuralist critique of humanism which, according to some, has heralded a profound shift in philosophical paradigm from 'modernism' to 'postmodernism'. Those attracted to postmodernist theory wish to dispense with universal categories – analytic tools like 'class', 'race', 'gender' (even 'woman'), stressing differences *between* women, for example, and construing power as 'decentred', localised and relational as between individuals.

I think extreme caution is needed where postmodernism is concerned. Always on the brink of collapsing into confusion, postmodernism comes in various guises. One book usefully distinguishes between 'affirmative' and 'sceptical' postmodernism, for example (Rosenau, 1992). My above characterisation of it would probably fit the 'sceptical' category. Since it is a position that requires giving up any hope of understanding the socially structured causes of oppression (a taboo word within its frameworks) it undermines any specifically feminist project (or any radical project) which allies itself with the interests of broad social groups, conceived as subordinated within capitalist, racist, patriarchal formations. (That last sentence should be enough to give any self-respecting postmodernist theorist heart-failure.)

On the other hand, I do think that poststructuralist insights can assist feminist theory and practice to the extent that they discourage efforts to explain (or get rid of) oppression crudely, in one fell swoop (see Pritchard Hughes, 1995). By replacing such understandings with an understanding of our lives as structured by a number of forces, including race and class, as well as gender, poststructuralism also insists that such forces are discursively as well as materially real. Foucault's model of power is important here and it is especially useful to feminists involved in education. For this reason I want to digress slightly from the main discussion in order to give a brief outline of Foucault's notion of power. (Readers who are so inclined can skip the following few paragraphs, under 'Power', without losing the main plot; on reading further, however, it may be usefully returned to.)

Power

Liberal and Marxist theories see power as a possession, held by individuals and groups, and as operating, at least potentially, repressively. For Foucault, modern power is productive: it 'produces' and 'normalises' bodies to serve prevailing relations of dominance and subordination. To understand how such power works requires two conceptual changes, Foucault believes (Foucault, 1979, 1980). First, we have to stop thinking of power as a possession of individuals and groups and see it instead as a network or dynamic of non-centralised forces. Second, we have to recognise that such forces are not random but assume certain historical forms in which specific groups and ideologies do have dominance. Techniques of power are 'captured' by institutions and colonised by privileged groups. However, such dominance is not maintained 'from above' but through multiple 'processes, of different origin and scattered location' which regulate the most intimate aspects of personal and social life. Where power works 'from below', prevailing forms of subjectivity, including gender, are maintained, not mainly through coercion (although that may also be present) but chiefly through *self-discipline*: 'Just a gaze. An inspecting gaze' is all that is required (Bordo, 1993, p 27; see note 3).

In proposing this relational and *productive* model of power – power as process – Foucault does not deny the existence of centralised (eg state) power. He just thinks this model of power as a possession, as centralised and flowing from top to bottom and as potentially repressive is not adequate to capture those forms of power which make centralised, repressive power possible: the myriad of power relations at the micro-level of society (Sawicki, 1991, p 20). As emergent, this power is produced in concrete sets of relations; importantly, it is produced in 'certain co-ordinates of knowledge'. These are the practices of disciplinary power which he sees as emergent from the rise of the human sciences in the nineteenth century. There are, Foucault says, 'no power relations without the constitution of a field of knowledge, nor any knowledge that does not presuppose at the same time power relations' (Foucault, 1979, p 27).

Foucault believes that the Marxist location of power in class obscures how power is also 'capillary', how, that is, it invests the body and soul. For Foucault power is all-pervasive: it is always there and always dangerous. Understanding how power works, he thinks, is a key to organising resistance at the local everyday level. It is power relations at the micro level which make possible class power and domination, but 'where there is power there is resistance'. Modern power relations are unstable; dominant forms and institutions (pertaining to adult education as elsewhere) are continually subject to penetration by knowledges and values which have been developing and gathering strength 'at the margins'.

I do not believe that all domination and subordination can be best understood in terms of Foucault's model of power. For example, women are frequently financially trapped in degrading jobs (as are many men) and violent relationships. We certainly cannot abandon a concept of power as repressive and concentrated in identifiable centres of power to a notion of power as productive and dispersed; nor can we deny the existence of systems of class, race and gender domination. Not at all. But we need also to see the social field as dynamic, not static. Otherwise we fail to see possibilities for change in the present. The advantage of seeing power as process rather than as a possession of individuals, groups and institutions is that it allows for the conceptualisation of ongoing transformation and change. The trouble with traditional Marxist accounts is that they tend to operate within a binary logic which is limiting. Such accounts (which I shall show, have influenced my own past research) tend to portray capitalist and patriarchal power in monolithic terms and the process of social change by conceiving of it as the *negation* of the present, rather than as emerging from possibilities in the present. For this reason they may limit our political imagination and keep us from looking for ambiguities and liberating possibilities in the present (see Sawicki, 1991).

They are also *methodologically* debilitating. This is because they seem to insist on separating social structures on the one hand and 'discourse', language and meaning on the other. This tends to result in regarding social structures and institutions as real and discourses and meanings as confined to the 'cultural' realm (and less real). We need to challenge this distinction and regard both as (real) social practices and processes. Thus, in this book, I regard adult education – my object of study – as something which emerges in different historical instances from the interaction of many different practices and processes, as part, that is of 'a thoroughly heterogeneous ensemble consisting of discourses, institutions, architectural forms . . . laws' (Foucault, quoted in Kuhn, 1990, p 6).

Theory and practice

I indicate below the significance of Foucault's model of power to the main project of this book. For now, in the context of my discussion of the changing nature of feminism and the recent influence of postmodernism and poststructuralism on feminist theory, I want to make two points. First, I believe that many feminists in the 1970s already had a quite complex and nuanced understanding of the way power works from their experiences in the Women's Movement and associated collective practices; they didn't have to await developments in poststructuralist theory for this. However, I do think that some of us, myself included, did not always apply this nuanced understanding – acquired through experience and political practice – to our more theoretical (academic) work. This theme of the split between theory and practice is taken up in this book (see Chapter 5 especially).

Second, an important aspect of feminism is its inclination to critique itself (unlike more dominant modes and traditions of thought). So, to the extent that poststructuralist arguments have tuned into this and resulted in feminism critiquing its own class and race biases, for example, they are welcome. The influence of poststructuralism is also evident in recent examinations by feminist educators of how race, class and cultural difference affect dynamics in the classroom (see, eg, Ellsworth, 1989; Lather, 1991; also see Chapter 7). All of this is important. However, it is important to remind ourselves that sensitivity to 'difference' and 'subjectivity' (themes central to theoretical feminism of the 1990s) emerged, not out of theoretical, *academic* debate, but as women engaged in *concrete* struggles around housework, childcare, trade unions, poverty, immigration laws (issues which have gone missing from much recent feminist writing). I make these points to make it clear that I distance myself from the postmodernist theoretical project (and associated feminist positions) according to which there are only different points of view, endlessly shifting and fragmentary, none better or more justifiable than any other. Instead, I position myself and the project of this book alongside those feminists who in the last 10 years or so have moved on from *criticisms* of traditional (or patriarchal) systems of knowledge for their exclusions, elisions or denigrations of women's lives and experiences, to an examination of new ways of thinking about knowledge. In this more *creatively* focused discussion, narrow notions of what is worthy of the term 'knowledge' are questioned; 'subjugated' knowledges are focused on and new definitions of 'objectivity' proposed (see Chapter 8).

All of this presupposes that it makes sense to talk about *developing* knowledge and seeking *better* understandings – something disallowed within postmodernist theorising. I ally myself with those who believe that people can develop better understandings of their social world through more democratic knowledge-making practices and structures than are current at present; and they can work to transform it. A central motif of the book is that adult education, specifically, feminist adult women's education, has already developed useful models for such a democratic knowledge-making project. That is, for achieving in practice what feminist epistemology theorises about (see, especially Chapters 3 and 7).

Subjectivity

Another theme of the book is my own growing disillusionment with sociology as a discipline – or at least with its dominant theories, modes of knowing and conceptual schemes. In the words of one past practitioner who has 'gone over' to film and cultural studies, sociology 'too often downplays imagination and understanding, detaching itself from its own ways of knowing and treating its objects – very often . . . the working class – as in some way other, curiously one-dimensional specimens' (Kuhn, 1995, p 101).

Here, the criticism is that sociology pays scant attention to how class or gender or race is actually lived, to how they inform our inner worlds as much as condition our life chances; indeed we have to look to literary and cultural studies for such attention. Carolyn Steedman's *Landscape for a Good Woman* (1986) is a case in point. This study is a beautiful illustration of a sociologist's insight that class is 'something in the blood, in the very fibre of a man or woman: a way of growing, feeling, judging, taken out of the resources of generations gone before' (Jackson and Marsden, cited in Kuhn, 1995, p 97). But the book's analytic tools are drawn, not from sociology itself but from psychoanalysis and literary theory as well as cultural studies. Steedman criticises that British (more accurately, English) tradition of cultural studies – of Richard Hoggart and Raymond Williams – for its privileging of class over other aspects of identity (gender, for example); its implicit attribution of psychological simplicity to working class people and its failure to represent complex desires which seek satisfaction *within* the dominant culture (see also Felski, 1995).

Exploring the complex subjectivity of Steedman's own mother – with envy the main interpretive device – the book's mode of address, too, is very different from the all knowing narrative voice which still dominates in much sociology (and philosophy). This voice, I shall suggest, also dominates much of the radical tradition of adult education with its roots in working class education (see Fenton, 1997). It is one of the aims of this book to leave that voice behind as a distant voice.

An aspect of what has been called the postmodern condition by some (Harvey, 1989), the condition of modernity by others (Giddens, 1990) is that there has been an increase in 'self-reflexive' accounts by social researchers of the processes and problems of doing research. This growing self-consciousness among the social science research community (evidenced by an increase in autobiographical writing and research which promotes 'putting oneself in the frame') has scarcely touched adult education research (Wendy Ball is a notable exception here; see Ball, 1992). In other spheres, for example, among North American teacher educators, feminist researchers have already made an important contribution to the trend (see, eg, Berlak, 1988, 1989; Ellsworth, 1989; Lather, 1991; see, too, Acker *et al.*'s retrospective analysis of their research, 1983).

Such reflexive social scientific research writing has its critics, drawing accusations of navel-gazing and self absorption and of being, often, a kind of 'vanity ethnography', an excuse for narcissism. Those who are drawn to it, on the other hand, see the effacement of self which is the norm in most research reports as a kind of sleight of hand, obscuring from the reader (and, indeed, the author) the interpretive devices, contingencies and compromises which have gone into their construction.

My own view – which is reflected, I think, in this book – is that exclusive concern with writing reflexive texts which display their own modes of construction constitutes a narrow view of reflexivity which should also pay attention to the social structures and processes under which knowledge is produced and legitimated. This precludes analysing texts alone. Both aspects of reflexivity are involved in this book, as the following framework – already sketched in above – indicates.

Stories and ideas

The structure of the book is chronological, a chronology provided by three case studies of research on adult education which I carried out between 1979 and 1993. The book unfolds around three core chapters in which I present research reports/texts written at the time the research was carried out. These chapters are entitled: 'Adult education by stealth'; 'Counselling by stealth'; 'Really useful knowledge?'. In the three case studies I move between the research reports and present time, re-assessing them, in companion chapters, in the light of current concerns and ideas which were not available at the time. The case studies, constructed around the selected historical texts or 'products', include an account of the research approach I adopted at the time; reference to the wider institutional and political context of the research; the views of the people involved and the main theoretical frameworks on which I drew, including those of feminism and adult education.

In the book, the changing context of research is focused on, as is the changing nature of feminism and adult education during the historical period concerned. A central theme is what constitutes 'feminist research', as is the relationship between theory and practice. The issue of memory, for example, the influence of current preoccupations and frames of reference on what is remembered, is picked up in the course of the account. The whole book represents a personal journey. But I have also included two specifically autobiographical chapters – Chapters 2 and 3. My final case study draws on material included in the draft of a recent book, written with Lynda Birke (Barr and Birke, 1998).

The book (re)presents my research as emergent, subject over time to reformulation and reinterpretation. It concerns the evolving relationship between my work in adult education, women's education and research on the one hand,

and changing social and cultural conditions, adult education policy and practice and feminist theory and practice, on the other. It should be seen as a whole,
the meaning of each chapter depending in large degree on what comes after it.
In returning to earlier work, however, I make no assumption that what I say
here and now is therefore an advance on what I said then. I do not see the
development of my work as moving towards 'the right answer'. Rather, the
way in which what is construed as the appropriate approach tends to shift – an
illustration of a broader epistemological approach which challenges the notion
that the context of knowledge is irrelevant to questions of truth.

What I present in this book is not, then, just a personal narrative of the
experience of doing research on women's education. Nor is it purely
deconstructive. Susan Sontag's preferred way of writing about cancer and the
mystification surrounding it is to present a theory, an idea, in order to explain
aspects of her own and others' experience of cancer. She resists the temptation
just to tell her own personal story: 'A narrative, it seemed to me would be less
useful than an idea' (Sontag, 1990, p 13). The idea she proposes is that the
metaphors and myths surrounding cancer kill: we must beware of the seductiveness of metaphorical thinking. In *Aids and its Metaphors* (1990) Sontag
describes her purpose in writing the book as being to 'deprive something of its
meaning', to argue 'against interpretation' because

> the metaphoric trappings that deform the experience of having
> cancer have very real consequences; they inhibit people from seek-
> ing treatment early enough . . . The metaphors and myths, I was
> convinced, kill . . . I hoped to convince terrified people . . . to
> regard cancer as if it were just a disease . . . Not a curse, not a
> punishment . . . Without meaning.
>
> (Sontag, 1990, p 14)

This idea is interwoven with her personal story and helps explain aspects of her
own experience. She hopes her book will help save lives.

Likewise, though less ambitiously, I locate my book within a practical
project and like Sontag's, the account I offer of my research is informed by and
makes sense in the light of an idea. This is the idea that if we are to re-think our
practices as adult educators – as I believe we must, continuously, and never
more urgently than now – we must learn to distance ourselves from our
unreflective common sense as adult educators. Before we can change our practices as adult educators we need to understand our current practices better and
for this to be possible, I believe, we need to learn to cultivate greater self-
understanding. This cannot be done through introspection and navel-gazing;
self-understanding (whether on the part of communities or individuals) can
only be sought through social engagement and dialogue. And it cannot be
achieved once and for all; our knowledge of ourselves is fundamentally historical (Fay, 1987).

At a time of increasing professionalisation, adult educators – who are not
privy to any obvious body of specialised knowledge – have (perhaps for that
very reason) embraced with enthusiasm self-conceptions based on their expertise as 'facilitators of adult learning', meeters of individuals' 'learning needs'

and as 'human resource developers'. Increasingly, too, they are being persuaded through government rhetoric and more material injunctions to see themselves as 'enterprising workers' (see Edwards, 1997; see note 4). Such professional legitimations, in emphasising the technical aspects of the job, remove any obligation to make judgements about content and value. In helping adults learn, the question, 'But what about?' need never arise; 'What for?' 'Whose knowledge?' remain unspoken. And there is the danger that adult educators are being produced with no self-critical perspective about their field, no sense of history and little understanding of how our own practices are implicated within networks of power – not only repressive power, but power as process, as productive (see above).

The current context of adult education

Adult education in Britain has long been associated with an agenda for social change. But that agenda is changing. The past fifteen years have seen more legislation relating to adult education and training than the previous fifty. The agenda is clear, set by continuing government rhetoric that Britain needs a highly skilled, flexible workforce to be competitive in the world market. Vocationalism, 'enterprise skills' and accreditation are leaving other aspects of adult learning out in the cold. And research indicates that after a decade and a half of New Right individualism, the notion of the social purpose(s) of adult education is giving way among practitioners to notions of 'widening the market' where students are viewed as consumers (see Benn and Fieldhouse, 1995).

Some practitioners nonetheless believe that the current social and cultural context offers new possibilities for developing a radical agenda for adult education (Belanger, 1994). Sally Westwood, for example, maintains that the current emphasis on individualism in which 'the private is more and more privileged and the public realm of culture and society is denuded' actually presents the 'opportunity for [adult education] to become, in part, a space for alternative traditions where other discourses can be maintained and where a diversity of cultures can thrive' (Westwood, 1989, p 9).

Some adult educators, speaking more recently for the British radical tradition have called on members of the adult education community to put the politics of resistance and transformation back on the agenda (eg Thompson, 1993). Others try to ensure that adult education's past traditions of engagement with particular social groups and movements should not become part of our 'forgotten memory' as adult educators (eg Alexander, 1994). And there is now, in Scotland, a fledgling Popular Adult Education Forum which organises workshops and conferences with the explicit intent of refiguring that radical purpose.

A central focus of the book is on whether there can be a renewed role for adult education which, in drawing on some of its best past practices, can devise new ones which are adequate to changed realities. I am interested in adult education in a particular historical period – the past 15 to 20 years; more specifically, my interest is in women's adult education during this period. Putting the focus on different historical cases of adult education practice and research, as this book does, allows us to focus on the various practices and processes, institutions and discourses, relations and meanings which both constituted them and brought them about. This means acknowledging the *time and place* of political ideas (like feminist ones) and adult education practices. And it means refusing current fashions in theorising which reduce the history of a field of study (like adult education) or of a social movement (like feminism) to a history of abstract ideas and their refutation – a refusal, that is, to see them in terms of the evolution of merely *academic* theory and debate. I shall keep returning to this point in various guises throughout the text.

The past twenty years have been a period of great uncertainty – even struggle – over the means by which adult continuing education is to be understood, defined and regulated. This is particularly true of womens education. Twenty years ago, in the heyday of 'community development' approaches to adult education, it was the meaning (and struggles over the meaning) of 'community' and 'development' which helped to determine much adult education practice (see my first case study, Chapters 4 and 5). Now it is 'human resource' and 'development' (see Jackson, 1995). An aim of the present inquiry is, then, to seek an understanding, with hindsight, of some of the forces at work in all of this, so as to understand better the possibilities for change in the relations of power which are involved. For this, we require different modes of understanding and analysis – sociological, philosophical, cultural – understandings which must remain partial, incomplete and uncertain (see Kuhn, 1990). That, too, is a central theme (see Chapter 2).

Education for freedom – heroic tales

'Critical' sociology of education (eg, Dale, 1989) posits that education systems should be construed as 'sites of struggle' between reproducing and transforming processes; that the state is not homogeneous; that education, too, is internally divided and has relative autonomy *vis à vis* state control. This relative autonomy means that alternative agendas can be introduced. The identification of 'subversive space' is, too, a theme of the 'radical' tradition of adult education literature (see, eg, Alexander and Martin, 1995; Ball, 1992; Johnson, 1988).

Paulo Freire in particular has offered a vision of how adult educators can use their relative autonomy to develop education for liberation. He developed his dialogical method while working with peasants in South America. His 'critical pedagogy' can be located within a critical social science framework (see Chapters 2 and 5). According to this approach, people are ignorant of their needs and the true nature of their social relationships under capitalism and patriarchy and this ignorance helps oppressive social conditions to persist. This 'false consciousness' is to be removed by the intervention of the critical educator and through such increased self-consciousness, achieved through reflection on their social conditions of existence, participants will change the conditions. Freire's educational method rests, crucially, on developing with people a notion of themselves as subjects, able to determine their situation rather than being mere objects of it; it rests, too, on seeing the 'oppressor within the oppressed', so that the oppressed secretly admire their oppressors or accept the legitimacy

of their position. Such beliefs are the source of resistance to the critical educator who, understanding how such 'resistance' operates, has to work dialogically
with the students, basing the content of education on their concrete problems
and experiences.

Critical pedagogy rests, crucially, on people acquiring new identities – new
self-conceptions; critical educators have to help the oppressed overcome a 'culture of silence' in which they cannot see that their situation could be different and
that they could intervene in their social world to transform it. In Freire's
'dialogical' educational programme a central role is given to reflection in individual and social transformation, thus placing the burden for social change on
rational enlightenment – consciousness-raising ('conscientisation') through education. It is indeed precisely because the power of the oppressor is not entirely
independent of people's self-understandings that development of critical self-
understanding on the part of those 'below' is a weapon against it. Adult education on this model can help empower people to overcome oppression – political
education being a crucial element in this struggle (see Gramsci, 1971, especially).

Radical adult educators throughout the world have used *Pedagogy of the
Oppressed* (Freire, 1972) as the theoretical inspiration and justification for their
work, myself included. However, as will become clear in the unravelling of this
book, I have become less thirled to its central assumptions and more wary
about what I now regard as its overly rationalist ontology (see Chapters 6 and
7). Further, the assumption of *Pedagogy of the Oppressed* is that in struggling
against oppression the oppressed will move towards true humanity.

The problem – I now think – with such an abstract, universalised (and
again, gender-blind) notion of humanization is that it fails to address the different forms of oppression experienced by different groups – the man who is
oppressed by his boss oppressing his wife; the white woman oppressed by sexism oppressing the black woman. As such, it does not consider the possibility
that different groups might propose different – even conflicting – definitions of
'humanization'. In its simple oppressor–oppressed model of power and its
implicit assumption that when the oppressed perceive themselves in relation to
the world they will act together to change it, it fails to acknowledge the possibility of a contradictory experience of oppression among the oppressed (Weiler,
1991). Moreover, as books such as Paul Gilroy's (1993) *The Black Atlantic:
Modernity and Double Consciousness* and Rita Felski's (1995) *The Gender of
Modernity*, argue, we need to expand our understanding of the inescapably
plural nature of modern subjects.

A personal agenda

My own views on what constitutes 'emancipatory' adult education have indeed
shifted over the years, as will become apparent in the flow of this book. That,
too, is a central theme. Briefly, I have moved from a belief – however implicit –
in the potentially transformative power of adult education and critical social
science to a belief in a much more modest project, namely, to seeing both in
terms of their contribution to what Susan Bordo depicts as 'the messy, slippery,
practical struggle' to 'create institutions and communities that will not permit

some groups of people to make determinations about reality for all' (Bordo, 1990, p 142). In this, I have been struck by something Michele le Doeuff has said – that the 'major contradiction of our times' is the loss of language among the learned (through poststructuralist underminings) and the need to articulate urgent problems with people other than academics (Le Doeuff, 1991, p 179). Knowledge is in the end based on acknowledgement. We 'know' as social beings, as members of interpretive communities. And we do not all have access to the 'rhetorical spaces' where authoritative interpretations are made (see Code, 1995, p 231; note 5).

A chilling scene from Muriel Spark's novel, *Memento Mori*, makes this point better than I can theoretically. Charmian, eighty-six and thought to be potty, has been left alone for the afternoon by her housekeeper, Mrs Pettigrew, who has gone out. With tremendous effort, vividly and painstakingly detailed in the text, Charmian has made her own tea and carried everything, one item at a time, to her chair in front of the fire. The scene begins with her husband, Godfrey, returning home, blustering:

> 'I say, you couldn't have made the tea and brought it in here. How could you? Mrs Pettigrew brought in your tea. Now think. You've been dreaming'.
> Charmian turned to Mrs Pettigrew. 'You have been out all afternoon, haven't you, Mrs Pettigrew?'
> 'Mabel', said Mrs Pettigrew.
> 'Haven't you, Mabel? I made my tea myself and brought it in. Godfrey won't believe me, he's absurd.'
> 'I brought in your tea', said Mrs Pettigrew, 'before I went out for an airing . . .'
> 'You see what I mean?' said Godfrey to Charmian.
> Charmian was silent.

Donna Haraway observes that 'struggles over what will count as rational accounts of the world are struggles over *how* to see' (1991, p 194. Emphasis in original). But, suggests Lorraine Code, struggles over how to hear and be heard may be even more complex (see Code, 1995). In fact my interest now could be described in terms of assessing adult education and research programmes in terms of how well they enable the articulation of 'views from below' (see Chapters 7 and 9) – not because by virtue of being from below they offer truer more accurate accounts of the world (although this, on some accounts, is what 'standpoint epistemology' maintains; see Harding, 1986, 1991) but because, in identifying and making available spaces where alternative ways of thinking and being can be worked up, such practices increase the possibilities of knowledge – that is, knowledge which is useful to those who generate it (6):

> 'Knowledge will never be complete', says Lynn Nelson,
>
> but the experiences and stories that have in their claim to universality excluded and mystified other experiences and knowledges . . . in reflecting the experiences of privileged men . . . have been partial in terms of what it was or is *possible to know* in given historical, social and cultural contexts and further

qualified in terms of divisions in experience brought about by
social relations (eg gender, race and culture) – a point that alludes
both to how things are and our ability to know it'.

(Nelson, 1993, p 151, my emphasis)

I regard adult education as a cultural and intellectual project. As such – a kind of public dialogue – it has the radically democratic development of knowledge at its heart. This entails the engagement of many progressive and excluded 'publics' in the generation of knowledge. It means foregrounding the question which was so important in the informal education of the women's movement: whose knowledge? And it means seeing adult education's current task primarily in intellectual and cultural terms rather than institutional and organisational terms, in which public debate on matters of concern to citizens is a central purpose.

This way of seeing adult education – that is, in terms of its critical and creative role within the wider culture – does not fit easily with current policy priorities. It is about new meanings and knowledge and its emphasis is on the conditions and means through which these can be developed – rather than on simply increasing access to existing knowledge. David Alexander has commented that it is precisely in allying itself with the development of socially critical and mature cultural understandings and with the grasp and development of 'really useful knowledge' as defined by different social groups and movements (rather than experts) that adult education in Britain has earned its reputation as a democratising force (Alexander, 1994). It is that project which defines this book.

To re-cap briefly on the central thrust of the book: in presenting the three case studies as historical events it is in the hope of contributing to our self-understanding as critical and creative adult educators and researchers. The philosopher, Richard Eldridge, suggests that we must attempt 'to find ourselves in cases'. Self-understanding is, centrally, an ongoing social process 'bound up with criticism and conversation' (Eldridge, 1989, p 20). And it is never completed: We must, said Wittgenstein, plunge into the waters of doubt again and again in our efforts to come to terms with ourselves. With this in mind the next chapter offers an autobiographical account of some of the influences on my development as an adult educator and researcher.

2 From certainty to uncertainty

The *Oxford English Dictionary* defines autobiography quite simply as 'the writing of one's own history'. Yet it is anything but simple and straightforward. Any autobiographical account involves selection, shaping and memory – a complex interplay between the self writing now and the self 're-called' then, at different stages of personal history. These stages are themselves constructed through the preoccupations, conceptual lenses and emotions (conscious and unconscious) of the present interpreting self (this is further complicated if we take seriously the poststructuralist notion of the fragmented self – that there is no one coherent self doing the interpreting).

Feminist autobiography (a genre in itself) seeks to offer specific and consciously political perspectives on women's lives; in so doing, it reveals what is a feature of any personal biography, however consciously acknowledged: it is never – indeed cannot be – merely personal (see Felski, 1989, Heilbrun, 1989). Since one of the arguments of this book is that ideas, beliefs and research practices are shaped and formed within their specific cultural and historical context, I hope that the autobiographical narrative which forms the substance of this chapter (and which mainly, though not exclusively, charts an intellectual journey) is read in that light – as an attempt, that is, to locate my own ideas within their specific historical and cultural context – rather than as an instance of self-indulgent 'vanity ethnography'. As a kind of critical autobiography I resist the seductiveness of the confessional form; in being personal I make use of theory as well as individual experience *and* a process of reflection which attends to politically and historically situated perspectives (Griffiths, 1995).

I was trained as a philosopher. Writing personally involves a mode of writing that does not come easily to me. That training also taught me not to pick up the pen (or switch on the wordprocessor) until I had marshalled my thoughts and worked out a well-ordered argument clearly and concisely. Plainspeaking was the order of the day. There is no doubt in my mind, however, that how we are expected to write affects what we can write about.

The main body of the book follows a chronological, more or less linear, pattern, in which matters of personal biography are introduced as and when relevant. In this chapter and the next I want to sketch in (in a necessarily schematic form) some aspects of my personal biography which are not covered by the main body of the text. In trying to write about myself in earlier approaches to this chapter I discovered that I could not do it chronologically. This is of more than theoretical interest to me. For if there is one uniting theme to my personal biography, it is that I tend to approach things indirectly. To be consistent with this self, in most of this chapter (having already begun the book at the beginning: 'I was born . . .') I shall pursue a more tangential, less direct path – more like a web – which will go off in different directions, criss-crossing at various points. This, indeed, has been the pattern of my working life to date. In my various jobs – all in education in one form or another – I have tacked between theoretical and practical concerns, trying to keep both moving together in tandem but, often, failing. The relationship – and, sometimes, split – between theory and practice which has been a theme of my personal biography is also a theme of this book.

The two constant intellectual and emotional influences in my life have been socialism and feminism. Living in Glasgow, being left-wing is more or less taken for granted. I have probably always been a 'feminist' although I didn't have a name for what was experienced as a deep-seated inclination until second wave feminism, in the form of the the Women's Liberation Movement, took off in the late 1960s. I have also spent most of my life involved in education in one way or another: as a school pupil in the 1950s and early 1960s when I attended my local primary and co-ed senior secondary schools in the South Side of Glasgow; as a teacher training college and university student for most of the 1960s; as a parent (of a son, born in 1970); as a schoolteacher (briefly); as a lecturer and researcher in higher education for most of the 1970s; as a manager, tutor and lecturer in adult education in the 1980s and 1990s.

For me, now, feminism (like socialism) has four dimensions:

- political – it is a movement to improve the lives of women of all classes, ages, races etc; thus it can't just be concerned with gender alone
- critical – it involves a sustained critique of dominant (male-defined/patriarchal/capitalist) systems of knowledge and practice
- praxis-oriented – it is a practical project of change involving the development here and now of more ethical forms of social and personal practice
- utopian/creative – it involves imagining and envisaging possibilities for a different (not just more equal) society from the present.

(*Note*: I have borrowed and amended and added to the dimensions of feminism laid out by Gaby Weiner, 1994).

These different aspects of feminism have been more or less present and given varying emphases at different stages in my life and in the various projects in which I have been engaged, including the research projects which figure in this book. Thus, as an adult educator (something I did not begin to define myself as being until the end of the 1970s/beginning of the 1980s), I started out very much with a social/political equality agenda, shifting towards greater concern for issues of curriculum development later on. Most of my intellectual work has taken the form of critique although my more policy-oriented work in adult education – particularly as a manager in the WEA in the 1980s – was more clearly directed at making change possible and with creating feminist and egalitarian practices, structures and processes. I believe that it is perhaps the fourth – utopian/imaginative – dimension which needs special emphasis now.

This is because we are in the throes of neo-liberal economic policies of an especially pernicious global form of capitalism which has not only resulted in such 'things' as the feminization of poverty, and the fragmentation of lives, but has been accompanied, too, by an especially pervasive ideology (encouraged by the downfall of various communist regimes) that 'there is no alternative'.

Throughout my life and work, the frameworks, practices, political projects and imaginings provided by feminism have, then, been central, but in different ways at different times. The same goes for socialism which has remained, too, an important influence. What has changed, I think, is my faith and growing distrust in any one political theory, any one categorial framework or discipline – and a growing scepticism, generally, concerning the role of rational understanding in changing ourselves and the world. In Chapter 1 I indicated that there have been corresponding shifts, too, in my views on what constitutes a radical adult education agenda. More than ever before, I think, an attitude of doubt towards our favoured theories and categories is essential for a dynamic politics. Such a politics, in contesting the injustices experienced by different social groups, has to remain open to change, diversification and reinvigoration by the ideas, ways of knowing and practices of those groups who are at present excluded from these processes. Until more people are involved in determining the terms of current debate we cannot know what possibilities exist for thought and action. It is that belief which is now absolutely central to my work.

I want to tell three stories of how I have come to where I am now. The first is factual (I resist the obligatory quotation marks), historical (hence fairly chronological) and discursive. The second is shorter, more personal, moving backwards to move forward, weaving a slightly more complex web. The third, the subject of the next chapter, selects a couple of strands from the web, moments in time which, with hindsight I now view as pivotal in my emerging identity as an adult educator.

First story: Life and work

I came to teaching sociology indirectly (of course), from philosophy. It was a growing field. It is probably not surprising that when I started teaching sociology at Strathclyde University in 1969 – my first real job and just one year after completing an honours degree in philosophy – I turned to the more 'philosophical' figures of the sociological tradition – George Herbert Mead, Alfred Schutz, Max Weber, Wilhelm Dilthey, Georg Simmel – even Erving Goffman. Ethnomethodology, phenomenology, symbolic interactionism – all stressing the subjective and 'socially constructed' nature of social reality – these were my favoured frameworks.

Indeed, I began my life as a sociology lecturer using Peter Winch's *The Idea of a Social Science* as my text (Winch, 1958). This argued the analytical philosopher's case for the conceptual, meaningful, discursive and non-causal nature of social reality. In this book, Winch reproduces a Kantian 'two world' view – a world of things which is the subject of natural science (and explainable in causal terms) and a world of meanings which is the subject of the human sciences (and understandable only hermeneutically and non-causally). The modes of study and knowledge appropriate to the *Naturwissenschaften* (Natural Sciences) and *Geisteswissenschaften* (Human Sciences) are seen here as radically distinct (1).

In the current intellectual climate – summed up, as I have already indicated, as involving the ambition to dispense with 'things' and to value 'words' more; and faced with the broad shift in feminist thinking – summed up by one commentator in the terms: 'difference, multiplicity, heterogeneity' (Kuhn, 1994, p 249), as well as a lack of faith in 'scientific' narratives – I am acutely aware of fighting against the temptation to (smugly) believe that it's all been said before and that all that is afoot just now is a re-cycling of old debates in new terms.

After all, my bookshelves heave under books with titles such as *Reflexive Waters* (Elders, 1974), *Meanings and Situations* (Brittan, 1973), *Dilemmas of Discourse* (Wootton, 1975); and titles of chapters of books written by feminists today re-cycle titles of books from 20 years ago. For example, 'Words and things' is the final chapter of a recent book of readings charting changes in theoretical feminism over the last 20 years. It is also the title of a well-known book by the (decidedly non-feminist) philosopher, Ernest Gellner, written about 20 years ago.

My sense of *déjà vu* is profound. In this connection it is perhaps instructive to recognise that history shows us philosophical 'moods' which differ greatly from one another. Michele Le Doeuff identifies two classic ones – the one architectonic, concerned with building theoretical systems, the other corrosive, aiming to criticise and demolish. Sometimes these come together but sometimes one dominates and suffocates the other. Over the last 20 years or so, observes Le Doeuff, interest seems to have lain in the possibility of destroying all language and undermining all speech, and although affirmatory works 'about something' have been produced, such production has tended to go unnoticed – because of the mood of the time (see Le Doeuff, 1991).

The 'mood of the times' in the 1970s was certainly very different from today. I returned to teaching sociology and the philosophy of the social sciences in 1973, at Glasgow College of Technology, following a year in Italy with my husband and year-old baby. There I had gone on strike marches with factory workers and been introduced to the works of Gramsci by my friend Orietta – an artist, and the only female member of the Partita Proletaria on the local council. (One of my most treasured possessions is a gift from that time of a hardback copy of Gramsci's *Prison Notebooks*).

On my return from Italy, in addition to my lecturing job and a young child to care for (assisted greatly by my mother and the availability of nursery school places for local authority teaching staff) I worked with my husband on the production of an 'alternative' left wing newspaper, *Glasgow News*. This was based in our home. For two years we did not sleep from Friday night until Sunday night, distributing the paper to pubs and shops on Friday, editing and varityping the next issue during the rest of the weekend. All of this at a time when Bowlby's theories concerning maternal deprivation and the damaging effects on infants with working mothers was still a powerful guilt-inducing force. In the case of my own son, I think, he benefited from the presence of several doting adults and an atmosphere of commitment, energy and engagement. He is now a journalist, producing social issue television programmes.

My recollection of much of the 1970s is one of exhaustion and exhilaration. Throughout much of the decade I was an active member of the Women's Movement in Glasgow and involved in a number of single issue campaigns: the National Abortion Campaign, the Legal and Financial Independence Group, the National Childcare Campaign and the Scottish Women's Charter Group. In addition, I was an executive member of the Scottish Immigrant Labour Council, a body largely dominated by Communist Party members, set up to promote the rights of the largely Indian and Pakistani immigrant population of Glasgow and the rest of Scotland.

Knowing the enemy

The agenda was social change directed towards equality. As feminists, we knew the enemy. We united against our opponents who argued against social change – against women's liberation – on biological grounds; so we stressed the environmental and social instead. We tended to see femininity as a distortion of women's potential and many of us shared an androgynous vision (like Simone de Beauvoir and Mary Wollstencraft). As socialist feminists (and most Glasgow-based feminists saw ourselves as such, unlike our Edinburgh-based sisters whom we derided for their radical feminist separatist politics) we stressed social structural causes of women's oppression (capitalist and patriarchal institutions). We were critical of liberal feminists for their individualism, their analysis of oppression in terms of role-socialisation theory and for their faith in equal opportunities and access to education as ways forward. Most of us believed in the power of consciousness-raising to reveal what oppressed us and believed that it was through a rational understanding of the social causes of their oppression that people collectively would bring about progressive social and political change.

During this period I included some of the early texts of second wave feminism in my teaching, both at Glasgow College of Technology and with adult education classes with women's groups which were organised under the auspices of the WEA in and around Glasgow. These included Kate Millett (1971), Shulamith Firestone (1970), Sheila Rowbotham (1973), Juliet Mitchell (1971) and Germaine Greer (1970). My personal recollection of that era's feminism (up until the fairly late 1970s, that is) is light years away from the theoretically crude, over-generalising programme that recent caricatures of it would suggest. As socialist feminists (including many working class women and a handful of black and Asian women) we emphasised the connections between sexism, racism, class, imperialism, heterosexism, consumer culture and so on. The list was long. Black and Asian feminists in Glasgow, though few in number, taught us to keep issues of British imperialism and colonialism to the fore (as Scots, too, we had our own specific understandings of these). We knew from experience, from listening to other women and through collective campaigning that there was no such thing as 'woman's' experience: it depended, for instance, on one's class, race, age, cultural and ethnic background and sexual orientation. We did not need abstract poststructuralist 'anti-essentialist' theorising to tell us that this was so. From that period of feminism in the 1970s stems my abiding belief that although there are important differences between women, there is also much structural common ground and shared experience.

Nevertheless, we did have a tremendous sense of being right. We believed in 24-hour nursery provision; that housework and 'care' had to be socialised (laundrettes were our model) and that women who did not agree suffered from false consciousness and a lack of understanding of correct revolutionary theory.

The kind of writing which I did during this period was highly political and popular. For instance, I helped in the production and publication of a small book which focused on the institutional racism experienced by immigrants from the Asian sub-continent who had come to Glasgow from the 1950s onwards. The publication concentrated mainly on the experiences and job prospects of school-leavers and was distributed widely within schools and various communities, as well as in local shops. I also wrote pieces for publication in *Glasgow News*, the *Scottish Women's Report, Glasgow Women's Liberation Newsletter* and other left-wing publications, of which, at the time, there was no shortage.

A taste for abstraction

On the other hand, most of my academic teaching during this period – courses in sociological theory and the philosophy of the social sciences – was highly theoretical and abstract – dominated by questions like: 'What constitutes an adequate theory/explanation?' 'Are the human sciences scientific?' 'What is the meaning of *verstehen*?' (Max Weber's notion of the distinctive kind of understanding required in sociology) and 'How does hermeneutic understanding relate to causal explanation?'. After my earlier inauguration into the sociological community and and my realisation that to be a phenomenologist (Schutz etc) was beyond the pale – positively the worst thing to be – I had by then adopted critical social science as my favoured theoretical orientation and, through involvement in the growing Women's Movement, a socialist feminist worldview. There was little room for doubt in all of this. Doubt and uncertainty are now, on the other hand, *de rigueur*.

In the broadest terms, 'critical social science' is an attempt to acquire a rational understanding of the oppressive features of society, an understanding which will thereby enable those who have this understanding to transform their society and so liberate themselves. On this view an emancipatory politics or education depends on a realist science; freedom consists in emancipation from oppressive structures of power and in knowing and being able to act in accordance with our real interests. A necessary condition for such emancipation is the enlightenment which a realist, critical social science and an education based on it may bring. I believed passionately in the rational enlightenment made possible by Marxist social science.

However, all of this exceedingly meta-theoretical cogitation went on quite separately from my political work and from my feminism which was very practically focused. And my high valuation of abstract theorising sat uneasily with lessons I should have been learning from my experience of the Women's

Movement and of the informal educational work which grew up around it during the 1970s and into the 1980s. For what that taught me – but only at a subliminal level at the time – was a view of knowledge and a form of education which rests on the development of new knowledge through dialogue and the collective sharing and analysing of experience. The kind of educational practice based on that view of knowledge recognises and takes seriously – concretely, not just in theory – both the emotional component of learning and knowledge and the social and political interests which invest it. I am in no doubt that my own predilection for highly abstract thinking was itself emotionally invested.

It could also become obsessive. It was this obsessiveness which lay behind my decision, towards the end of the 1970s, to leave my job and to seek a research post where I might be able to apply my theorising and philosophising to an area of direct relevance to my feminist politics. By this time, the sister-hood which had moistened my eyes in the earlier part of the decade had begun to show cracks. The Glasgow Women's Centre which had seemed to be a place for a diverse range of women broke up over tensions between socialist/Marxist feminists and radical and lesbian feminists who felt that their interests and experiences were not adequately catered for within a socialist/Marxist feminist framework and agenda.

Reforming the welfare state

The year I took up my post as an evaluator on the Pre-school Evaluation Project (1979) – the subject of the first case study of this book – was the year Margaret Thatcher took up her new post as Prime Minister. That year inaugurated a new brand of right conservatism which, along with wider, global processes of eco-nomic, social and economic restructuring, was to profoundly affect education at all levels. However, the pre-fives/parent education project I evaluated was one of a myriad of community schemes which were popular in the 1970s, a result of importing the policies and practices of community development into working class neighbourhoods: policies and practices which, as Cynthia Cockburn had convincingly argued, were built into the corporate management of change in cities and were therefore as much (or more) to do with controlling the direction of change in communities in a state of crisis as they were with enabling people to take more control over their lives (Cockburn, 1977).

I saw such schemes as having a strong element of 'blaming the victim' and as being imbued with a culture of poverty approach which disgusted me. In refusing to adopt the newly-minted 'utilization-focused' evaluation approach to the project (Patton, 1978) – an approach which evaluates schemes in terms of their usefulness according to criteria set by policy makers and project origina-tors – I was refusing, as I saw it, to endorse the role of evaluation as a tool of the state. I chose instead to align myself with the interests of the women in the community who were the objects of the project and to use the evaluation as a tool for the representation of their needs as they saw them.

From the 1960s until the mid-late 1970s there had been a whole plethora of central and local government reports and policies, which, as a result of the 'rediscovery of poverty' were directed at tidying up the edges of the welfare state. These had included the Plowden Report on primary education, the Skeffington Report on town planning, the Seebohm Report on personal social services, the Russell Report (in England) and the Alexander Report (in Scotland) on non-vocational adult education. None of these considered the possibility that the problems they sought to solve might be manifestations of a much more fundamental crisis in the political economy. The consensus which had dominated public policy since the 1940s was not put in doubt by any of them: namely, that the basic problems of a capitalist political economy had been resolved, with the state acting as a means of regulating the economy to ensure full employment and social justice. It was indeed this view of the welfare state which was the source of my father's pride. A safety net; and it was this post-war consensus which was to be so effectively challenged by a radical right, politically quiet in Britain in the 1970s, which, in an international context, had been developing the ideological attack which was to dominate in the 1980s (see Jackson, 1995).

The Workers' Educational Association

When I had completed the evaluation (see Chapters 4 and 5), and after a temporary one year appointment as Staff Tutor in Educational Studies for the Open University in Scotland, I took up the post of District Secretary of the West of Scotland District of the WEA, in 1982. Thatcherism was beginning to bite by then and for the remainder of the 1980s when I worked for the WEA the District was subject to the whims of short-term changes in government funding mechanisms, frozen Scottish Education Department grants and cutbacks on Local Authority spending. The District's work was greatly influenced by Strathclyde Region's Community Development Strategy in Areas for Priority Treatment (APTs) – largely because of its financial dependence on the Region for teaching funds. As chief executive of the District, responsible for its day-to-day management and for advising its lay management committee on matters of funding and policy, I found myself embroiled in the many contradictions which such a position of responsibility brings with it.

I discovered that despite the paternalistic policies and practices of the Region and its own Community Education Service, it was possible, with committed tutor organisers (in collaboration with some community education workers) to devise really useful educational work. Such work involved, primarily, working with already established groups in the communities – women's groups, credit unions, tenants' associations, unemployed groups, people with learning difficulties or with physical or sensory disabilities – and devising curricula arising out of the issues which were of concern to them. Writers', History and Drama Workshops developed alongside one another and groups from different areas came together from time to time in joint residential events. Women's education was central. What united this work was an insistence on the social as well as individual nature of experience and a privileging of experiential and creative forms of learning over, or at least alongside, more abstract forms (see O'Rourke, 1995).

All of this provision had to be nurtured and developed on a shoestring, and a shortening one at that, as Conservative policies towards voluntary organisations started to erode grant support – both directly, through standstill or reduced revenue assistance for administrative costs, and indirectly, through squeezing local authorities' expenditure on non-statutory provision like adult education. Community-based adult education of the sort we were engaged in depended, crucially, on building up relationships of solidarity and affection. It took time – much more than was paid for in salaries and tutor costs. Much of my time during this period was taken up with political lobbying and fundraising. It was crucial, I believed, to maintain the kind of provision the WEA represented, in the face of the other sort of educational offerings in deprived areas. In a journal article which I wrote at the time (not endearing myself to Local Authority Community Education officials or Scottish Education Department officials, on whom we depended greatly for financial support) I claimed:

> There is a kind of community education for the 'disadvantaged' which sells people short by concentrating on 'life adjustment skills and diminished cognitive content'; it is part of the ameliorative, social conscience tradition. . . . This happens, I believe, less through conscious intent than through the workers involved not having the orientation or skills which are necessary to develop learning programmes from the issues raised by participants. . . . [Any] adequate education practice must be explicit about educational content and underlying ideologies [and the] . . . curriculum open to negotiation, challenge and change. It should also be underpinned by adequate provision for tutor training. The amount of education with adults in Scotland which fits the description is minuscule – and shrinking. Not surprising, given the absence of a sensible framework for adult and continuing education, the lack of resources devoted to it and the poverty of policy.
>
> (Barr, 1987)

Given my strong views about ameliorative community education and on the necessity for tutors to be aware of the social and ideological implications of any educational work, it was with a sinking heart that I was enlisted (or, more accurately, co-opted) onto the Scottish Community Education Council's (SCEC) new Community Education Validation and Endorsement Committee (CeVe). The task of the committee was to devise a competency-based framework for the vocational preparation of community education workers. It was driven – quite clearly, in my view – by a managerial agenda for change, dominated in this case by key local authority officials whose rhetoric of democracy blinded them to their own controlling tendencies. 'Value for Money' (VFM) and 'Total Quality Management' (TQM) were the terms in which the new functional definition of community education was to be devised.

I recall the extreme embarrassment with which I sat through a session, bought in from SCOTVEC (the Scottish Vocational Educational Council, a rising star at the time) in which the intricacies of 'functional analysis' were explained to us: our task, we were told, was to break down the role of community education workers into its constituent parts ('elements'); to spell out the 'competencies' required for these; and to specify means of measuring that they had been acquired ('performance criteria'). Endless hours were spent discussing the values needed to be a proper community education worker and how to measure these. There was a minority voice of resistance which pointed out the conceptual confusions and maskings of power which were involved in the exercise, an exercise which was designed to portray education as merely technical. Because of the powerful managerial lobby in the committee, such expressions of disquiet (sometimes made in the form of outbursts of frustration and almost hysterical mirth at the lunacy of the exercise we were engaged in, as much as in reasoned argument) were easily contained.

It was with little regret that I relinquished my place on the committee when, in 1989, I left the WEA for a year's time out to pursue further study and to take stock. I was physically and emotionally exhausted and had developed a debilitating illness which caused me extreme pain. My mother had just died.

After my MA year out at Durham University, where I wrote my dissertation on women's education in the WEA (the subject of the second case study of this book), I returned to the WEA and attempted to make my post a job-sharing one. Meeting resistance to this from National Officers and some other District Secretaries (but not from my own District) I resigned, and returned to a post in higher education, this time to university-based research in Adult and Continuing Education. At Warwick University, as a Senior Research Associate in the Continuing Education Research Centre, I joined Lynda Birke in a University Funding Council sponsored investigation into 'women's perceptions of science'.

Changing fashions
in feminism and adult education

After several years of having time to read only sporadically, I now had the opportunity to immerse myself in feminist theory once more and to engage with its new epistemological turn which had been on the ascendant for some years, in the writings of, mainly, North American feminist academics (see Chapters 8 and 9 especially, my third case study). And what I found there deeply disturbed me: a new feminist methodologism, a kind of feminist theoretical correctness, eschewing any generalisations about gender on *a priori* grounds, as 'essentialist'.

Yet the real agents of the challenges to the 'old' feminism of the 1970s were those women who felt excluded from it. These were the 'women of colour' in the USA (I don't think it was quite the same in Britain because of our stronger tradition of socialist feminism and black feminists' important contributions to that tradition: see Brah and Hoy, 1989; Brah and Minhas, 1985), lesbians and others who found their own histories and cultures ignored in prevailing discussions and actions over gender. Another aspect of this new theoretical turn, I felt, was that, whereas 'race' was foregrounded, 'class' seemed to have dropped out of much of the discussion.

The important point I want to make here is that such challenges to the mainly white women's movement arose out of *concrete experiences of exclusion* – not out of a conception of *adequate theory*; and what is demanded by these challenges is certainly not a theoretical response but practical institutional and intellectual change – and respectful listening. Postmodernist feminism – for such it was on the ascendant – reminds me of my philosophy undergraduate days where the lesson learned was that you were wrong to speak whatever you had to say. The new feminist theoreticism, in which problems of racism and ethnocentrism, for instance, have become tied to *methodological* concerns about the legitimacy of making any generalisations about gender at all, is an aspect, I think, of the growing professionalization of feminist thinking which I alluded to in Chapter 1. It manifests and suggests an increased incorporation of feminism into the academy, into institutions of knowledge and power which are antithetical to feminism as a movement of cultural resistance and transformation (see Chapter 10).

Almost 10 years before my return to the higher education sector, I had written about the integration of feminism (in the form of women's studies) within universities in the USA, contrasting this project with the situation in Britain where fears of co-option were traditionally stronger and where the strongest early developments of women's studies took place within Adult Education. I wrote:

> Many are cynical about such efforts [the US project], seeing in
> them the route of co-option and reasoning that if we really believe
> that radical social change is necessary to change the position of
> women in society we can't really expect our ideas to be accepted in
> the mainstream – especially universities which are very firmly
> embedded in the present social structure. They would suggest
> (a) Women's Studies must retain its status as an outsider to some
> extent and (b) that there should be more involvement of Women's
> Studies in the community on the ground that if it is confined to
> universities and colleges it cannot touch the lives of the majority of
> women.
>
> (Barr, 1984)

When I moved back to Scotland, following the Warwick research, to take up a university lectureship in adult and continuing education I also found a very different adult education context from the one I was used to. Here, quite different interests and assumptions operated from those underpinning my previous work in the WEA. In this new context, part-time degrees, Access courses, management training, measurement of competencies and accreditation dominated. Issues of policy and purpose, teaching and learning, curriculum development and equal opportunities, which still framed practice and discussion when I left the WEA, were scarcely touched upon.

Understandings and approaches which I had taken for granted for over a decade and which I had expected from my own staff in the WEA – which, indeed, I regarded as built into being an adult education worker – were not required of me. There was acceptance that provision would only meet a small section of the community; efforts on my part to widen access by increasing contacts with the local community were positively discouraged – seen as time-consuming, even self-indulgent. Tried and tested forms of provision which worked – 'second-chance' courses for women, for example, with an open agenda and creche provision – were 'old hat' (see O'Rourke, 1995). What was required were 'monuments on the landscape' (a quote from my new boss) to improve the market position of the University and the profile of my Department within the University. I left after three years.

In my current work at Glasgow University I seek to contribute to the arresting of the forgetting of adult education's more radical agendas and purposes. In this work I am guided by a metaphor bequeathed by Hannah Arendt. We need to cultivate a form of thinking, suggests Arendt, which, though located in the past, is directed at the future:

> This thinking, fed by the present [may work] with the 'thought
> fragments' it can wrest from the past and gather about itself. Like
> a pearl diver who descends to the bottom of the sea . . . to pry
> loose . . . the pearls and corals in the depths . . . this thinking
> delves into the depths of the past – but not to resuscitate it the way
> it was. What guides this thinking is the conviction that . . . in the
> depth of the sea, into which it sinks and dissolves what once was
> alive, some things suffer a 'sea-change' . . . as though they waited
> only for the pearl-diver.
>
> (Arendt, 1969, pp 50–51)

Certainly, 'old' traditions of radical adult education grounded in notions of a male working class and rooted in an impulse to politically educate will simply not do.

In fact I now believe that during the 1970s, when I was involved in several 'left-wing' endeavours, I accommodated my feminism far too much to a socialist/Marxist framework. Women were 'victims' of capitalism and patriarchy – powerless. Working class women were doubly oppressed, black women triply and so on. There was little room in this model for agency; in particular, it ignored both women's collusions with patriarchal culture and their frequent attempts to resist it (my own included). It also rested, I now believe, on a notion of being 'fully human' which, though seemingly genderless, actually presupposed within its Marxist framework a thoroughly male and patriarchally derived norm: the autonomous, self-directing, rational individual, empowered to take part in the public political arena by the removal of all that bound 'him' to the body and the kind of caring, productive work required to sustain life (see Hart, 1992). Thus, a feminist friend, recalling from memory, can now quote with gentle irony the words of William Morris which inspired her at an earlier stage:

> These things shall be, a loftier race
> Than e'er the world has seen, shall rise
> With flame of freedom in his soul
> And light of science in his eyes

It is this (supposedly genderless but actually highly gendered) ideal of being

human – derived, first, I think from reading philosophy – which I import unconsciously into my research on childcare (see first case study – Chapters 4 and 5).
The same notion lies behind my disdain for Carol Gilligan's book, *In a Different
Voice*, when it first appeared in 1979: I (mis)read her book as a simple (even
simple-minded) celebration of traditional femininity and of 'female' values of
caring, empathy and connectedness, rather than as a critique of the sexual division of labour which consigns 'female' values to a separate, 'private', domestic
sphere while keeping the public male sphere a bastion of autonomous selves
(see Bordo, 1993). It is a conception which continued to influence my intellectual work until much later, despite my own experiential learning. It is, for
instance, embedded in the form and content of my research on women's education in the WEA which I conducted in 1989 (see the second case study in
Chapter 7).

In the 1970s, I did not doubt for a moment that I knew the right (Marxist
feminist) theories and that if enough people knew them too, then, together, we
could – indeed, would – change the world. For much of the 1970s as I have
indicated I was a (very philosophical) sociologist and I can see myself – the way
I was then – in the following depiction in a recent book. In the book, the
writer's mother, Poppy, gently chides her sociologist daughter for her literal-
mindedness and reliance on 'thinking' to the exclusion of imagining. The voice
in the book is the daughter's:

> 'How could you swallow all that stuff about choosing
> happiness . . . as if our lives are lived outside things like poverty
> and unemployment and patriarchy and Thatcherism and Nato?'
> The list was long. 'It depends how you look at it', Poppy said, a
> line of argument that struck me then as feeble . . . Pressing her [I
> was] told when I was unhappy, it was not because Nato was to
> blame.
>
> (Modjeska, 1990, p 292).

Second story: The sociological imagination

I now want to re-trace some of the steps depicted above and by a slightly
different route tell a slightly different story of how I have come to define myself
and my work now as an adult educator. It is, in a sense, a conversation between
myself as a feminist adult educator and my selves as philosopher and sociologist.

To re-trace my steps . . . I came to teaching sociology, indirectly, from philosophy, in the late 1960s and early 1970s. Then (and now) I found in C Wright
Mills' 'sociological imagination' something inspiring and humane which was
missing from my undergraduate and postgraduate studies in philosophy. The
idea of a kind of imagination or way of knowing which is based on understanding the invisible social forces which influence people's ordinary lives struck me
as a compassionate and much needed counter to the abstractions and individualising impulses which featured so strongly in my philosophy studies. I still

begin a number of my courses through Mills' imaginative understanding so as to encourage a habit of thinking which moves beyond the narrow confines of self and personal experience and psychology and yet connects back to personal biographies. I continue to see the value of sociology as lying in its debunking possibilities and strategies. These arise from its commitment to getting behind appearances to what is going on – especially the operations of power and deeply rooted relationships which explain more apparent phenomena.

I therefore accept much that is contained in critical social science's agenda as outlined, for example in Brian Fay's book, called, simply, *Critical Social Science* (Fay, 1987) and I am in agreement, too, with the main aims of critical social research as outlined by Lee Harvey in his book of that title (Harvey, 1990; see Chapter 5). However, the voice of certainty which sometimes booms out of such work and its central metaphors – 'digging beneath the surface', for example – seems inappropriate to its central methodological and epistemological stance, namely, that our knowledge of the complex underlying structure of advanced capitalism is always conjectural and indirect; reality is opaque; the existence of deeply rooted relationships which explain superficial phenomena is only evident in certain clues and signs which have to be 'read' and interpreted (see Ginzburg, 1980). That is to say, epistemological caution seems the only stance to adopt in the face of 'critical' social science's ontological boldness (Bhaskar, 1989, p 186).

Philosophy and the voice of reason

I had come to philosophy by an indirect route too. I was one of the girls Valerie Walkerdine discusses in *Schoolgirl Fictions* (1990), among whom she counts herself: girls from working class and lower middle class families who went to training college to become primary school teachers. Like Walkerdine, in 1968 I (briefly) became a primary school teacher following three years at Jordanhill College of Education. Like her, I had read *How Children Fail* (Holt, 1969) and like her I believed in the romantic promise of progressivism in education. I, too, occasionally found myself weeping at 4 o'clock, tears of exhaustion and frustration: how to bring order to 40 restless nine- and ten-year-olds in a school in a peripheral housing scheme in Glasgow was not self-evident – despite my abstract grapplings with issues of discipline and punishment in my philosophy of education course at training college.

Rather eerily and by a neat coming together, it was two essays, one entitled 'Discipline', the other 'Punishment' which set me off on a path which led me to take an honours degree in philosophy at Glasgow University and, some time later, to my reading of Foucault's *Discipline and Punish* (1979). ('Docile bodies', his chapter on the disciplining of bodies can still make me shiver). In my first essay, written at training college, I argued that the only discipline deserving of the name is self-discipline. I blush now at the smug certainty with which I wrote it and at the belief in willed, rational self-control which informed it. I learned, much later, through personal experience and through reading, that the self-discipline for which I argued is by no means free of the play of power, that education and learning involve the disciplining of bodies and passions as much as minds and that reason itself is a product of things other than itself. Yet even now I can still recall, almost like a taste, the pleasure of these early forays into philosophical thinking.

Philosophy, from the outset, resonated with something deep inside me. Or so it seemed. Although it did not form part of the school curriculum (despite Scottish education being relatively broadly based) I came to it with an odd sense of recognition. I do not know why. What I do know is that the desire to 'do' philosophy, once I had discovered it, came to me as a revelation, with utter clarity. Despite later dissatisfactions with what passes as philosophy in practice – its abstract academicism; its concern for examining assumptions behind all other systems of thought and frameworks besides its own; its respect for academic authority; its emphasis on critical thinking over/against creative work; its astounding male domination – it can still give me immense pleasure.

What I regard as philosophy's basic stance – never taking anything for granted, questioning all authorities, irreverence – is shared, I think, by feminism and is part of the reason, perhaps, for my attraction to both. Yet what can so easily turn into an overly critical stance – at least the kind of philosophy which held sway when I studied it in the late 1960s – I now see as a severe limitation and source of intellectual arrogance: the viewpoint of critical critique, ceaseless negation, carried out as if from nowhere can itself become a kind of uncreative, dog-in-the-manger stubbornness which, in seeing value only in learning to criticise, has often little positive to say. It is a stance which underlay countless conversations I had at the time with philosophers and non-philosophers alike. 'How can you say that?' 'What do you mean?' 'How do you know?' were typical conversational moves and in taking up this posture as my own I was simply perpetuating the typical philosophical practice of the time which, crudely, boiled down to establishing that one is wrong to speak, whatever one says.

It has been suggested that there is such a thing as a dogmatism of the impasse, doubt or void which is harder to root out than dogmatic conviction (Le Doeuff, 1991). How can you argue against a position which refuses to assert anything? We were being taught 'how to think' – what about was often neither here nor there. It may be for this reason that when it came to writing our 'Credos' – a final year tradition in the Moral Philosophy Department – some of us had not a great deal to say.

Nevertheless, the kind of question which dominated much of my waking life then and later, when I taught the philosophy of the social sciences in my first lecturing job – questions like 'Can reasons be causes?' (what kind of question is this?) – forced on me certain habits of thought which have proved useful in trying to come to terms with and fathom meatier matters. Wrestling with such abstractions could even bring a surprising elation, like the brief moment when I understood 'Godel's Proof'. Proof to me that, if only for an instant, I could grasp the most 'difficult' of ideas. Experiences such as these taught me not to underestimate the pleasures of thinking or the sheer joy of understanding. School gave me none of that. And when I decided on adult education as my sphere, in the 1980s, I took with me the conviction, not only that adult education should be about enlightenment and understanding rather than remediation and comfort, but also, that its worst sin would be to short-change people in the name of relevance or in order to be true to their own experience.

Thus in 1984 in a keynote address presented at a conference on women's adult education, and drawing on the feminist theorist, Mary Evans, I could say: 'To despise theory because of worries about elitism suggests an uncritical and reactionary acceptance of a society in which access to higher education and to critical thought is denied to most people. Political engagement to change these arrangements is required – not the retreat from the difficulties of political struggle which is implied by this anti-theory stance'. In the speech I referred to Jane Austen's reference to 'the horror of mean understanding' – living in a circumscribed world constantly in the presence of over-developed opinions and under-developed understanding (Barr, 1984).

What strikes me now about such statements is my rather touching faith in the 'reason' of official knowledge and my somewhat arrogant blindness to ways of knowing other than those valued and given recognition in seats of learning – in the mainstream. As if knowledge which springs from everyday life and which is directed to some useful purpose is not therefore knowledge and as if the only theory that deserves the name is inscribed in books.

Healing the breach – knowledge from above and below

I have become fascinated with the idea of knowledge 'from below' and the need for adult education – any education – to give recognition to ways of thinking which do not fit within the narrow parameters set by our culture's dominant notions of rationality and intelligence (see Chapter 7 especially). Knowledge from below, common knowledge ('You have absolutely no common sense, Jean' was a constant rebuke from my mother and her friends, one which I no longer bear with pride), is often trivialized and patronised as female intuition, old wives tales or folklore. Carlo Ginzburg speaks of this knowledge, which is rooted in the senses and everyday life but is not irrational – as typically the property of those in a given society who are not in positions of power – indigenous people and peasants, as well as the working classes of industrial societies, particularly the women among them (Ginzburg, 1980). This notion, coupled with Gramsci's distinction between 'common sense' and 'good sense', is, I think, infinitely suggestive.

My continuing choice of adult education as my field is now fuelled by the will and desire to transcend the divide between ways of knowing and forms of knowledge which in our culture are separated off from one another – knowledge 'from above' and knowledge 'from below'; cerebral and emotional; literal and imaginative; scientific and literary. I retain my attachment to philosophy. And I do not believe that in my continuing attraction to it I am simply being a dutiful daughter who has learned her lessons well. I may be deluded, of course. As a Scottish schoolgirl who was both cheeky and brainy and whose mother was often brought to the point of extreme rage – 'If you give me any more of your lip I'll take my hand off your face' (and sometimes did) – I was not only subjected to what Walkerdine has described as subtle regulation into normality at home and at school (Walkerdine, 1990). Control and coercion were often overt and quite unequivocal. At Primary School in the 1950s I was belted with the tawse every other day and, too, in the early months at Secondary School. Maybe I was, indeed, beaten into submission for talking back. Or maybe, in studying philosophy and learning its corrosive and irreverent ways, it was because I had accounts to settle with those in power and authority (see hooks, 1994).

Certainly, recalling such brutalisation and humiliation now I am bound to believe, perhaps more than some, that a purely rational approach to adult learning and education with any liberatory pretensions at all – whether, 'liberal', 'critical', 'feminist' or whatever – will not do. We learn as much with our bodies as our minds. And for those of us who have learned to hold our tongue through those and similar humiliations (often located in our class, gender or race positioning) and however thirled we come to be later on to a life of the mind or critical consciousness and the quest for knowledge, the hardest thing of all is to find a voice; not the voice of super-conscious self-assertion which speaks from a position of overview (the voice of my philosophy undergraduate days) but a voice which in 'summoning the resources' of the place we come from 'can speak with eloquence of and for that place' (Kuhn, 1995). I now see the task and promise of adult education as lying precisely in helping to identify and open up spaces where such a summoning up of resources can take place. Where, that is, what has been called 'responsible knowledge' can take root and grow (Haraway, 1991a; Code, 1989, 1995). I hope that this book, too, will be judged in these terms.

In the next chapter, I want to tell a third story which relates this current project of 'writing the self' (2) to an experience which not only marked me but was part of an historical moment which opened up many 'spaces of enunciation' for the development of responsible knowledge.

3 Becoming an adult educator

Third story

In this account – my third story – I want to trace some connections between my emerging notion of myself as an adult educator, my experiences of women's education, and my changing views on useful research. Most of the first part of the chapter concentrates on informal women's education as it arose out of the women's movement and its formative influence on me. The second part of the chapter focuses on my emerging self-definition as an adult educator (crucially influenced by those experiences) and the kind of research interest this engendered. However, I begin by locating the account of women's education which figures in the first half of this chapter in relation to recent debates within feminist theory concerning 'feminist research' and 'feminist epistemology' and to the dearth of feminist (or, indeed, gender-related) research in adult education.

Feminist research

I believe that informal women's education/women's studies as this grew out of the Women's Movement in the 1970s and early 1980s in Britain can be seen as a practical precursor of a later highly abstract debate within academic feminism about feminist knowledge production (concerning feminist research and feminist epistemology) which has been underway for the last decade or so. For it provided a context which was a seedbed for many and varied 'epistemological communities' engaged in numerous knowledge-making projects which arose out of women's lives and sprang from their need for 'really useful knowledge'. Crucially, it challenged the notion of knowledge as something produced solely by experts and refused to separate the development of abstract knowledge from the emotional and social lives of people.

When I started doing empirical research and when I carried out the research which features in the first case study of this book, between 1979–81, on the Headway Pre-school Community Project, (see Chapter 4) the notion of specifically 'feminist research' as offering a distinct methodological and epistemological standpoint (or standpoints) on the world, and implying a shift away from research on or about women to research for women, had scarcely been enunciated. (But see Oakley, 1981; Roberts, 1981; Smith, 1979; Stanley and Wise, 1983.) Prevailing concerns regarding 'feminist research', such as they had been articulated, were mainly reactive and critical, rather than actively challenging and creative. The aim was to expose the sexist bias of the social sciences and to seek to remedy this, for example, by getting rid of sexist language and by exposing the gender blindness involved in the prevalent practice of basing generalisations about humans on data about men.

To the extent that I saw myself as engaged in 'feminist research' in Headway I'd have probably defined this to mean research on women, by feminists and carried out in a sisterly, egalitarian, democratic way. In some vague sense I would have regarded qualitative methods as more 'feminist' than quantitative ones, an assumption which has been questioned and, I think, rightly, rejected, by several feminist critics (eg Jayaratne and Stewart, 1991). Such a preference suited, too, my anti-positivism, my antipathy to 'treating social facts as things', explainable in ways which by-passed conscious meanings and agency.

Since then there has been a spate of writing on feminist methodology and epistemology; over the past ten years, especially, this literature has been developing, largely written from a highly abstract and academic point of view, and mainly written by feminist academics for other academics, who are also mainly (but not exclusively) North American. These theorists have moved on from critique of the sexism of social science and other disciplines into a less reactive, more positive project – that of exploring what specifically 'feminist' knowledge might look like, and, relatedly, raising questions about women as agents rather than objects of knowledge. This, I believe, is precisely what women's education/women's studies as it developed within British adult education in the 1970s and early 1980s was about in practice – at least, some of it. Very little of this work has been documented – a fact which relates to the general dearth of research in this area.

Adult education research in Britain is stubbornly gender blind – with a few notable exceptions (eg Ball, 1992; Keddie, 1981; McGivney, 1993; Thompson, 1983). This is probably partly due to the tendency of educational research to explain educational privilege in class terms; partly to the fact that there is little policy interest and hence few funds available (except, for instance, in relation to women's access to science education; see SHEFC, 1995); and partly to resistance to the idea that there may still be gender inequality in adult continuing education (the assumption here is that women have 'caught up').

Veronica McGivney asks an important question: 'Why has research in adult and continuing education, which otherwise draws heavily on insights from sociology and psychology, been so unresponsive to and made so little of the impact of the women's movement and the changing social and economic position of women?' (McGivney, 1997, pers. com.). Little seems to have changed since Hayes' (1992) analysis of British and North American journals over a 23 year period. This showed how little research referred to feminist influences, reported the gender of students, used gender as a variable in data analysis, or included a discussion of gender differences (or lack of them) in the interpretation of findings. This silence reflects the deafening silence concerning feminist theory and practice in standard textbooks in adult and continuing education – a feature which is as true of the narrower sphere of radical and popular education as it is of the mainstream. Indeed, the lack of impact of feminist popular education on the 'discipline' of adult education, even within the narrower sphere of radical education, is one of the reasons behind a recent collection of readings on gender and popular education, edited by Shirley Walters and Linzi Manicom (1996). They point out that much of the evidence for feminism's impact exists in the form of workbooks and 'how-to' manuals.

The story of the impact of feminism and the significance of gender on adult and continuing education has to be told again and again if it is to be heard, as Miriam Zukas observes (1997). This is quite remarkable, given that on some estimations 90 per cent of participants in popular education programmes are women. The failure to be heard is probably not un-related to the fairly mundane fact that the vast majority of published theory which informs work in adult and continuing education (like most other fields of study) is produced by a small elite of usually (though not exclusively) white university based men. Despite its marginal status (maybe even because of it) theory here is becoming increasingly abstract and subject to academic fashions and power struggles. And, of course, those who traditionally have power (and time) to write books and define what is to count as worthwhile knowledge tend to assume that their audience is pretty much like themselves. Building on this assumption – of shared, but actually very culturally specific experience – effectively keeps most others out of the conversation (1).

The dearth of publications is also partly due to the fact that women working in feminist women's adult education in the 1970s and 1980s, in programmes designed by feminist women for women (see below), have themselves largely failed to document this work. The reasons are understandable. Most of it took place outside the formal sector and in the least well resourced adult education sector (the WEA, local authority-provided and extra mural provision) and was carried out by part-time tutors with little time or resources to write and theorise about their work. Most of the material which emerged from the work was practical, including the manuals and tutor workbooks already referred to. This particular gap was partly remedied in a series of pamphlets produced by the WEA's Women's Educational Advisory Committee during the 1980s. By documenting some of the work in women's education/women's studies over the past decade, this series, *Breaking Our Silence*, not only challenged prevailing forms of adult education provision (for men as well as women); it also challenged prevailing research methodologies. In its accounts of women's education, it rejected academic research in favour of involving students themselves in the research; and in so doing it offered a useful example of how the practice of women's education can be linked to the development of feminist theory (see especially, Aird, 1985, Marshall, 1984; see also Taking Liberties Collective 1989). The series is now out of print and this whole body of work is in danger of becoming part of our forgotten memory as adult educators.

I want to partially remedy this here. That period marked me. It also marked an historical moment when a new space for 'naming the world' was in fact carved out and when many and varied (feminist inspired) groups co-existed in relatively harmonious tension with one another. Towards the end of this period (whose significance as well as consequences can, of course, only be judged with hindsight), Jane Thompson, quoting Pam Annas, was to write that women's studies had by then made the transition from a 'precarious' to a 'permanent marginality' (Thompson, 1983). Thompson also stressed that women's studies did not arise simply through a rational awareness of sexism in existing bodies of knowledge but was brought into existence by political movements which continue to struggle for legitimacy.

I want to outline some of the main features of this moment as I see it, before moving the narrative on to 'becoming an adult educator'. I do so because of the dearth of research already noted and because it offers models of adult education and research which emphasise the creation of new knowledge and which challenge, rather than just reproduce, existing theories. This is a theme which – as I suggest above – is also being played out (in a highly abstract way) in recent academic writing in 'feminist epistemology'. This, too, is the theme of the recent collection of essays edited by Walters and Manicom, referred to above. While not downplaying the importance of theory – indeed the book is a clarion call for good theory which connects with and illuminates people's lives – it is primarily a book of stories. Fourteen women from different parts of the world reflect on their experiences as feminist popular educators. In the process, they engage with issues of theory and practice in ways which challenge dominant modes of theorising, defy conventional scientific paradigms of social research and act as an antedote to the self-confident, abstract tone of much of the literature of popular and 'critical' education (Apple, 1993; Giroux and McLaren, 1994). In structure and content the book assumes a readership characterised by complex subjectivities and certainly by much more than abstract rationality.

The origins of women's studies in Britain

First and foremost, women's studies was the direct consequence of the re-emergence of feminism and the development of the Women's Liberation Movement, which was a seedbed of many educational activities – study-groups, conferences, newsletters, consciousness-raising. It developed primarily as a strategy for social change, specifically aimed at ending women's oppression. Significantly, while in the USA the strongest women's studies networks were developed in Higher Education, in Britain, to a significant degree, women's studies grew up and acquired its distinctive methods and approaches in Adult Education (see McNeill, 1987), that is to say, in the least well-resourced, most marginal sector of education and the only sector where women were in the majority. Nell Keddie has described British Adult Education (as it was then) as a women's education service, studented by women, serviced by women – and run by men (Keddie, 1981).

Adult education, before the sweeping changes of the past 15 to 20 years, seemed to many British feminists in the 1970s and early 1980s to be a fruitful place for the creation of spaces in which groups of women could 'name the world' in their own terms. Many feminists, inspired by the educational developments of the Women's Liberation Movement – its study groups, conferences, consciousness-raising – were attracted into adult education (the WEA, University Extra-Mural Departments, Local Authority Adult Education) by its rhetoric of empowerment and by its non-hierarchical organisation. Adult education's involvement in social change provided a space for tutors to experiment and develop, helped by being removed from the disciplinary policing of academic boundaries, academic objectivity and intellectualism of the university. The moral and political ground occupied by adult education in the 1970s and, to a degree, the early 1980s (see Westwood and Thomas, 1992) made it possible to have and occasionally win the argument for resources (see O'Rourke and Croft, 1994).

The argument for the development of women's education in the 1970s was certainly hard won, and other reasons (besides a social change/justice agenda) lay behind its development: quite simply, there was a market for it. Moreover, within adult education organisations, the argument was not won primarily on a radical agenda of social change. One tutor who played a central role in political lobbying for resources for women's education within the WEA in the 1970s comments:

> We didn't really win the argument. Or at least, we've always won it on a liberal compromise. We've always tried to ride two horses at once. I kept wanting not to allow into the debate notions of 'disadvantage'. You can't carry this idea and the idea of serious, structural inequalities of power. You can't deal with the latter as if it was the former. And we've never tried the other alternative hard enough. We didn't in fact win the argument, yet work in women's studies was able to go simply because the WEA needed it. Where else were the new students to come from?
>
> (Sue Gardener, pers. com.)

However, in the 1970s, small groups of feminists exploited the rhetoric of adult education to establish a base for women's studies and for different kinds of women's education from the usual diet of, on the one hand, subjects related to their domestic role and on the other 'selective admission to a system of knowledge which is defined, theorised, and controlled by men' (Blundell, 1992, p 200). I think that this flowering of women's studies and women's education can be seen as a clear example of the growth of new 'epistemological communities', engaged in the creation of new knowledge (Nelson, 1990, 1993). The hybrid term, 'women's studies/women's education', was often used. This signalled a central feature of the development, namely, that it was not purely the creation of academic critique. On the contrary, it was diverse, changing, and multifaceted, concerned as much with the processes and institutional trappings of education – creches, context and timetabling – as with its content and pedagogy.

Adult women's education/women's studies had many of the features of a popular education movement. Influenced by different feminisms, much of it took place in local neighbourhoods; alliances were built between working class communities and community groups and with the Women's Health, Trades Union and Peace Movements, as well as with the wider women's movement. A key element of this popular women's education movement was autonomous black and Asian women's groups which had formed to oppose specific kinds of oppression being faced by different categories of black women, and to challenge racism within the broader Women's Liberation Movement.

Women's education and really useful knowledge

To give some examples from my own experience of such educational projects, the WEA Trade Union and Basic Education Project in Manchester, consisted of groups of Indian, Pakistani and Afro-Caribbean women discussing together their different and common experiences of colonialism. In doing so, they arrived at new understandings which went beyond the sum total of the knowledge and experiences of individual members – and that contained in books (see Barr, 1984, 1991). Women's education groups – which met in various community centres and unemployed workers centres in very deprived housing schemes throughout Glasgow (under the auspices of the WEA) formed a joint action group which resulted in the first locally based women's centre in the country. In another development, a group of Asian women (Indian and Pakistani mainly), having taken an English language course, took part in a cultural exchange with other adult education groups based on their writings about early childhood. And in Northern Ireland, groups of Protestant and Catholic women developed new knowledge and insights about the workings of sectarianism. Some of this work led to publications, conferences and, generally, to a circulation of ideas which challenged official knowledge.

Learning through active engagement with groups has been central to feminist pedagogic practice. Through consciousness-raising groups, women (ideally) shared understandings and learned both to respect each other's knowledge and to construct their own. They 'made visible what had been rendered invisible' (Luttrell, 1989). Most such groups were fairly general; some focused on 'specialist' areas such as health – or science (see Brighton Women and Science Group, 1980). Self-help health groups, in particular, produced a kind of knowledge about medical phenomena different from that provided by medical science and experts – knowledge and skills which drew on women's own experiences and needs (see Bell, 1994; McNeill, 1987). They, alongside environmental and third world science movements, have pointed the way to how lay people have actively participated in constructing really useful knowledge around science (Shiva, 1989).

Women's education as it developed in adult education thus challenged, in concrete, practical ways, the notion of disembodied knowledge, recognising that knowledge is not neutral but always socially situated: there is no 'God's eye view', no 'knowledge from nowhere' (Haraway, 1989). By taking an explicitly partisan approach to knowledge it re-valued the place of experience in its generation and positioned 'the learner' in an active role (O'Rourke, 1995). It was, in short, a thoroughly political process which self-consciously acknowledged the need for gender politics in adult education and feminist politics in knowledge production (see McNeill, 1987).

Questions concerning the relationship between theory and practice were to the fore – 'Who and what is adult education for?' 'What is really useful knowledge?'. It was fired by a belief in the possibility of personal and social change.

And the capacity to engage in self-critique, to challenge usually taken-for-granted ways of feeling and thinking and the source of these in social organisations and relations was a central assumption of the collective sharing and analyses of experience which was a feature of groups and which they shared with the consciousness-raising groups of the women's movement. Feminist popular adult educators in Latin America still work actively to integrate the emotions, intellect, body and spirit – all seen as integral to 'conscientization', using story-telling, human sculpture and play as well as more recognisably educational practices (Walters and Manicom, 1996).

Throughout most of the 1980s I was one of only two female District Secretaries in the WEA – the chief executive role in the WEA's organisational structure of 21 Districts – and my District already had an established tradition of women's education. This stretched back to Jean McCrindle's collaborative work with the Co-operative Movement in the 1960s and her pionneering 'women's studies' classes held in the afternoons for working class women in Lanarkshire (although they were not so named at the time). These classes even provided childcare – an aspect of provision which was not enshrined in WEA national policy until some years later (see Miller, 1978).

From the mid 1970s, women's studies courses were mounted by the District in Areas for Priority Treatment (APTs) in Glasgow using money released by the new Strathclyde Region in line with its social deprivation strategy. The Alexander Report (1975) on non-vocational adult education also encouraged the WEA to develop work with disadvantaged groups in deprived areas. The neighbourhood-based educational programmes for working class women which were made possible by these financial and political encouragements differed greatly from the clandestine variety with which I was to take issue (see below). They were developed by tutors who were also involved in the women's movement in the West of Scotland at the time. These tutors drew many of their ideas and educational practices from their experiences in the campaigning and consciousness-raising groups which were active at that time and from the workshop-based conferences which were then a fairly regular feature of feminists' lives.

It was women's education/women's studies not 'education for the disadvantaged' in which they were engaged. And it was a form of women's education which was defined as much in terms of class as gender. Groups focused on themes – the family, welfare, employment, sexuality for example; curricula developed out of the women's own lives – making connection with literature, the law, social and historical studies as and when required. The aim of such discussion groups was, broadly speaking, to examine the shared condition of being women, an examination arising out of but moving beyond the context of the women's own lives. I think this community-within-a-city context within which women's education grew up in the WEA in Glasgow and the West of Scotland was important. This can be illustrated by means of an example: concurrently, the recovery of women's history as part of 'people's history' was being attempted by feminists, mainly in England, within the History Workshop Movement whose journal, *History Workshop Journal*, founded in 1976, presupposed an adult education context (indeed, the adult working class learner was the preferred reader addressed by the journal). However, that reader was almost invariably assumed to be male; and, further, the Marxist theory of the journal did not require either women's history or feminism as central components. As Terry Lovell has observed: 'Marxism permits feminist history, but without necessarily permitting it to make a difference' (Lovell, 1990, p 25).

In contrast with this, in Glasgow, slightly later (the late 1970s) a Glasgow Women's Studies Group was established as a workshop which linked together academic feminists, grassroots feminists and women's networks in peripheral housing schemes in Glasgow. Glasgow's WEA tutor-organiser was central to its work. By setting its own terms from the outset the Group was able to research and produce a book on past and contemporary history of women in Scotland which, in looking at history from the point of view of (mainly working class) women's lives, did not feel in any way compelled to construct 'women's history' as a sub-plot within the real thing.

On the contrary, the publication, *Uncharted Lives* (now out of print), showed, first, that a proper understanding of history demands an analysis of gender divisions; second, that exclusive concern with the 'domestic labour' debate is insufficient to understand women's lives; and third, from the standpoint of women's lives, new definitions of politics, too, can emerge. Yet, as the WEA tutor organiser who contributed to the book observes: 'When women discuss "the treatment you get from the doctor these days", "waiting for operations", "damp in the back bedroom" and "the price of a loaf", they are more likely to be perceived as immersed in idle gossip rather than political comment. The trade union member who complains of "treatment from supervisors", "fumes in the paint shop", "cold on the shop floor" and "cuts in wages" is viewed rather differently' (Phillips, 1983, p 133).

The original aims of women's education in the West of Scotland District of the WEA in the 1970s (as reflected in District Annual Reports of the time and in later writings of the then tutor organiser in Glasgow) were consciously to do with empowering women. The assumption was that through increased knowledge and critical reflection women would be better placed to make more choices in their personal lives; through coming together to discuss their shared concerns and to make connections between their own lives and social, economic and political conditions they might become part of a movement for social as well as individual change.

Personal experience was central but 'sharing experiences' was not the point and purpose. Ideally, dialogue rather than simply discussion was the point (see Allman, 1987). People involved in discussion share knowledge they already have; often this is a series of monologues where each person expresses their views. Those involved in dialogue help each other examine their understandings of the world, develop more complex understandings and, through identifying and clarifying problems and new questions to be asked, thereby create knowledge.

One of the first video series on women, *Women in Focus*, was made by the WEA with women in the Vale of Leven. This concentrated on work, childcare and images of women and became a resource for women's studies throughout the country. I have already said that a major problem with this kind of informal educational work, so far as building towards something substantial, repeatable and improvable is concerned, is that it is seldom documented or written about. Another important feature of this work in the West of Scotland District of the WEA was women's dayschools which were organised to bring women together from different areas. These day schools generated many of the groups with which the District worked for the remainder of the 1970s. 'Awaydays' were then started – whole groups or members of different groups going to a residential adult education college in the country for whole day or weekend workshops. Most groups met in large housing schemes – in nursery schools, community centres (and later, unemployed workers centres and 'family centres'). From being initially discussion groups, some developed into drama groups or writers and readers groups; some provided a stepping stone into other forms of education and qualifications or into various forms of community and political action.

The new professionalism

By the mid 1980s there was a growth in self-defence courses and in practically focused courses in, for example, women's health and assertiveness training – reflecting the growing trend towards finding private and personal solutions to what were largely public and political problems. By this time, with a few exceptions, the social change-coupled-with-personal development agenda of this work had given way to personal development goals. Tutors began requesting training in counselling skills and I remember worrying that the educational point of the tutors' work was becoming subordinated to a counselling role and that relationships based on solidarity, trust and friendship were in danger of being replaced by professionalised notions of counselling.

Counselling had indeed become institutionalised in Britain in the 1980s, in health and social services as well as education. The growing faith in counsellors coincided with a waning of belief in politics and social movements as forces for change. Some commentators suggested that it signified a new strategy for social control – a means of achieving discipline through self-discipline (see Fairclough, 1989; Foucault, 1979). And feminism itself fragmented, with 'therapeutic' and 'cultural' feminism taking greater hold. Thatcherism effectively forced the most political forms of British feminism – socialist and radical feminism – underground.

Now, in the late 1990s, there is very little of the radical kind of women's education left and few written testimonies to it exist. Women's studies as a field of academic study is now fairly well entrenched in the academy but it has tenuous and often incidental links with grassroots feminist politics. The demands of 'professionalism' are powerful for all academics – including feminists. Tensions have developed between women's studies (explicitly feminist, with its distinctive methodology and subject areas) and women's education, masking the latter's feminist antecedents and increasingly concentrating on assertiveness-training, access, new opportunities and vocational preparation courses (see O'Rourke and Croft, 1994). The two strands which used to co-exist in adult

education – women's studies and women's education – provided feminist scholarship more generally with a dynamic intellectual community which was not
primarily academic but was constituted by a much wider educational, cultural
and political project. Crucially, this was defined – to a significant degree – by
pressures from 'below', rather than by educational priorities set from 'above'.

With hindsight it is to that period and experience that I owe my self-
definition as an adult educator, as, that is, a cultural worker, concerned primarily with the business of the production and reproduction of knowledge. Not a
'counsellor', 'trainer', 'human resource developer' or 'learning needs meeter' or
any other of the favoured self-categorisations dreamed up in the last decade by
those involved in adult learning. Issues of curriculum; who owns knowledge
and the social arrangements through which knowledge is developed and legitimated are my primary concerns.

That, too, is the central concern of what has come to be known as the
'epistemological debate' which has been underway within theoretical feminism
for the last decade (see Rose, 1994; and Chapters 8 and 9). A basic aim of that
debate is to contribute to the expansion of democracy in the production of
knowledge; and its basic premise is that knowledge(s) should be useful to those
who produce it. But that dialogue about knowledge has so far been conducted
at a highly abstract level, among a small group of feminist women academics
and scholars. It is, however, implicit in this dialogue that there will be little
progress towards the goal of 'really useful knowledge' until such abstract debates
about knowledge are brought down to earth and practical spaces opened up for
democratic knowledge-making:

> If we wish to empower diverse voices, we would do better . . . to
> shift strategy . . . to the messier, more slippery, practical struggle to
> create institutions and communities that will not permit some
> groups of people to make determinations about reality for all.
>
> (Bordo, 1990, p 142)

It is precisely such a practical space for the democratic development of knowledge which, I am suggesting, was opened up by women's education/women's
studies as this developed within British adult education during the 1970s and
early 1980s. Central to it was an emphasis on women as agents of knowledge;
so, too, was the insight that what we learn is influenced by how we learn.

What I now regard as having been particularly important for me from
those experiences involved learning a new notion of 'rigour'. The kind of rigour
which infused women's education/women's studies was the opposite of the safe
self-censoring (and always ready to censor) puritanism I learned from my philosophy training, according to which the right to speak seemed to require the
assertion of oneself as a kind of super-consciousness with an overview of everything that had been thought or written up until now. In the sort of women's
education I have described, on the contrary, everything is brought in (life stories, jokes, dreams, improvisations, free writing, group poems) to undo the
often prohibitive learning which many girls and women have acquired from
their past educational experiences.

Such prohibitions on girls are often indirect, conveyed in a tone of voice as much as in what is explicitly said; and they are emotionally charged. As such, they act as a force which 'unsettles our understanding', says the philosopher Michele Le Doeuff who, as a schoolgirl, came across a work of Kant. Overwhelmed by it and wanting more, she asked her teacher where she might get a copy of Kant's *Critique of Pure Reason*: It was, she was told, in word and gesture, 'much too hard' for her. That such 'prohibitions' continue to unsettle our understanding in later life seems borne out by the fact that this professional philosopher still has not read it (Le Doeuff, 1991, pp 142–47).

Becoming an adult educator: Education as ordinary

In the remainder of this chapter I concentrate on the middle period of the chronology sketched out in Chapter 2, when I was, that is, becoming an adult educator. That self-definition impinged on the research which figures in my second and third case studies. When I was involved in Headway on the other hand (first case study) I did not see myself as an adult educator by any means, but as a feminist academic (quite philosophical) sociologist. I offer here a sketch of the development of my adherence to a radical agenda for adult education and adult education research, particularly in relation to womens's adult education. This agenda puts the emphasis on the development of 'really useful knowledge' through the articulation of problems, interests and desires with people other than academics. That conviction has arisen primarily out of my involvement in women's education as I have already said. But it also owes a lot to my wider (overlapping) experiences in the WEA and to my engagement with international movements in adult education, primarily through the International League for Social Commitment in Adult Education (ILSCAE) which taught me that some of the best, most sustaining learning we do does not require a shared language.

It was through ILSCAE's activities that I came to see myself as part of an international educational movement, and that to make a contribution to struggles for social justice, the work of adult educators has to move beyond isolated pockets and classes to becoming a dimension of the work of wider social movements – working class, women's, disabled, environmental. Through conferences, workshops and study circles in ILSCAE, I learned about popular education in Latin America in the 1960s and 1970s; about the educational work of Chilean educators in exile and, through this, of the political street theatre of Augusto Boal and the potential of drama and song to provide a more celebratory and joyful dimension to adult learning. Through John Benseman, an inspirational adult educator from New Zealand, I began to incorporate Maori social rituals into some of my classes.

I learned too about education in social action in Zimbabwe and South Africa; about Aboriginal adult education work in Australia; and about Folk High Schools in Scandinavian countries. I was introduced to the work of Myles Horton and the Highlander Folk School in the American South where education has been provided for trades unionists, civil rights workers, unemployed activists, women's groups and environmental activists for over 60 years. It was here that I came to understand the meaning of 'dialogue' as an educational method and that the basic starting point for any democratic education is a deep respect for learners' life experiences – to 'start from where they are' and to discover with them 'where it's worth going'.

In Horton's words:

> One of the things we have to do . . . is to learn how to relate our experience to theirs and you do that by analogy, you do that by storytelling. You don't get off and say: 'Look, here are some facts we're going to dump on you'. We say: 'Oh you might consider this. Now this happened to someone kinda like you in a different situation.' So we get them to do the same thing, with each other – get peer teaching going.
>
> (Myles Horton, quoted in Foley, 1995, p 49)

The tutors and tutor-organisers with whom I worked in the West of Scotland WEA knew that the people with whom they worked in the most deprived areas of Glasgow and other places would have fled at the first hint of condescension. They recognised the inevitable invasiveness of their work in areas where people were used to having a 'cavalry of community workers' sent in instead of jobs (see Chapter 4); they knew too – and were so inclined – that their efforts to support and provide learning resources for learners which would challenge and extend them had to be based on relations of solidarity, not patronage (Foley 1995; Head, 1977; Miller, 1987).

Another important influence on how I came to see myself as an adult educator was Raymond Williams. To mis-quote him, Williams believed that 'education is ordinary', that it is, before everything else, 'the process of giving to the ordinary members of society its full common meanings, and the skills that enable them to amend these meanings in the light of their personal and common experience'. The 'test of cultural seriousness' is whether we can redefine and rethink the content of education 'to the point of full human relevance and control'. Williams defined himself as a cultural worker whose work as a tutor in the WEA had to be judged in terms of its contribution to the creation of an educated and participatory democracy. (Williams, 1993, pp 98–9).

Such a vision, in its simplicity, clarity and stress on commonality may seem out of step with postmodern celebrations of difference; and Williams' notion of 'full human relevance' does suffer from unconscious gender blindness in equating human with male experience (a criticism levelled by feminists against most of adult education's 'founding fathers'). His ideal of a common culture is certainly more common to some people than others as Julia Fenton suggests (Fenton, 1997). Paul Gilroy maintains, too, that there are even traces of a 'morbid celebration of England and Englishness' in his work (see Gilroy, 1987).

Nevertheless, those of us who have chosen adult education as their field (rather than fallen into it by accident – although, for myself, it was the result of both) would agree that the central passion which is the groundspring of Williams' work is the same motivating force behind their own. They will want to replace a pedagogy, in which the concept of 'catching up' is the key idea –

with a pedagogy through politics, in which public debate on matters of concern to citizens and the democratic development of learning and knowledge, are central (Griffin, 1983; Le Doeuff, 1991).

Becoming an adult educator: History and biography

The period of women's education which I described in the first part of this chapter pre-dated and overlapped with my employment as District Secretary of the West of Scotland District of the WEA (between 1982 and 1989). For most of this period I was concerned less with teaching and research than with matters of policy and management.

At the time I undertook the Headway evaluation – before joining the WEA – little or no research had been done on adult community education in Scotland. I was later to write about this in a journal article. The central argument of the article was that since the Alexander Report was published in 1975 adult education in Scotland had been subsumed under the general heading of 'community education' which had led to its virtual disappearance as a distinct service with its own policies and resources, and to the provision of 'adult education by stealth'. My area of responsibility at that time included the huge Strathclyde Region whose 'Social Strategy', coupled with the Government-sponsored Alexander Report had encouraged a 'community development' approach to adult education in Areas of Priority Treatment (APTs) since the mid 1970s.

As a result of this policy, I wrote, 'the vast bulk of the "educational" work which is undertaken by working class people, particularly women, remains hidden from view, unrecorded in the statistics and seldom the subject of systematic research, appraisal or evaluation' (Barr, 1987). In the article I refer to Jane Thompson's scathing indictment of adult education of the 'low profile' variety introduced by stealth into community centres, mothers and toddlers groups and gatherings of women on housing estates and where significance is attached more to the women's influence on their children's or community's development than to the needs of the women themselves for their own intellectual or creative progress:

> Slipped in between the afternoon cuppa and the organisation of
> the jumble sale . . . fearful of being seen to be serious and as a
> result failing to take seriously the educational needs of the women
> involved.
>
> (Thompson, 1980)

The dearth of research in this area largely continues, although there have been two studies (Alexander *et al.*, 1984; Highet, 1991) which reach similar conclusions to my own. Alexander *et al.* conclude from their research on community education in a number of local authorities in Scotland that much community education for the 'disadvantaged' – the vast majority of which involves women, although not by design (see Tett, 1995) – sells people short by concentrating on 'life adjustment skills and diminished cognitive content'. And Highet, in her study of the ideology and practice of informal community-based women's education in Glasgow, criticises three of the four projects examined on the grounds that they contributed to 'the socialisation of women into accepting differential societal roles' (Highet, 1992, p 155; see also Barr *et al.*, 1996).

When I became District Secretary of the WEA in 1982 one item high on my agenda was to try to do something about the sort of 'ghetto mentality' which seemed to be being encouraged by the Region's funding policies. Funding (including Urban Aid) for adult education was increasingly being tied to very specific geographical areas: local groups, communities (and WEA staff) competed with each other for cash. To counteract this we put in place structures and processes which would connect together groups and individuals in different areas and, in addition, encouraged the development of courses and conferences in which class, gender, culture and race were central organising themes and principles. Another top priority was to develop policies and practices in the District which would counter the kind of apologetic education for women which I believed to be prevalent in community-based schemes.

My experience of evaluating Headway was formative in all of this (see next chapter). It contributed to my contempt for adult community education in which education is downgraded or not even mentioned and it helped consolidate my passionate commitment to a type of adult community education whose role is not to 'facilitate' and contain but to help people engage in critical analysis (see Barr, 1984 and 1987). It is to that critical period that I now turn – the first of my case studies.

4 Adult education by stealth

In which a socialist-feminist, ex-lecturer in Sociology and the
Philosophy of the Social Sciences finds herself evaluating a pre-
school community project in a working-class area of Glasgow . . .

Background to the research

Between 1979 and 1981 I was employed as an evaluator of a pre-school community project ('Headway') run by the playgroup movement in an Area for
Priority Treatment in Glasgow. I had just relinquished a lectureship in sociology and philosophy of the social sciences in the belief that I ought to undertake
empirical research. This I hoped would serve as an antedote (as I saw it) to the
excessive theoreticism of sociology (and myself) and at the same time engage
me in work which was relevant to my socialist feminist aspirations. I wanted
especially an opportunity to 'apply' methodological principles with which I had
so far grappled only theoretically. These principles derived from a new 'critical
social science' paradigm which was emerging at the time in opposition to both
'positivist' and 'interpretative' traditions in sociology (see, eg Bhaskar, 1973;
Fay, 1975; Keat and Urry, 1975; and Chapter 2).

Throughout the 1970s, as I have already indicated, I was involved in a
number of single issue campaigns in the Women's Liberation Movement and
heavily involved in an 'alternative' newspaper which was produced from the
spare room in my house. I was very much committed to social progress through
social reform and practically immersed in such political work (although I really
thought a Marxist feminist revolution was necessary – and, indeed, possible – if
deep change were to take place). I also taught the nascent Women's Studies
which was beginning to filter into Sociology and at the same time lent my
support to feminist-inspired women's education being undertaken in Glasgow
housing schemes by the Workers Educational Association. These were heady
(and exhausting) times; we thought we had right on our side and people were
judged to be 'in' or 'out' depending on their views on whether or not they
thought Russia was a 'state capitalist' or genuinely socialist society.

As a member of the National Childcare Campaign, a feminist organisation
committed to universal pre-school provision, I believed that the ideological glo-
rification of motherhood existed alongside actual social and economic discrimination and that the absence of decent childcare provision acted as both cause
and consequence of the second class status shared by women and children. I

believed too that the outlook for the extension or even maintenance of current childcare facilities was, under the newly elected Margaret Thatcher-led Government, dismal (despite an earlier promise from her, as a Minister, that every five-year-old would have a nursery place). No other European country had such an abysmal record in pre-school provision, as several research reports had clearly demonstrated.

I suspected that one of the reasons for this might lie partly in what has been described as a 'uniquely British disadvantage' – playgroups. The playgroup philosophy leaned heavily on the concept of 'maternal deprivation', derived from a particular reading of Bowlby's work which was in vogue in the 1950s, and according to which even short periods of time away from their one mother figure on a regular basis are damaging to young children. Such theories, I believed, had helped successive governments avoid addressing the issue of care for the children of working mothers. Critical assessments of Bowlby's theory by other researchers in child development had no apparent effect on Government policy – the provision made for children appearing to be determined less by concern for their understood needs and requirements than by still pervasive ideologies concerning motherhood, the family and welfare.

I believed, too, that at a time of cutbacks such ideologies had particularly disastrous consequences for children and for women and that instead of feeling angry – as they should – women often felt guilty instead. Believing that there was an urgent requirement for a radical re-shaping of policy in the pre-school field and, consequently, a need for energetic public debate on issues surrounding childcare, I seized on the advertised pre-school evaluation project job as an opportunity to contribute to this debate and development of policy.

My evaluation was to form part of a national study of pre-school provision commissioned by the SSRC in 1979 and described by the SSRC's Working Party on Pre-school Education as 'an information-gathering exercise to remedy the lack of objective feedback on current programmes and practices'. The Pre-school Evaluation Project (PEP) was an outcome of official concern in the late 1970s to find low-cost alternatives to state-financed care and education for under-fives. It was recognised that widespread expansion of provision for the under-fives was likely to prove costly. There was therefore an interest in comparing low cost voluntary provision with more expensive statutory services.

It was envisaged by the SSRC Working Party that the findings from PEP, in addition to providing feedback to fieldworkers, would be widely disseminated and that the schemes, if favourably evaluated, might be replicated in other parts of the country, In the course of a feasibility study the research director selected fourteen established schemes for possible evaluation. Four evaluators were appointed, based in London, Glasgow, Southampton and Bradford and for practical purposes the number of schemes for study was reduced to nine.

The four evaluators were responsible for drawing up their own evaluation research designs under the general coordination of the research director. Team meetings were held quarterly to discuss progress. During the planning stages of the research a number of problems arose, centred on the question of values. The evaluation project – as can be seen from the above SSRC Working Party quote – was conceived in the 'neutral' tradition of research. Yet in reality particular values were implicit in the criteria used to select schemes, schemes which were explicitly defined from the outset in the feasibility study as cases of 'good practic' and innovation. This might be seen as loading the dice against the possibility of negative findings and it implicitly discourages critically examining the schemes' own objectives and assumptions. At least, that is how three of the four evaluators interpreted the situation. Three of us, that is, believed that the schemes should not simply be evaluated in their own terms, because of the highly controversial nature of preschool provision as an area of social policy. Appealing to Michael Scriven's writing on evaluation I insisted that 'if it is to have any reference to goals at all . . . evaluation proper must include evaluation of the goals'.

The project director saw the main task of PEP as demanding evaluations of the various projects in terms of their own objectives; the three of us felt that the projects had to be scrutinised from the point of view of the theoretical and ideological assumptions underpinning them. That such scrutiny had to be from some other point of view was not something which I or the others explicitly acknowledged. This now seems bizarre and somewhat forgetful, given my (then as now) theoretical rejection of the possibility of 'value neutrality' in research.

I was however clear about one thing: that studies of preschool provision, like preschool provision itself, cannot be divorced from the social and political context of their production. It seemed obvious to me that one of the main hoped for outcomes of PEP was to be able to present a range of mainly low-cost options to politicians and policy makers at local and national level: it followed that to question the objectives of the schemes was to challenge political orthodoxies and the expectations of the funders. It was also to risk seeing the findings of the substantially funded evaluation project dismissed or ignored. The Project Director wanted the evaluators to adopt a 'utilization focused' approach which would examine projects from the point of view of their utility to the various interested parties involved (funders and politicians mainly). I decided to adopt an 'illuminative evaluation' approach, examining the project from the point of view of its various participants but (because I spurned value neutrality) dismissing as naive the notion of the evaluator as 'honest broker' (MacDonald and Parlett, 1973).

I decided to immerse myself in Headway and to 'progressively focus' on themes which emerged in the course of this immersion. I decided to use a combination of methods: documentary analysis; participant observation of the process of the project, including attendance at various project meetings; semi-structured interviews with project leaders and participants as well as with members of the local area. Thirty-five 'uninvolved' families were selected for interview, as were a number of local community development workers, social workers and other local workers, including nursery school staff; in addition to one-to-one interviews, fairly impromptu group discussions were held with project participants to tease out the meanings and significance of the project for them.

Few traces of the research process remain. I have no archive in which to delve. Various changes of job and house moves meant that I ditched all of the notebooks and diaries in which, as the research progressed, I recorded daily plans and events as well as personal reflections, thoughts and feelings. I am left with only one fragment, a yellow scrap of paper which is headed 'Team Meeting, Bristol, 6/3/80' and consists of my own scrawled preparatory notes for the meeting and a few other notes in shakier handwriting (subsequently penned, possibly on the train going back home).

The notes suggest some of the (relational and conceptual) tensions involved in the research process and provide a clue to the state of my mind at the time. Listed on my notes to report to the meeting is the following:

> *Feedback – How much and with whom? Suspiciousness of M and J [SPPA project leaders] Have expectations which aren't being met by me. Links with question of control – meetings with SPPA to discuss evaluation periodically. Question of relevance. How an evaluation is affected by worldview of project designers and practitioners – no distance between – how I conduct eval has to fit in with their project ie treat people as they do – mothers as 'groupies' etc – name of game is 'participation' (that I have a different notion of what this means) I prefer to approach them as individuals not as mothers or groups at different 'stages' of development. Each time I've been other than a fly on the wall or a sympathetic ear all hell is let loose.*

My subsequently scrawled notes to myself include the following fragment:

> *Question of common theoretical approach/framework puzzles me – my more macro concerns difficult to reconcile with concentration on subjective values – feel need to link w. wider processes and view as ideological.*

None of this doubt and uncertainty appeared in the evaluation report which I produced in January 1981.

The evaluation report

The remainder of this chapter consists of extracts from this evaluation report. In Chapter 5 I will 'deconstruct' the report. The idea is that by viewing the research product as 'data' I may learn something about my own evasions and (self) deceptions as well as about other contingencies of its production. It may well be that: 'Interpretation reveals the interpreting self much more than the world it seeks to explain' (Stronach, 1989, p 26).

The only change to the original evaluation is in the names of the project, the area in which it is housed and the names of all participants and interviewees for the simple reason that I have not sought permission to use the evaluation in this book. An ellipsis indicates where I have edited – omitted – sections of the report for reasons of space.

Headway Pre-school
and Community project – 1981

Introduction

Headway is a community-based project for under-fives, set up by the Scottish Pre-school Playgroup Association in some of Strathclyde's poorest working class areas. Funded by Urban Aid, the project is an attempt by SPPA to show that a family-based approach to pre-school provision is appropriate in such areas. The objectives of the project (paraphrased here from the Urban Aid submission) are:

1   to establish local projects where the aim is to encourage mothers to play a responsible part in the development of their under-fives through creating community groups concerned with the play and care of young children and to enable parents to gain confidence in skills as parents and as responsible members of the community
2   to help the development of community organised groups eg mother and toddler groups, playgroups, lending libraries
3   to find ways in which the needs of pre-school children can be provided for with parents involved in the process
4   to offer project leaders training to develop skills like knowledge of theory and practice of play and the ability to relate to workers concerned with other aspects of community development, education and social work
5   to contribute to the regeneration of communities, focusing in particular on young families and to encourage local leadership and self help . . .

In 1975, Strathclyde Region, the Local Authority which administers Glasgow, in which areas with the highest concentration of problems in the whole of Europe had been identified, selected 114 Areas of Priority Treatment. Although the number of such areas has fluctuated, the policy of the Region since then has been to concentrate resources in them. In practice this has meant trying to protect them from the effects of cuts by directing Urban Aid to them . . .

Prior to regionalisation, SPPA in Glasgow had received Urban Aid funds to pay for playleaders in 30 playgroups. This money was due to run out in 1977 and a radical rethink of its work in disadvantaged areas was necessary. In January 1977 an application for Urban Aid was submitted. Part of this submission was the proposal for the Headway Pre-school Community Project. It was to cover four areas in Glasgow, described in the submission as: 'areas where problem families and children are many . . . where parental responsibility for children can be minimal; where a dependent attitude of the adults on the help and support from the state is the norm; and where taking responsibility for their community is accepted by only one or two outstanding individuals' . . .

Underlying rationale . . .

Underpinning Headway there are various assumptions, stated and unstated theories and values. On the basis of a reading of background material, conversations with project leaders and other SPPA members, the following elements of its rationale have been drawn out. They are not exhaustive and most are related to some notion of 'needs' of children, parents and communities.

1   Parents should have a bigger say in the education of their children as a right. But:
2   Attitudes of dependence are prevalent in places like Lochend: attitudes bred through people's relation to the Welfare State and bureaucracy. A greater sense of responsibility can be developed according to the maxim 'Nothing breeds responsibility faster than experiencing it' although it cannot be achieved quickly and stepping stones have to be built towards it.
3   Communities like Lochend are 'adultcentred'. Many mothers cannot meet their children's needs because their own developmental needs were not met by their mothers when they were young. In order not to repeat the 'cycle' they have to learn different standards of childcare and, in addition, experience play of which they were deprived.
4   The needs of mothers and their children can be met together as the possibility of mutual growth exists for mothers and their under fives through SPPA's middle way: for, 'if mothers take part in the provision of play for their children . . . their own growth as individuals takes on a new impetus'.
5   If mothers are encouraged to hand over their children to professional child carers motherhood will represent just another failure for many. The role of project leader is to facilitate a process of growth towards a state of maturity whereby mothers will accept responsibility and become actively involved with their children. Although they may not want this to start with they cannot know what they want until they have experienced the alternative.
6   This approach will help stem family breakdown and so contribute towards the regeneration of the community.

There is, then, some talk about 'rights' but this is subordinate to the dominant frame of reference which concerns 'needs' and 'stages'. There is a definite tension between the democratic principle expressed in 1. above and the emphasis on changing what are seen as culturally induced attitudes and beliefs. Indeed, this was a source of a number of strains in the practical working of the project. Right from the start 'how do you put into their hands what's theirs and they don't want?' (project leader) the paradox involved in moving into an area to meet needs not voiced by the people themselves, needs which did not necessarily match the felt needs and wants of the people, did not go unnoticed . . .

Any interventionist project faces certain problems before it even starts. It brings with it its own theoretical background which may conflict with the realities of the situation; it may, for example, have a view of what people need which does not entirely match the felt needs of the particular area . . .

The community living in Lochend

Lochend is one of the 45 Areas for Priority Treatment which were singled out in 1976 by Strathclyde Region for 'positive discrimination'. With a population of around seven thousand, it is part of a larger scheme of interwar housing which resulted from a comprehensive redevelopment programme aimed at eliminating the notorious slums, but which also had the effect of breaking up working class communities.

Places like Lochend have now acquired their own notoriety, coming top of Europe's league table for multiple deprivation. The statistics which indicate high unemployment, a high incidence of 'problem families', single parent families and so on say nothing about the flora and fauna of the area: 'At one time there were more rats than people running through the closes. Beetles and cockroaches and wee white things that move like lightning in the bedroom.' A man went to the housing department to inquire about a particular mould growing on his walls. 'What would you say this is?' he asked. The official examining the sample said 'Mmn, I'd say it looks like orange peel.' 'In that case', the man said, 'You'd better put up my rates. I've got a f... orchard in my house.' A woman remarked, mock sorrowfully that all her mushrooms had died. Residents' opinions regarding the Headway project are divided between, at one extreme, the uncomplimentary remark made by one resident: 'Their heid's got a zipper up the back.' and other comments like 'It's the best thing that ever happened to Lochend.' And, not criticising the project but the Region's Strategy: 'We needed jobs and they sent in the cavalry of community workers.' . . .

Although the area is a working class community, it is clearly not homogeneous. No sense of class or community identity unites the people . . .

There is, however, one uniting factor – the lack of money. Poverty, or at least the threat of poverty, dominates most people's lives. All the other problems facing them are caused, or at least aggravated, by the lack of money.

Family life

In Lochend, despite high male unemployment, it is the women who are visible pushing prams, going shopping, queuing outside Social Security, Housing, Social Work Departments, visiting schools, taking children to the doctor's surgeries. As one local resident community worker said: 'Women run life totally here.' Women provide the ties binding extended families, which still exist in Lochend and which many regret having passed away in other areas. But more often than not in Lochend the extended family means grannies and aunties looking after children so that their other female relatives can work . . .

Women in areas like Lochend work, or would like to work, for several often intertwined reasons. Economic necessity is the most obvious, but economic independence is another. Margaret F. points out, that running a household is work and male unemployment can actually increase this workload. She explains her reasons for going out to work: 'There's no man's going to treat me as if he's keeping me. I've been told so often "I'm the breadwinner", I get mad. I've as much a job as he has and I've to spread the money out. At one time I had three men in the house, all unemployed. I was going daft. And I just told *him "You keep the house". After a week of it he agreed to give me more money. But now I'm going to get a job and get some money I can call my own.'*

Although the kind of work available to the women is often menial cleaning and factory jobs and often during the twilight shift, it does at least provide an element of social contact for women who might otherwise feel isolated. In fact, in some cases, there is practically no economic rationale for work, but it is still prized. One single mother, for example, continued to work in a bar two nights a week even although the combination of low pay and travelling expenses (by taxi, for safety) meant she was almost working at a loss.

When both parents do work, the cost in terms of family life can be high, and the woman, in particular, may have to accept work well below her qualifications.

Christine D works as a cleaner. She has to leave the house at 4 pm and a babysitter watches the three children for an hour until their father comes home. Christine gets back at 10 pm at night. She used to work as an office bookkeeper, but now, even if she could find an office job she doubts if she would have the confidence to cope with it. Mr and Mrs B both work full time. Together, they bring home £80. He works nights and looks after their two year-old and three year-old during the day. He sleeps most of the time.

Informal child care arrangements are common with a relative or neighbour and sometimes paid. Such arrangements often break down when the minder herself gets a job or when the practical logistics or strain of having two jobs, one at home and one outside, become too much for women. Despite a publicity campaign by Strathclyde Social Work Department there are no registered childminders in the area. This can mean a depressed single parent, Janet, who cannot herself get a place in the day nursery, looking after her neighbour's under fives as well as her own to enable the neighbour to work. Her own 2 year-old begins to stutter in the company of other adults and she feels she is 'sleeping her life away' and has 'no patience' with the child.

The nuclear family is not always kind to women or children in the area: Jean H: 'Until I had C (her youngest child) I always had black eyes. He'd bang me off the four walls. Until one night C got up and jumped on top of him when he had me on the floor. He got an awfie shock. He never did it in front of the children, you see.'

She, like other women in the area, invests heavily in motherhood: 'I've been told I look stupid without a pram. I go down the road now and I don't know what to do with my hands. I had a phantom pregnancy before I had the last one. I went the full nine months and the day I was due I went flat.'

Some women are not allowed out by their husbands, even to a women's night: ' "Who'd you rather go out with – them or me?" Often as not it's them but I cannae say that.' Some women walk out but come back because of the children. Others try a different tactic: 'I had his bags packed and he sits for two hours getting his shoes on. "My name's on the door," he says. So I says, "Well, take it with you and I'll get one wi' my name on it!".'

There is extensive use of tranquillizers, treating symptoms ranging from temporary boredom: 'If I get fed up I just get on my coat and go up the road to my mammie', to a state of almost clinical depression:

'I cannae see any future. I can't see how to survive here. I keep tae mysel'. The ceiling's falling doon, see? The kitchen's been flooded four times. I cannae take any mair. I'm in a big fortress with a big wall up, can ye understand? I'd be lost without E.'

Her three year old, E, has only one playmate: *'a lassie of 14 upstairs who insnae right'*. She keeps her in *'because of the stolen motors . . . they drive them around in the street and set fire tae them'*.

Mutual suspicion between families is fanned in some cases by fear of being *'shopped'* for working while on social security or, in the case of single parents, for having a man in . . .

Everything that could be called a childcare resource is filled to capacity and beyond in the area. The nursery school has a long waiting list as has the one day nursery which draws on Lochend. Recent letters in the local newspaper indicate a demand for more flexible provision . . .

Lack of suitable playspace both outside and inside homes is a major feature of life. There are no parks and many backgreens are unsuitable, containing in some parts, broken glass, burnt out cars and badly designed play equipment . . .

Characterising people in the area as having dependent attitudes and as lacking in responsibility for their children and community hardly squares with the lives and experiences of women in the area. Take three women, each of whom became progressively more involved in the project by different, but, in the end, similar routes.

Liz speaks of her children: *'Maist of the time it's them that counts. Maybe I'm just getting older. I've just resolved the only important thing in my life is my weans. It's all I'm interested in'*. She describes the birth of her first child and the state of her marriage:

> *'Then Jenny was born and she was beautiful . . . her lashes long and silky. They had tae cut me. It was a breech. I was stitched fae her tae here. I just said, "God, Liz, ye cannae even dae that right". When my husband came in he looked at her and said 'That's no mine . . .' He'd beat me up . . . no just bash . . . it wis feet, fists intae the stomach, face. I wis in the kitchen . . . he got me up against the wall, jumped on me and kicked me. Then I heard him clear his throat. Ye can take so much. And that wis it. I wis nothing, just his tae dae what he wanted with . . . When he finally left I just sat and cried and cried . . . just the relief. Jenny came up and said "Mummy I love you" and I said "I love you tae, hen. We'll make it all right".'*

Of work and dependence:

> *'I'd have worked if I could . . . I went tae the Security and they told me I couldnae work because the children were too young. I'd love tae get out and be independent and get off the Social . . . I'd an investigator in. I said if I'd a man wid I sit in this hovel? He looked about the hoose and asked how I got that and that. It's*

very degrading . . . But a job wid need tae be a full time one tae be worth it because the Social said I could only earn £6 so I couldnae get a job. Naebody wants ye at 40. So I've tae sit on the Social. I've thought of trying two jobs but it'd take everything oot of ye and ye'd have nae time for the weans.'

Helen, one of the area's 'weel kent faces', developed the cafe facilities in the neighbourhood centre part of the project . . .

In addition to the cafe, Helen had a job as a cleaner in the centre complex. So she worked from 6 am until late afternoon and was paid £21 in total, for her cleaning work. It is, she says, 'compulsory' now for women to work.

Regarded by leaders of the project as an inadequate, neglectful mother, who treats her husband badly, she speaks of her teenage daughter who refuses school: 'She's really screwed up. Three years ago she got attacked by six boys who're at the school. They stripped her . . . and . . . stood on her feet . . .'

Of her husband:

'He takes nae responsibility. He wis wrapped in cotton wool. I wis brought up strict. He'd just put money for the messages on the mantlepiece. Bills I'd never see. I thought he wis paying them. Then a man comes and says 'Right, you've got 28 days to pay'. By this time I'm cracked up completely. My mother died in February. I'd a miscarriage of twins and debts of £300 – £400 I'd nae idea aboot. And then he marched out. I didn't know what'd hit me . . . It wis just an existence day in day oot and work. I paid back the furniture money out of any wee job I could get. We're by that patch now. Now I've got some independence and it's taken years. It's made a difference. Now we sit and talk. But I'd every right tae treat him with the contempt he treated me with'.

Pat started her involvement in the project a few months after her mother died. She used to spend every day looking after her mother in her house, then back to her own house to look after her family. When her mother died: 'I just used to sit in the house. But I'm not in much now. My husband disnae mind me coming here [the project] but if I said I wis at Betty's say, I couldnae do that. There's no way I could get out on my own. Bingo's all right because it's a big crowd.'

She speaks of work, paid and unpaid and her husband's attitude to it:

'I didnae feed him for three months and didnae take money from him except to feed the kids. Once he asked for stew and paid for it. He widnae let me work when the weans were younger. I really wanted to, just to get out . . . even to clean up someone else's dirt. I wis a jack-of-all-trades after school. I was in a whisky factory for six years, packing, filling and wiring the cases. It wis a man's job. There wis naebody staundin over the top of ye. I'd like a job noo tae fit in with school but ye cannae get them. One wage isn't enough. I want tae gie them what I didn't get' . . .

Early contradictions

Headway speaks of 'contributing to the regeneration of communities' where others would speak of 'community development'. The subtle distinction perhaps marks the conscious dilemma which faced SPPA in 'moving into' areas to meet needs which the people themselves have not voiced. 'Regeneration' implies a process of indigenous growth from within, whereas 'community development' has connotations of an outside agency 'coming in' to actively make things happen and this does not square with SPPA's democratic impulses. In the area of interventionism where woolliness of phrase and vagueness of meaning are ubiquitous, rhetoric can sometimes provide a veil for contradictions or inconsistencies which are built in from the start but which are seldom consciously acknowledged. Sometimes they appear in the form of 'dilemmas' or 'double binds' in the practical applications of the theories and objectives.

Project leaders had to 'facilitate' the process of 'growth' on the part of the individuals and groups. Thus, in their view, members of the mothers' committee had to mature and learn how to function as a committee in order to understand the complexities of the situation facing them. This could mean that when women raised issues of concern to themselves they were deflected back to the objectives of the project leaders. In this way opportunities for discussion in the women's own terms were missed. At one meeting, for example, a disagreement between the Chair and another of the mothers over the presence of men at a forthcoming social was interpreted as an example of 'immaturity' and became a reason for mounting a course on being a committee – thus providing a lesson in democracy. At another meeting the possibility of the centre providing day care for the children of single and working parents was raised by a single parent member of the committee. 'It would', she suggested, 'help a lot of people an awful lot'. This too was postponed to get on to the real business of the meeting and did not reappear during the evaluation period.

Project leaders were in the privileged position, despite their conscious democratic intent, of being able to determine the framework for the development of the project and therefore to define the terms of arguments. 'They still see us as authority – though nice,' spoken with regret by an egalitarian project leader does not indicate a regrettable mistake on the part of women in the project but an accurate perception of the real relationship involved.

In fact, most women who used the centre were unaware of the objectives of the project. At the same time, tensions between its democratic intent and interventionist nature manifested itself in comments like: 'We're told we're the bosses, then they step in . . . and instead of coming straight oot wi'it, they go roon, aboot an' in and oot.' . . .

Inevitably, many of the larger issues are decided before a project like this gets under way. But some developments which occurred during the project were not disclosed to the mothers' committee until plans and negotiations had reached an advanced stage . . .

This issue of openness arose acutely over the small Family Centre which was opened in the most run-down area. Negotiations began towards the end of 1978 for the lease of a flat to be jointly run by SPPA and the Social Work

Department, mainly for the use of under-fives and their parents. The idea was to provide a small centre in the most deprived part of the area to be used by people who might have difficulty approaching the larger neighbourhood centre. A previous street group house in the same area had been closed, mainly because of vandalism, but this time the centre was to be more structured, with two part-time pre-school workers responsible for its day to day running and community management gradually phased in.

The mothers' committee first heard of this plan in the autumn of 1979, by which time the lease from the Housing Department had been arranged. It was explained to the committee that they could not discuss it earlier because they had to wait to hear from the Housing Department. The mothers had severe reservations about the plan. They all knew something of the history of the previous street centre, and one or two of them already involved in community action before the Headway project started had helped to clean and decorate it.

One of them said: 'This is where Kate and Ann [SPPA Project Leaders] are at a disadvantage. They've got great ideas, but we know the people. I suppose now it's decided we'll just have to wait and see how things go.'

The small centre finally opened in March 1980. In April it was twice broken into, first by vandals, then by burglars. The mothers who used the centre were called to attend the second half of a meeting of the centre management group on which they were not represented. Before they were called in, Kate expressed her concern that 'they can't go on feeling that we will continue to supply things. Responsibility rests with them; they know who did it and they've got to stop it happening.' And the same message was clearly conveyed to the mothers.

This was demanding responsibility on the part of the mothers without corresponding representation on the management committee. However, a few months later, the members of the management group discussed whether the mothers were not ready to play a part in managing the small centre. A paper on the aims of the centre had just been written by Kate, Ann and Gill, the full time worker in the centre. The paper was aimed mainly at health visitors who, they felt, were not taking the family centre and its work seriously.

At this meeting the team leader of Lochend Social Work Project wondered whether it was appropriate to distribute a paper on the Centre, which the mothers had not discussed or seen, while at the same time considering involving the mothers in the running of the Centre.

The paper contained remarks about the lack of play between parents and children in the area, about the 'unobtrusive example of the worker for the mothers to follow' and about the way in which, with encouragement, the mothers' confidence could grow. Kate was reluctant to let the mothers read this sort of thing . . .

It is, of course, extremely unlikely that women in the project would challenge this view of themselves and of their community and offer an alternative, even opposing 'definition of the problem' to that contained in the paper. To do so would require shifting the whole ground of the argument (as, in fact, some community workers in the area attempted to do by regarding 'cycle of deprivation' type explanations as misconceived and by seeing the project as reinforcing women's social role; according to this point of view it is their structural position as working class women which is the source of many of their and their children's problems).

Opposing arguments in the same terms, on the other hand, are relatively easy to mount like, for example, protesting that parents do play with their children (a view which was indeed borne out by the research although 'play' may have had a different meaning to that of project leaders). Similarly (although going rather further in challenging dominant assumptions and 'meanings' of the project), one woman, back from a conference on 'play' said to me:

> *'They kept talking about deprivation. Tae me it means weans wi'nae claes, nae shoes and a father who goes tae the boozer every night. There was this woman frae Blackhill who was gettin' really annoyed aboot it. One of the speakers said that deprivation is not being able to choose and that those parents are usually so deprived that they can't play with their children . . . they don't know how tae. I think it's not that they can't. It's that they don't want tae . . . and all the time wee Ethel wis 'duntin me as I wis tryin' tae write.'*

Not surprisingly, women who were involved in the project, either peripherally or heavily, were involved for reasons quite unconnected with the project's dominant purpose. Liz, for example, commented: 'Most of the voluntaries are here because for one reason or another they cannae work'. Of the most regular attenders, some live in poor housing conditions from which escape is in itself a relief. One younger mother who attends the small family centre lives upstairs with nine people in a four-roomed flat. These include her father who is 'done' at 50, her two-year-old son and several brothers and sisters. Some come, in part, to get away from unemployed husbands, others because this is the one place they are allowed to come. Some come because they are lonely or, quite simply, because they have nowhere else to go: 'If I didn't come here I'd know nobody'. 'If I didn't come here I'd just be sitting staring at four walls'. Or, simply, 'we come for the talk' . . .

It is clear that the question of openness is of central importance to the project. Without it, 'enabling' can move close to manipulating, as the unintended consequence of the mothers not knowing why the project is there in the first place and how it defines their needs and those of their community . . .

Individual growth and community action

. . . Project leaders believe that, if asked, the majority of mothers in Lochend would prefer a fully staffed, flexibly run Children's Centre, with or without parental involvement or control. It is equally clear that this runs counter to SPPA's whole philosophy based on the parent–child axis, and according to which, in choosing a Children's Centre, the mothers cannot be exercising a genuine choice because they have no experience of the alternatives . . .

On the basis of interviews and conversations with women involved in the project, including members of the mothers' committee, a majority believe that the greatest childcare need of the area is more flexible provision, including full *day care, for working parents. These same mothers who have been exposed to the alternative approach offered by SPPA would make use of such facilities in order to work.*

During a conversation with a group of mothers, one suggested that mothers using the neighbourhood centre should join up with the Nursery School mothers to put pressure on the authorities to meet this need. No such campaign materialised. This form of self-help is unlikely to emerge in a project whose rationale runs counter to it. The self-help principle in Headway means primarily that people in the community, with financial assistance from the state, provide and run facilities for themselves as an alternative to state provision. Voluntary or voluntary/paid work seems essential to that part of its rationale which is tied up with encouraging independence from the state – rather than with simply saving money per se.

A number of authors have spelled out the dangers in 'self-help' schemes. Related to this are criticisms of community development as a local government approach in APTs which contains a large self-help element (see, for example, Bennington, J. Community Development; Cockburn, C. The Local State. Wilson, E. Women and the Welfare State and the CDP pamphlet, Gilding the Ghetto). It has been argued, for example, that:

1   *Local self-help groups may provide an excuse for authorities to neglect their responsibilities to an area.*
2   *The self-help approach tends to focus on individuals and small groups within a community rather than on the structural aspects of the shared situation of people.*
3   *Notwithstanding the best intentions, professionals involved in self-help groups tend to control rather than facilitate development because they believe they know what the people need.*

It is argued too that although self-help in this form (brought in from outside to meet needs and solve problems) may provide short-term relief, it may unintentionally serve to perpetuate the very socio-political system that caused the problems in the first place, by, for example, reinforcing the definition of people as having disabilities in themselves. This is particularly paradoxical for an organisation like SPPA because of its conscious and public efforts not to underestimate the capabilities of people – something of which it believes other agencies to be guilty.

Parents and children

An emphasis on parent–child interaction is a central theme of Headway. In this it is part of what is now almost orthodoxy in thinking about pre-school education particularly in disadvantaged areas. Summed up by Eric Midwinter: 'The preschool problem, especially as it affects the disadvantaged child, can only be solved by treating the mother and child together as the unit of concern'. It is broadened to include both sexes by Bronfenbrenner 'it is by taking as its focus neither the child nor the parent, but the parent–child system that early intervention . . . achieves its staying power.'

   But Headway is not explicitly a compensatory project. It does not have a clearly structured programme where parents know the aims of the programme and are participating in its implementation. Rather, it focuses on changing the attitudes of parents to children and its approach to 'education for parenthood' is, correspondingly, an informal one. In addition, it conceives of the 'dual approach' as a way of meeting the needs of mothers as well as of children. This is of course the hallmark of PPA and SPPA. Both mothers and children should learn and grow through selfhelp groups . . . 'until they have the opportunity to catch up on the stages of development which they missed as children they cannot meet their own children's needs' (project leader). In particular: 'all the adults [in Headway] have stopped at a certain stage and so there's the need for someone in the project to take the children through the stages they've got to go through. They are just unaware of their children's needs' (project leaders).

   The reliance on developmental psychology in attributing causes screens out the extent to which constraints of economic hardship and poor living conditions may actually prevent parents fulfilling their own standards of childcare in Lochend, standards which may differ from those of the project. On the basis of interviews, these are causes which have considerable influence on the 'childrearing practices' of some families. In other cases reasons for not playing with the children are lethargy and lack of motivation, rather than inability or lack of knowledge that one ought to. One depressed single parent, recently moved into the area and not interested in meeting other women in similar circumstances, said 'I used to play with her but now I don't want to. I've just not got patience.' And although there were a few comments like 'I don't know what to do with her inside, she usually looks out of the window' most of the parents interviewed did to some extent play with their under-fives. Much of the play mentioned was horseplay and 'doing our exercises together'.

   What is important is how Headway defines problems and needs and its assumptions about the nature of deprivation. It emphasises the importance of women changing their attitudes of dependence and attitudes to themselves, like low self-esteem. It believes that if they do so they can thereby gain more control over their own lives and accept greater responsibility for themselves, their children and their neighbours. Headway looks to the individual to break 'the cycle of deprivation'.

   In doing so, and in regarding better parenting as a major part of the remedy, it runs the risk of equating emotional and material deprivation and of reinforcing the definition of people as having disabilities in themselves . . .

Adult education and Headway

Strathclyde Region has recently given support to the development of a number of Family Centres. Among other things, it regards these as providing appropriate local bases for various adult education activities, offering informal community settings for people who do not have a clear idea of what they want to do. The idea is that working class people are turned off adult education by its formality and that if parents are encouraged to come along with their children and 'taste' a variety of crafts, they will move on from there. The children play *in the same room generally, for another idea is that the mothers will pick up, informally, good parenting practice.*

There are some disquieting features in this model of adult education provision. First, informality can be an effective cloak for a hidden curriculum, about how mothers 'should' play with their children but which, because it is hidden, cannot be easily challenged or even discussed. (Lack of openness has been a central theme in my discussion of Headway.) Second, if most of the staff are craft-based and/or trained to cater for children's needs, the kind of curriculum that will be negotiated with the women is not likely to be very challenging, radical or exciting.

Jenny Scribbins has expressed some of the tensions involved in adult education for women and parent education in a a paper of that title. She nails her colours to the mast in her opening sentence: 'Women are an oppressed group in Britain . . . in that they are personally, socially and economically less likely to reach their full potential than men.' She points out that it is women's position, as parents, as the prime carers of their children, which, though often a source of deep joy and personal fulfilment, is also the tool of their continuing oppression.

Working class women in particular have few options of help with childcare and have few other routes to self-fulfilment 'in an initial education system that brands most as failures'. What should adult education do in the face of this? It should, she believes, try to do two things:

1   *recognise and value women's traditional work*
2   *'conscientize' women about wider aspects of what they do, enabling them to question their role and open up other possibilities. While there is a strong tradition of the first in Britain there is very little of the second in relation to women's traditional work.*

An attempt by the WEA to introduce to Headway some of the 'conscientization' sort of adult education never got off the ground. It was suggested by project leaders that the consciousness-raising aims of the class might be incompatible with the 'family-centred' approach of the project. In addition, and in line with its self-help philosophy, the provision of a creche for the purpose was regarded as the mothers' problem to solve . . .

Conclusion

It is fashionable at the moment to view current financial constraints as providing an opportunity for a more imaginative and broadly based approach to pre-school provision. This tends to mean a cheaper system for pre-fives with fewer professionals and a reliance on mothers in the name of community involvement . . .

The nagging suspicion, when this sort of stance is adopted, is that, in terms of present needs, both women and children are being shortchanged. Barrington Moore writes in Injustice, expressing an unpopular view: 'Those who seek to change the frequently indefensible barrier between human beings in modern society would do well to consider the possibility that, by and large, the destruction of the community may be the most valuable achievement of modern industrial civilization.'

Headway, as a community project, relies on women caring (for children and one another) but could also provide an excuse and rationalisation for not providing sufficient professional input to the area.

In the next Chapter I begin the process outlined in Chapter 1 – a return to and reappraisal, with hindsight, of the Headway research which has figured in this chapter.

5   Research as unmasking

Adult education as a site of struggle

Education has commonly been seen by feminists as an important arena for –
indeed, as integral to – the struggle to end women's subordination. Re-naming
reality in women's own terms was central to the consciousness-raising groups
of the Women's Movement; contesting patriarchal systems of thought and
understandings of the world (and of ourselves) has been central to feminist
education ever since. Adult education in particular (taking this to include the
kind of informal learning opportunities made available in community projects
like Headway) has been seen by some feminists as an especially, potentially
fruitful place for that struggle – as a 'site', that is, where the definition of what
constitutes knowledge may be radically challenged, as well as reproduced.

My interest is in both the politics of adult education and the politics of
feminism as these are played out in each of the pieces of research which are
reviewed in this book. In this chapter, in returning to my Headway research, I
employ two inter-related strategies. First, in line with the general project of the
book which construes adult education and adult education research as 'sites of
struggle', I view my case study of Headway and the sort of education for women
portrayed in it as historical events. With hindsight, the past 15–20 years can be
seen to have been a period of great uncertainty – as well as struggle – for adult
education. The same could be said for feminism. To return to the beginning of
that period could be instructive in terms of understanding the possibilities for
challenge and change in the relations of power which were involved.

Second, I view my written account as data: by examining it from the point
of view of the *how* of its production – putting some of the contingencies of its
construction back in – and by viewing it through the lens of ideas not available
at the time, I hope to learn something more which is not merely additive. A
'more', that is, which should contribute to qualitatively better, because more
responsible, research practice and knowledge. Some feminists insist that such a
reflexive strategy is necessary for more rational accounts of the world. Donna
Haraway, for example, regards notions of rationality and objectivity which
omit the knowing/writing subject as 'fantastic' views 'from nowhere'. Explicit
self-consciousness regarding the necessarily limited and partial stories social
scientists tell is a prerequisite of rational social research/writing (Haraway,
1991a; Jones, 1992)

A dream

Last night I had a dream: I am in a classroom of sorts. Someone is approaching from the distance. It feels very important to me that we meet. But I don't want her to see that I've got so many clothes with me. I try stuffing them into carrier bags and my very small briefcase and I take off the several layers of coats I'm wearing and start stuffing them away too. They seem to multiply as I discard them. I see her in the distance . . . she's going to come across me before I get them all away and I'll be found out. Just as she is about to happen upon me (she's waving) I wake up. The feeling tone of the dream is panic.

When I sit down now to begin writing, a memory comes to mind – an image of myself from over 15 years ago, sitting at the kitchen table, anxiously trying to impose some order on the mass of research material spread out in front of me. Even now, this remembered moment of extreme anxiety catches my throat and threatens to sabotage this present endeavour. The trouble with trying to cultivate a more open-minded, open-ended way of thinking and writing in preference to a self-contained, systematic account is that in the pursuit of such a project it is possible (even likely) to come up against some fairly uncomfortable personal insights.

If I keep the dream and the memory firmly in focus it seems clear to me that order, authority, (self)deception, criticism, concealment are among my 'glitter words': this is the term which Christa Wolf uses for those words which make adults' eyes glitter   words like 'not normal', 'alien blood', 'oversexed': 'One had to watch their eyes, not their mouths when they spoke, to find out which words one couldn't ask about' (Wolf, 1988, p 57): 'I can read you like a book, Jean', my mother used to say.

Following this through, I cannot avoid noticing the central root metaphors of depth and unmasking which permeate my Headway account: notions of concealment, masking and obscuring and, correspondingly, of digging beneath the surface, revealing and unveiling, are its central motifs.

The metaphors we choose to use, usually unconsciously since they are embedded in our preferred (and available) theories and methodologies, are in themselves revealing. When I review my own research and writing work to date it is clear that notions of masking and unmasking, implicitness and explicitness are central to much of it. One of the central processes in Headway is described by me as 'adult education by stealth'; so too, when I wrote my MA(Ed) dissertation on NOW courses in the WEA a few years later I describe some of these courses as involving 'counselling by stealth'.

It was indeed my hunch when I was researching Headway and before I identified myself as an adult educator that most of the educational activities engaged in by working class women in the West of Scotland took place in a myriad of community schemes such as Headway in which adult education was not the main activity but where the workers involved in running the schemes saw educational aims in some sense as an important, but unstated, part of their agenda. I was later to write about this invisible adult education on the basis of my experience running the West of Scotland District of the WEA (Barr, 1987).

Yet despite my obvious predilection for unmasking – in the case of Headway, of its hidden assumptions – I was reluctant to apply the same technique to my own work, standing safely outside each of the situations I comment on, leaving my own investments – theoretical and emotional – hidden from view. As if anyone, given enough information, would come to the same conclusions as I did – anyone rational and sufficiently disinterested, that is.

Yet, one thing which I did not acknowledge (even to myself) when writing up my evaluation report was the deep anger and disgust I felt much of the time when I was immersed in the daily workings of the project. Anger, that is, at how 'the mums' were positioned by the project – as objects of remediation and regulation by those who knew better. And that anger, I now believe, fuelled my account – evidence for me that in addition to being located socially, conceptually and historically, all efforts to understand and acquire knowledge have an emotional dimension.

To re-cap on the central components of my Headway account.

When I wrote up my evaluation report I wanted to present it as an illustration of the hidden assumptions of parent involvement schemes, even, perhaps especially, those which claim to be the least directive. Such schemes, which often rely on informal methods of parent education and encourage community involvement in their implementation, are seldom explicitly compensatory. Nevertheless, applied in deprived areas using Urban Aid to carry them out, this is precisely what they are. I was quite certain about my objections to such schemes, which can be easily summarised. First, because the educational element in schemes like Headway is largely hidden from view, carried out, as it were, 'by stealth', it is not open to challenge by those subjected to it; it operates as a hidden agenda.

Second, I believed that in an area like Lochend, women's needs and interests are not hard to identify and could be expressed very well indeed by the women themselves. I felt, too, that professional workers, in defining the needs of women and families, in believing they were meeting these needs and in disseminating this belief, actually obscured the women's own testimony.

Third, I believed that self-help/community development schemes such as Headway served to deflect attention away from the wider, structural sources of problems in deprived areas, especially for women and children. Instead of locating their source and solution in prevailing patterns of patriarchal and capitalist power relations, such projects (implicitly) locate them in the women themselves – in their 'wrong' attitudes and other lacks – and in their local community. In other words, they pathologise the people and the areas.

Critical influences

At the time I wrote my Headway evaluation, little or no research had been done on adult community education projects in Scotland. In the absence of any body of research of direct relevance to how I constructed my object of study I turned to other literature. There was a small body of critical political analysis on Community Development Projects (CDPs) in England – *Gilding the Ghetto* springs to mind – and Cynthia Cockburn and Elizabeth Wilson had produced Marxist-feminist critiques of, respectively, *The Local State* (1977) and *Women and the Welfare State* (1977). The focus of these bodies of work – on how the welfare state and community development strategies reproduce capitalist relations and uphold the traditional patriarchal family – influenced my prior thinking about Headway and the area of Lochend, directing my attention to how Headway might serve to reproduce capitalism and patriarchy.

A number of critiques of 'community' also existed, on which I drew. These included Sennet's *The Fall of Public Man* (1977) which indicted the 1970s' celebration of 'community' for fostering a ghetto mentality – an attempt to reduce the scale of human experience to the level of the local and intimate. I warmed then to Sennet's observation that building a sense of community at local level in a city, as opposed to re-awakening meaningful public space and public life in the city as a whole, serves a stabilising function by deflecting attention away from the larger political structures in society: 'The more people are plunged into these passions of community', he wrote, 'the more the basic institutions of social order are untouched' (p 309). And 'in a society which fears impersonality, identifying with strangers who may share one's interests becomes hard: who "we" are becomes a highly selective act of imagination' (see Iris Young, 1990, for a recent, similar critique but from a very different, more postmodernist, theoretical position).

By illustrating in my report the divergence in views about the needs of the Lochend women as identified by project initiators and by themselves, and by 'giving voice' to the women's point of view, I saw myself as engaged in revealing such disparities of power and material resources between social groups which, as I saw it, the conservative ideology of the project obscured and drew a veil over.

What I did not acknowledge was that in presenting the women's own testimony as if they were 'speaking for themselves' (my main rhetorical strategy) I actually obscured questions of subjectivity and agency: whose voice, point of view, interpretation I was actually articulating at any moment – mine, theirs, some theory's. I was clearly reluctant to appear as myself in the text, thus blurring the ways in which meanings emerged from our encounters. And I masked the ways in which my account was a construction out of my own theoretical and epistemological assumptions and values as well as a product of my material location and identity.

I expand on this below, beginning with my theoretical assumptions.

In Chapter 1 I indicated that what united feminists in the 1970s was the assumption that the central question for feminism concerned identifying the cause(s) of women's oppression: this was sought in society. This was a time when the influence of social science on academic feminism was unquestionably strong. Indeed, the Women's Movement itself has been described as an instance of critical social science at work – an 'enlightenment' project (Fay, 1987).

I was certainly immersed in both when I came to Headway but whereas Brian Fay sees the two as mutually reinforcing I now believe that my experience of the Women's Movement and its educational work lie behind the discomfort I felt – and which comes out in the yellow piece of paper – (see Chapter 4) – in trying to apply a 'critical social science' paradigm in my Headway research. I shall take up this point later. For now, I want to delve deeper into the idea of 'critical' social science.

Critical social science

The main features of critical social science have been helpfully enunciated by Brian Fay and Lee Harvey in separate publications. Fay's broad definition is worth repeating here:

> In the broadest sense, critical social science is an attempt to under-
> stand in a rationally responsible manner the oppressive features of
> society such that this understanding stimulates its audience to
> transform their society and thereby liberate themselves.
>
> (Fay, 1987, p 4)

The practical aspirations of critical social science are educative, says Fay, and rest on the belief that through rational enlightenment people will be enabled to change society. The kind of social research which arises out of a critical social science approach has been characterised in the following terms:

> Critical social research does not take the apparent social structure,
> social processes, or accepted history for granted. It tries to dig
> beneath the surface of appearances. It asks how social systems
> really work, how ideology or history conceals the processes which
> oppress and control people.
>
> (Harvey, 1990, p 6)

Critical social science and research based on it seek, then, to dig beneath the surface of historically specific, oppressive social structures in order to get at the unobservable underlying conditions which account for the experienced world of appearances and events. This contrasts with positivist social science which, according to critical social scientists, is concerned only with the level of appearance and with discovering factors which 'cause' observed phenomena (ie 'correlate' with); it also contrasts with phenomenological attempts to interpret the meanings of social actions (Harvey, 1990, p 1). A crucial part of critical social science's ontology (unlike positivism's) is the idea that the limits of the real (and causally determining) are not co-terminous with the directly observable or experienceable (see Bhaskar, 1978, 1989).

Critical social researchers have to ferret out what is really going on by following leads, seeking out clues so as to understand the circumstances within which anything occurs: how it is, say, that working class children get working class jobs, how it is that women make and re-make their lives under conditions of capitalist patriarchy (Harvey, 1990, p 197). Here, the concept of ideology plays a central role – conceived as concealing the 'contradictions' which inhere in specific oppressive social structures. Women's lives are inherently contradictory in this analysis. The critical analysis of history locates events in their social, political and economic context and engages with taken-for-granted ideological factors. It does this, says Harvey, not just in terms of the events themselves but also reflexively, in terms of the social situatedness of the researcher.

According to critical social science, social structures are maintained by the exercise of political and economic power. Such power is grounded in repressive mechanisms and legitimated through ideology: 'Critical social research thus addresses both the ostensive social structure and its ideological manifestations and processes' (Harvey, 1990, p 19). A central theme is the role of ideology in obscuring social processes: 'Ideology itself is transparent. It has to be made to appear' (Harvey, 1990, p 198).

No specific methods are entailed in critical social research although it has some preferred approaches, for example, 'critical case study' and 'critical ethnography'. The critical case study is always a means for referring beyond itself – a resource for exploring wider questions about the nature of oppressive social structures – like patriarchy and capitalism. What is important is that the study is designed to address critically contradictions or 'myths' at the level of actual practices that relate to broader questions about the operation of oppression. And in critical ethnography, which uses traditional ethnographic methods of in-depth interviewing and participant observation and is also reflexive (ie it locates the study in its social structural setting) the intention is always to move beyond the subjects' meanings to ask how these meanings relate to wider cultural and ideological forms.

In sum, critical social research involves 'keeping alert to structural factors while probing meanings' (Harvey, 1990, p 204). In common with all critical analysis it seeks out contradictions and myths: inconsistencies between what people do and what they say are transformed in such analysis from being mere anomalies into contradictions. For example, in a study by Weis of black college students it was discovered that what they had to say about time-keeping and what they actually did was anomalous. It became an 'analytic contradiction' for Weis, says Harvey, once it was explained in terms of the concept of 'white man's clock time' within the cultural context of the black man's urban ghetto. The students were paying lipservice to the white male meritocratic system while living in an everyday world which operated on a different sense of time (p 105).

Critical social research, then, has to build from the micro level to the wider social system level and relate people's experiences and felt needs to wider social structural features of capitalism/patriarchy/white imperialism. For the critical social researcher, political commitment is crucial, in contrast with the 'dominant research paradigm' – positivism – which prescribes an objective, value-free methodology.

Headway as critical social research

In the 1970s when I was trying to do critical social research, I'd have given my back teeth for such subsequent expositions of what I then conceived myself to be attempting. What I now hear is less comforting: a cut and dried, repetitive, rational voice of certainty clamouring for attention – and a kind of theoretical imperialism.

In line with this critical methodology, I used the Headway case study as a resource for exploring wider questions about the nature of oppressive social structures. I 'critically addressed' 'contradictions' at the level of actual practices that I saw as relating to broader questions about the operation of oppression.

Thus, in my analysis of Headway's underlying rationale I immediately focus on 'strains' and 'tensions' between the explicit democratic intent of the project and the actual attempt to change (through informal educational methods) what are perceived to be culturally induced attitudes and beliefs, suggesting that this contradiction was a source of strain in the practice of the project. Paradoxes become 'contradictions' when understood in terms of the real social relationships involved. I use snippets, edited quotes from conversations with project workers and participants in the project to illustrate this.

Thus, snippets like 'How do you put into their hands what's theirs and they don't want?' (project leader) and, later: 'We're told we're the bosses and then they step in . . . and instead of coming straight oot wi' it, they go roon' aboot an' in and oot' (project participant) are used to represent contradictions which derive from the social position of areas such as Lochend as objects of State intervention and which are rooted in wider social structures of power (eg class and gender/capitalism and patriarchy).

That is to say, I used Headway to illustrate a theory and I was practising the critical social research paradigm as enunciated later most fully by Lee. I believed myself to be armed with a superior theory whose concepts and explanatory schemes provided me with a powerful means of gaining a better understanding of what was really going on than was available from inside the project and the area.

The trouble was that the epistemological assumptions of the theory and methodology which provided my standpoint tended to see everyone else but myself as mired in ideology, unable to see reality clearly because of their 'false consciousness'. This came close to treating the women in Lochend as 'cultural dopes', victims of processes of socialisation which take place behind their backs, rather than active participators (actively colluding or resisting, for example) in these processes. I go into this below through a comparison of my socialist-feminism in the 1970s and now.

Feminist theory in the 1970s

A number of blindspots were created – I now believe – by the Marxist-feminist theoretical position which I adopted at the time of Headway. I shall illustrate by reference to my account. The early part of my report consists of a descriptive account of the area of Lochend entitled 'The community – living in Lochend'. The picture I present here is of women as victims of a monolithic welfare state whose policies and practices serve to reproduce patriarchal and class relations of power. The account is written around quotations from women living in conditions of material distress to illustrate the effects on their lives and their children's lives of the operation of these policies and practices.

The focus of the descriptive account is on the absence of adequate childcare facilities and the effects of this on the ability of women to go out to work.

Thus, I use Margaret F to illustrate women's will to independence in working: 'There's no man's going to treat me as if he's keeping me . . . now I'm going to get a job and get some money I can call my own'; Christine D to show how, in order to juggle with childcare in the absence of provision, women end up in jobs below their qualifications and Janet – who failed to get her own child into nursery and ended up, bored, sleeping her life away, and caring, too, for a working neighbour's child – to illustrate how children end up being cared for by reluctant carers. I also use a quotation from Jean C to suggest the violence which can inhere in the nuclear (patriarchal) family which the welfare state supports: 'Until I had C . . . I always had black eyes. He'd bang me off the four walls . . .'. And I present some of the psychological effects on women of living in such limiting and oppressive circumstances through the examples of Jean H's 'phantom pregnancy' and another woman's depression: 'I cannae see any future. I can't see how to survive here. I keep tae mysel'.

It is notable that in this depiction of the area and women's lives the edited highlights I present tend to be ones in which the issue of paid work is prefigured and made central. This centrality was undoubtedly conditioned by the categories which were central to feminist theory at the time: the 'domestic labour debate' which dominated much Marxist-feminist literature in the 1970s (an outgrowth of the Marxist construction of economic relations as the origin of all power relations) lies behind my central motif. In line with that literature I operated with a notion of productive work as paid work (and as crucial for women's empowerment and economic independence) and I regarded childrearing work done by women at home as reproducing labour power, as, that is, functional for the capitalist–patriarchal state.

Moreover, when I wrote Headway, the State had just become an object of theoretical concern to feminists. In this early theoretical work, Marxist feminists tried to graft an analysis of social reproduction, the family and gender on to a Marxist analysis of the capitalist state (see for instance, Cockburn, 1977; McIntosh, 1978; Wilson, 1977). The focus of this literature on the welfare state was thus on how it reproduces capitalist modes of production and upholds the traditional patriarchal family.

I cannot go into the complexities of this debate now. I bring it in here because I want to focus on just one aspect of that 1970s debate which has been highlighted in recent writing from within the same basic socialist-feminist framework. And the reason I do so is because of the light it throws on the features of women's lives which my Headway account obscured and left in the dark.

Contemporary feminist critiques: The marginalisation of women within Marxism

For example, writing recently from within a socialist-feminist framework, Barbara Ehrenreich has suggested that the problem with the early Marxist feminist 'capitalism-plus-patriarchy' paradigm was that it was too deferential to Marxism (see Ehrenreich, 1992). In trying to grant women agency within a Marxist politics, the theory, paradoxically, depersonalised women. Importantly, it had no room within its categories for caring on the part of women. The possibility that, indeed, some would prefer to care for their children than 'work', given decent circumstances; that some might even regard 'women's work' as more productive than other work, because sustaining of life, was not a theme I pursued in the course of my research. My categories would have been inadequate for this purpose.

Indeed many feminists now believe that the effort to extend theories like Marxism to women's lives is misconceived because such theories (liberalism too) are not just superficially sexist (that is, with a bit of cleaning up they can be made to fit women's lives too) but intrinsically so. The claim here is that their sexism is built into their discursive commitments (see eg, Gatens, 1992). Some feminist theorists go further, calling for what has been dubbed 'essentialism with a difference' (Braidotti, 1994, Spivak, 1988) and claiming women now must take 'the risk of essence' in order to think differently. The argument here is that because women share a 'discursive marginality', knowable only as similar to, different from, or complementary to 'man', the assertion of 'the feminine' – that is, of the values and priorities, powers and capacities which women have developed in their specific cultural and historical contexts – may be an important political strategy (Pringle and Watson, 1992). This is a tricky position to maintain (1). However, in the context of my present discussion, the point which has to be underlined is that once the work and investments involved in childrearing have been reduced to 'reproducing labour power' – once, that is, 'women's work' is reduced to processes which help perpetuate existing society – women (within this account) actually lose their autonomy and subjectivity. There is no place in this story for desire (even, pleasure) or resistance; nor is there room for emotion, the body, personal relations – aspects of personal and social life neglected (even repressed) within Marxist categories:

> Trying to fit all of women's experiences into the terms of the market didn't work, and adding on patriarchy as an additional 'structure' didn't help.
>
> (Ehrenreich, 1992, p 145)

The point here is that feminism does assert the unambiguous reality of women's oppression (in liberal versions, their 'disadvantaged' position) and tries to do something about it. It can't therefore be 'against theory' or 'against reason'. But it has to be against narrow notions of theory and reason which, for example, split it off from emotion, context, embodiment. Feminist theorising has to use various forms of argumentation and critique which can take into account aspects of personal and social life which tend to be neglected in Marxist accounts, and which can remain receptive to what is most specific about female experience (see Felski, 1989).

As it was, the 'oppressor–oppressed' Marxist-feminist model with which I operated not only effectively screened out the women's agency, collusion and resistance; it also prevented an acknowledgement that power and pleasure do not cancel one another out (as the pleasures of caring for young children testifies). Complex notions of power are necessary to understanding this (as well as other aspects of the women's situation in Lochend and Headway). But I was tied to a restrictive notion of power.

Locating power

The implicit model of power with which I operated was undoubtedly one-sided – power conceived as centrally located in large structures of the economy and the state, class and patriarchy – and as only repressive in its effects. Such a location of power implies political struggle (with a big P) and resistance at the level of the economy and state. Indeed, my text sought to represent the interests of the women in Lochend over 'against the state' – a state whose operations I saw reflected in the Headway project, conceived as reproducing capitalist and patriarchal structures of power (2).

And I would still go along with the main thrust of that analysis, overly crude as it then was. The structures of capitalism and patriarchy persist and continue to be reproduced – albeit in different forms – and they crucially shaped the conditions of life of the women in Lochend and Headway. Nevertheless, although I would not abandon that analysis altogether or the idea of central-ised power contained in it, I now believe that we *also* need a notion of power as dispersed and emergent. Residing in all social relationships, such power is exer-cised (rather than possessed) in a myriad of locations, events and relations of people.

In my own deference to Marxism I was insufficiently attentive to the fem-inist insistence on the personal nature of the political – to how, according to Foucault, power is also 'capillary', operating productively (not just repres-sively) at the level of everyday life and at the very heart of human beings, their desires and pleasures. Understanding this is a key to organising resistance at the local and everyday level. Power as it is lived out is lived out in uneven and fragmented ways between different categories of people and also within the experience of any one individual. In the parlance of poststructuralist feminism, there is a range of 'subject positions' which women (within each woman and the group 'women') may engage and women both re-produce and resist the subject positions historically available to them (Jones, 1992). For, to repeat, 'where there is power there is resistance' (see Chapter 1). Prevailing power relations, that is, however dominant, are never seamless or static but are always spawning new forms of subjectivity, new contexts for resistance and change.

Thus Foucault's own 'genealogical' method proposes – as a method of resistance – a way of facilitating an 'insurrection of subjugated knowledges': 'naive knowledges, located low down in the hierarchy . . . particular, regional, local knowledge' (Sawicki, 1991, pp 26–28). Genealogical critique may be con-strued as Foucault's alternative to traditional revolutionary theory. It seeks to free us from the oppressive effects of prevailing ways of understanding our-selves which we have inherited.

I have already suggested (Chapter 1) that the advantage of seeing power as productive in certain ways and as an active process rather than as a possession of institutions is that it allows for the conceptualisation of unevenness, resist-ance, ongoing transformation. And the advantage of Foucault's genealogical method is that it focuses on the 'subjugated knowledges', common knowledge, 'intuitions', knowledge 'from below' which Carlo Ginzburg speaks of as rooted in the senses and everyday life and which is typically the property of those in a given society who are not in positions of power – positions occupied, most clearly, by women in Lochend.

Using my research to encourage ambiguity and to create spaces for 'subjugated knowledges' was not part of my agenda in 1979, however. The name of the game was interpreting the women's experiences and the goals of the project in terms of my own favoured theories – theories whose categories were, I now believe, inadequate to understanding the women's situation.

Had I pursued a more open approach, the story I told might have been more ambiguous, complex and contradictory, less about 'victimhood' and more, perhaps, about the pleasures and power of mothering, for example. Carolyn Steedman talks about girls' contradictory relations of power and powerlessness in relation to the home and child-rearing and asserts the possibility of using an awareness of this to produce change (Steedman, 1980). By regarding the women in Headway and Lochend as, quite simply, powerless, as not 'having it' I was not in a position even to consider this possibility.

And because of the position I took up in my research and writing – as spectator and narrator – I effectively denied the women's own agency and knowledge, and, paradoxically, my own. I shall go into both of these mutually reinforcing aspects of my research stance below. First, I explore the notion of using research as a 'space of resistance' in the sense suggested above.

Resistance

Returning to the anger which I felt much of the time when I was immersed in the day to day workings of the Headway project, what enraged me most was the way in which I perceived 'the mums' to be positioned in the project. As, that is, completely 'other', objects of remediation and regulation by those who 'knew better'. They could never really get it right. Kate, especially, represented for me the middle class English colonialist come into an area to put it to rights. I instinctively identified with the other women in the project – the women from Lochend – whose warmth, sense of humour, toughness and absence of deference matched the qualities which were familiar to me from my own background. In the Headway project, 'the mothers', as well as their children, were portrayed and treated as having 'missed out' in their stages of natural development (the mothers, because they hadn't had the requisite nurturing environment themselves and were 'repeating' this with their own children); they, too, were seen to be in need of maternal nurturing of the correct kind – by some kind of corrective therapeutic practice (Kate indeed moved on to become a therapist for adults later on).

Walkerdine (1990) and Walkerdine and Lucey (1989) have since written provocatively about child-centred pedagogy and child-rearing practices (and the notion of natural child development enshrined in them) as practices of normalization; intervention into the lives of (usually) the poor, the working class, ethnic minorities becomes justified to re-assert the normal. I had not of course read their accounts at the time of my research. Reading them later put a fresh gloss on what I experienced at the time of Headway as a gut feeling of antipathy and contempt for the prissiness of Kate's ways, which I found patronising. I also believed in the superiority of sociological over psychological understandings.

The women (as well as the children) in Headway (and Lochend, more generally) were constantly being seen (positioned) as beings without agency and autonomy, not least by being read by the middle class project leader as not 'getting it right', as not knowing how they should behave (3). And what is particularly important in the context of my present discussion, namely, my lack of attention to 'subjugated knowledge' and 'resistance', is that the women saw this and resisted. Or, at least, some of them did. Yet I scarcely seem to notice this; to the extent that I do give any space in my text to challenges arising out of the women being positioned by the project's definitions of them, it is, as it were, in parenthesis.

An example of the challenges and resistances which were actually present in the mundane day to day life of Headway but which, I suggest, my account actually obscured is indeed discernible in a paragraph which follows my tale about the small family centre. It will be recalled that in my report I present the leaders' reluctance to show the paper on the family centre to the women involved (because of the language used in it to describe them) as an illustration of the structural contradictions involved in interventionist schemes such as Headway and of its pathologising constructions of parents in Lochend. I then follow this with a discussion, reprinted below:

> It is, of course, extremely unlikely that women in the project would challenge this view of themselves and of their community and offer an alternative, even opposing 'definition of the problem' to that contained in the paper. To do so would require shifting the whole ground of the argument (as, in fact, some community workers in the area attempted to do by regarding 'cycle of deprivation' type explanations as misconceived and by seeing the project as reinforcing women's social role; according to this point of view it is their structural position as working class women which is the source of many of their and their children's problems).
>
> Opposing arguments in the same terms, on the other hand, are relatively easy to mount like, for example, protesting that parents do play with their children (a view which was indeed borne out by the research although 'play' may have had a different meaning to that of project leaders). Similarly (although going rather further in challenging dominant assumptions and 'meanings' of the project), one woman, back from a conference on 'play' said to me:
> 'They kept talking about deprivation. Tae me it means weans wi'nae claes, nae shoes and a father who goes tae the boozer every night. There was this woman frae Blackhill who was gettin' really annoyed aboot it. One of the speakers said that deprivation is not being able to choose and that those parents are usually so deprived that they can't play with their children . . . they don't know how

> *tae. I think it's not that they can't. It's that they don't want*
> *tae . . . and all the time wee Ethel wis 'duntin me as I wis tryin' tae*
> *write.'*

Although I acknowledge (in parenthesis and almost grudgingly) that 'one woman' went some way towards challenging dominant assumptions and 'meanings', it is *my* theorising which is foregrounded (albeit through the mouthpiece of 'some community workers in the area' – thereby, preserving a veneer of 'neutrality'). I contextualise other comments from participants in the project in a similar way. Returning to the observation of one woman that, 'We're told we're the bosses, then they step in . . . and instead of coming straight oot wi' it, they go roon' aboot an' in an' oot', I use this quote to illustrate tensions between the project's democratic intent and its 'interventionist' nature. That is, as grist to the mill of my theory about structural contradictions *rather than* an illustration of the participants' awareness of and resistance to the project's ways of positioning them.

As the text stands, it is of course open to the reader to take that meaning from it too. But what of all of the other instances that never even reached the page – even in parenthesis? The point is that in creating my account, I muted, if not quite silenced, the 'subjugated knowledges' inside the project and in so doing I masked the possibilities for challenge and change which actually inhered in the day-to-day workings of Headway. These were obscured – at least in part – by the limited and limiting notion of power with which I operated.

Feminist standpoints

I failed, too, to see my own theories' dominating tendencies. That is to say, in taking up the Grand View as observer and narrator, I, too (like the project which I was criticising) constructed the women as 'other'. This comes through I think in the way I display the women's accent. My spoken English is not much closer to 'correct' written English than theirs but I embed their vernacular within academic prose, thus distancing myself from them. In reporting some of their words and practices I engage legitimated theorists (or other authoritative community officials) to explain them. In consequence, I missed an opportunity to help 'heal the breach' between my favoured theories and the women's own interpretations.

At the same time, I masked my own emotional investments and responses; these were kept safely hidden from view, as were the relationships of friendship I formed with the women. It is indeed possible that had I used my anger as a clue and a resource (part of my own 'subjugated knowledge', perhaps?) I might have focused my account more precisely. Had I not dismissed my own gut, emotional response, treated it as an impediment to objectivity, to be quashed or ignored, I might, that is, have learned something about the day-to-day operations of power and the contradictions which inhere in relations between women based on class. I would certainly have had to acknowledge that my own West of Scotland class position (not just my political, theoretical and methodological perspectives) influenced how I perceived the project and how I was perceived in it. For class like gender doesn't just condition our life chances. It is part of the 'fleshy material identity' we bring to our research, influencing our most deeply rooted ways of feeling and judging and responding. As such it is an epistemological factor: it shapes our knowing (Alcoff, 1988, 1995). And it is just possible that some social locations – for example, working class women's lives – may provide a starting point for asking new, critical questions which simply do not arise from other standpoints or 'from above'.

This, in essence, is the crux of 'feminist standpoint' approaches to knowledge. Feminist standpoint epistemology argues for a feminist research 'not only located in, but proceeding from the grounded analysis of women's material realities' (Stanley and Wise, 1990, p 25); an analysis which takes up the standpoint of women 'as an experience of being, of society, of social and personal process which must be given form and expression within the culture' (Smith, 1978, p 294). 'Standpoint epistemology' (Harding, 1992, 1994) rests on two assumptions: first, that knowledge is not neutral but socially situated; second that 'knowledge from below', in its capacity to transform ways of looking at and understanding the world, may contribute to changing the world we see and live in.

Standpoint theory has drawn criticism since it is obvious that certain feminist standpoints, for example, those of white, middle class, academic feminists, have clear predominance over others. In fact those feminist theorists, like Sandra Harding, who write most about the need to prioritize 'marginalized lives' in standpoint approaches to research do so from a highly academic perspective and do not engage in empirical research.

It is possible that had I possessed the notion of 'standpoint epistemology' when I carried out the Headway research, my account would have been more consciously constructed from a specifically Scottish working-class, feminist vantage point – to stand alongside those other 'silenced feminist standpoints' of black and lesbian epistemology which have been enunciated recently (Stanley and Wise, 1990; Collins, 1990).

As it was I engaged in a number of rhetorical (and other) strategies which actually masked my personal and theoretical standpoint. My chief strategy was to give the appearance of representing the 'natives' point of view': 'Giving voice' to the people of Lochend regarding their lives and more specifically, regarding childcare facilities, was a major objective of my evaluation report. And this was anything but straightforward.

First, we cannot assume any correspondence between a life as lived and a person's narrative about it; a personal history is not something possessed by every self; 'testimonies' do not lie around inside people waiting for someone to come along and ask the right questions: they are constructs, moments when we reinterpret ourselves, structured by unconscious as well as conscious processes (Linden, 1994). Moreover, the context in which such 'stories' are recounted matters. For example, most of my interviews were one-to-one; had more use been made of group discussions I am in no doubt that the material derived would have differed since the kind of experiences, thoughts and feelings expressed (as well as the power dynamics) would have been different.

However, as it was, my interviewing, observational and interpreting skills lay, as I saw it, in making coherent sense of the rational and non-contradictory accounts I thought the women were giving me – and in relating these to my own rational account. Listening to, responding to and interpreting accounts of personal experience are capacities which are learned. The need to exercise them responsively and responsibly is necessary for any approach which purports to retain continuity with that experience and which moves only cautiously in the direction of interpretation. One thing we can be sure of is that there can be no uniquely true story, nor any uniquely right interpretation (Code, 1989).

Second, just as listening responsively and responsibly are learned capacities, so too with writing. I had learned that a proper research account required me to distance myself from the women and their situation and to bring in academic and other legitimated authorities to interpret and explain. Thus, in writing my text I do not appear as myself in it. None of it is in the form of conversations or dialogue in which I appear in the conversation. Parts of my text in fact feign to be a mere vehicle – a transparent mouthpiece as it were – for the women's stories. This is so in the case of Liz, Helen and Pat, for example.

My three 'life stories' of Liz, Helen and Pat are in fact trimmed and edited around my favourite themes. I create the illusion of the women simply speaking for themselves by producing snippets from conversations with them, prefaced with a reference to a written report by project initiators about the 'dependent attitudes' of people in the area. This reference is to the original Urban Aid submission for the project which I quoted at the start on my report and in which areas like Lochend are described as 'areas where problem families and children are many . . . parental responsibility minimal . . . a dependent attitude of the adults on the help and support of the state the norm . . . where taking responsibility for their community is accepted by only one or two outstanding individuals'.

The quotations I chose were specifically designed to contradict and falsify this portrayal of people in Lochend. Thus I chose snippets from conversations showing how Liz coped with a violent husband, a degrading and poverty-inducing social security system and dearth of full time jobs but still managed to keep her head above water and care for her children. I show Helen, 'a neglectful mother' according to project leaders, managing against all the odds to pay off debts left by her feckless husband and secure 'independence' for herself. And I portray Pat, caught in an exhausting cycle of caring for her mother and children and a husband who refuses to 'grant' her any autonomy, yearning after the kind of job she once had, where 'there was naebody staundin over the top of ye'.

More obvious strategies which masked my own position included deference to authorities in the critical self-help/community development literature which backed up my own stance. Another was to make reference to 'community workers in the area' to voice what were, in effect, my own views, as, for example, in my account (referred to above) of Kate's dilemma over the language used in the paper written by project staff on the newly opened small family centre. At another point in the text I refer to 'an attempt to introduce a

WEA class' into the project which was stillborn, but omit to mention that I initiated this attempt.

Responsible knowledge

It might be objected that I am labouring a point here, that how I wrote up Headway is the name of the game in many research reports. Everyone knows the text is crafted, involves selections, editing out and so on. So what? There are three points which I want to make.

The first point is that if we genuinely want to pursue responsive and responsible knowledge-making projects then we would do well to draw attention from time to time to the processes and contingencies of textual production. Good adult education practice similarly draws attention (sometimes, not obsessively) to processes going on in the group and between the tutor and other participants which might hinder learning. The point here is that how we know (flexibly, dogmatically, pragmatically) reflects how we learn. Producing research reports (or 'lessons') which are closed accounts, with all of the contingencies of their production sanitized out, reproduces and perpetuates a notion of knowledge as certain and fixed which is illusory.

Second, when I came to Headway I was immersed in traditions of sociological theory and cultural criticism which, to the extent that they were interested in working class lives, either ignored issues of subjectivity or, in Carolyn Steedman's words, celebrated a kind of psychological simplicity in working class people. I think that my account of Headway was complicit to a degree with this refusal of a complex psychology to those living in conditions of material distress (see Steedman, 1986). The likely rejoinder, 'But that's not the business of sociology . . .' is to miss the point which is precisely that it has to be. Otherwise, it produces one-dimensional figures, unrecognisable to most people – not least the very people who are the subjects of research.

Third, I now think that my primary rhetorical strategy of 'allowing' interviewees to speak in their own voices was not innocuous but blurred the ways in which meanings emerged from our encounters: it obscured whose voice, point of view, interpretation I was actually representing at any moment – mine, theirs, some theory's. Mostly, it was mine/some theory's.

This now strikes me as bizarre. I acted as an invisible, neutral observer in my written account of Headway, producing, as it were, a view 'from nowhere'. Yet I would not have defended any notion of value-freedom in theory. I rejected orthodox notions of value-freedom which prevailed in sociology at the time and which derived from Weber and, for instance, Gunnar Myrdal. According to this notion, one's personal values always influence one's choice of subject and interest in the matter, but as long as one states these at the outset, the objectivity of one's analysis is unsullied, just so long as one follows 'proper' scientific method; according to this view, values are influential only in the 'antechamber' or 'context of discovery' of science. I believed this view to be wrongheaded and naive. For this reason, perhaps, I believed that nothing would be served by preceding my account with a litany of political and value commitments.

I believed that the more important influences on social studies were usually unconscious ones, socially induced ideological presuppositions which operated implicitly and undetected in one's main categories and methods of analysis. I think that because my own theoretical orientation 'saw' this, I thought that by using my theoretical toolkit I was in a more privileged position to see how things really were (aka Althusser for whom the mistake lies in the fact that ideologies are not based on true, scientifically based knowledge).

Or maybe, like Ian Stronach, I just thought I was politically right and claimed an objectivity in practice of which I denied the possibility in theory – bizarre, but probably not an altogether uncommon position (Stronach, 1989). I 'knew' that research accounts were never neutral, yet I seem to have written mine according to some expectation that mine could be.

Postscript

A friend, who worked with me in the WEA, reading what I have just written above, comments

> Is it because the view you are trying to have validated by the research is itself 'subjugated knowledge' set against the powers that be and their knowledge? That is, trying to evade the problem of being accused of being political by an establishment that denies its politics? Therefore you were trying to be subversive by dissembling your viewpoint – the only eyes you were trying to pull the wool over were the eyes of the establishment – because to nail your colours to the mast would mean instant dismissal of everything you had to say – playing the game by the accepted rules in order to get across something that implicitly undermines these rules.
>
> (Alison Miller)

Well . . . maybe.

Expert knowledge

I was certainly thirled to theory with a capital 'T'. My card index system covering this period of my life offers ample evidence of this; Althusser, Bhaskar, Bowles and Gintis, Bourdieu, Fay, Keat and Urry, the Open University course units on Education and Society – together with a host of British academic socialist-feminist writing: Barrett, Mitchell, Rowbotham, Segal – far outnumbered any other, more descriptive or literary texts.

This reflected, of course, the state of sociology (and British academic feminism) at the time but it also reflected my own privileging of certain ways of seeing and, too, my deference to academic authority (though, thankfully, not all male). I privileged theory produced by professional social theorists whom I viewed as experts on the 'real meaning' of social experience and behaviour. As a result, I positioned myself as an expert on and over the women in Lochend's and Headway's experiences and I presented carefully selected snippets of life to exemplify my theoretical projects (see Stanley, 1990; Stanley and Wise, 1990).

Before going on I want to pause to make something clear. The direction of my writing here may appear to be moving towards an anti-theory position. This is not my intention. Nor is it my intention to deny the importance of critical social science's project (and that of critical theories like feminism) – that is, to seek out the underlying, often concealed, but real, conditions and consequences of actions (although I would now extend this to the personal unconscious as well as social) and to examine critically the seemingly self-evident truths of everyday life. But I do think that it is elitist (and reductive) to think that only highly specialised, intellectual work can 'pierce the veil' of ideological mystification. This is to locate all critical thought outside the practices of everyday life. Such a position ignores the complex, contradictory nature of human subjectivity (and the 'good sense' which Gramsci locates in everyday lived experience); and it discounts the differing degrees of dissent, resistance and potential for change which exist in specific social and historical contexts – like Headway and Lochend, for instance (see Felski, 1989).

It also contradicts Dorothy Smith's concept of a feminist sociologist as someone who inhabits the 'same critical plane' as the women whose 'everyday world' she investigates. Smith is a materialist sociologist who believes that research must treat women as agents of knowledge – as knowledgeable subjects and constructors of meaning whose experience and practical knowledge of their everyday lives must form the starting point of a 'sociology for women'. The academic mode of production of traditional sociology, she believes, renders women's lives *invisible*. While the sociologist's special skills lie in moving beyond that local, experienced world in order to disclose wider social relations which impinge on it, it is the standpoint of women's lives which provides the topics and relevances of a sociological research programme for women.

A 'consciousness-raising' element akin to Freire's notion of 'conscientization' is suggested in Smith's recommendation that research must 'provide for subjects the means of grasping the social relations organising the worlds of their experience' (Smith, 1987, p 153). But she insists that there is a need for methods of enquiry and writing sociology that 'organise the relation between the text and those of whom it speaks as "co-subjects" in a world we make together' (p 141). As I read Smith (and there are various, conflicting ways of reading her work) this is not a call for feminists to engage only in a form of action research. Smith is insisting that the knowledge and discourses created by social scientists are not different in kind from anyone else's. The theorising that some of us do as scientists isn't different in kind from what we do as laypersons – or even as philosophers – and 'expert knowledge', though granted special epistemological authority in our society, is not the only sort that deserves the name. On the other hand, who is regarded as 'knowing' matters, crucially, to what comes to count as social scientific knowledge (see also Nelson, 1990).

Had I regarded the women in Headway as 'co-subjects' of the research I might have learned an important lesson in how to allow the women's experiences to shape and reshape my own favoured theories. This might have made an important contribution to my *own* conscientization as a result. And had I taken my own anger seriously my research report might have been less about the project's power to define them and their needs and more about their own wisdom and 'good sense' to take these constructions on board, to partially challenge them (as in the 'play' example and 'they tell us we're the bosses and then . . .') and yet still take what they could from it ('we come for the talk'). In other words, they knew very well indeed how they were expected to behave; they were not ideological dupes and they had their own investments in the project – a route to paid part-time work, the warmth and support of other women, a safe place for their children, for example – and maybe, even, respectability, as Skeggs (1997) found in her research on working class women studying 'caring' courses at college. It now seems to me very likely indeed that the hidden agenda of learning to be better parents may have been something of which some of the women were well aware but chose not to challenge openly.

Noting the problematic nature of the notion of 'false consciousness', Marjorie Mayo quotes Bina Agarwal's comments on meetings she attended in rural India:

> At these meetings I learnt more than any single book on feminist theory could teach me. In particular I learnt about peasant women's numerous ways of resisting gender oppression that disprove the assumption that women suffer from false consciousness . . . Even the most outwardly compliant women often resisted covertly . . . From these interactions I thus learnt that for poor women's empowerment, what is needed is less the raising of consciousness and more the strengthening of their ability to overtly protest and mobilise for change.
> (Agarwal, 1994, p 254, quoted in Mayo, 1995, p 4)

As it was, in the way I conducted the research and wrote my account, it was as if the women's own accounts of their lives and their experiences of childcare, the project, living in Lochend etc and my social 'structural' interpretation were two separate stories, moving along in tandem but seldom connecting. And when they did connect, I 'read off' their meanings in terms of my macro sociological account. I think I was just very concerned not to participate in anything which smacked of phenomenology – the reduction of the social world to people's experiences of it.

New learning

I said at the outset that I wanted to learn something from this return to past research. What, then, have I learned? First, not to stand outside of what I say, to take seriously my own feelings of discomfort and anger and to give space to 'subjugated knowledges' which may not be brought into focus by the categories I bring to any enquiry. My own 'conscientization' has involved to a degree precisely a consciousness of the role of the emotional underside – of gut feelings – in the generation of knowledge and that to deny this is to court both self-deception and a potentially important source of new understanding and insight. In adult education, too, failure to offer such a space can lead to an overly rationalist approach which in failing to acknowledge issues of complex subjectivity fails people, particularly women, whose experiences do not fit well into traditional divisions of knowledge.

Second, to be less anxious about order and theoretical unity. It may be that in my anxiety to impose structure and order in my account I did not encourage ambiguity sufficiently. Resistant voices and subject positions did peep through to a degree but as somewhat distant voices. I could not, therefore, claim that my work on Headway went much 'beyond critique [to] help produce spaces for the emergence of subjugated knowledges and the organisation of resistance' (Lather, 1991, p 83).

To sum up: in writing myself back into the original Headway text, I have suggested ways in which it masked my own ideological and emotional investments, as well as my theoretical and epistemological assumptions. Had I been more open about my own theoretical standpoint and political commitments in the processes and writing of the research, participants might have put their finger on my (and my theories') blind spots, denials and contradictions, just as I was keen to do with the project's. Explicit incompleteness and partiality coupled with greater tentativeness leaves space for others to enter the conversation. It is more accessible, inviting a response rather than simple acceptance or rejection – the only possible responses to accounts written as if 'from nowhere'.

Nevertheless, I would still broadly stand by my original critique of the Headway project. That is to say, I believe that, whatever my reluctance to 'appear in the text' and acknowledging there is no uniquely right interpretation, some are better than others. Just as we cannot absolve ourselves of the responsibility to listen and interpret responsively we cannot, either, absolve ourselves of the need for judgement and choice of political and theoretical perspective. This is so, even as we grant that what we say is never quite what we think we say, every discourse generates its blind spots and our specific position in society and history limits the range of ideological, political and theoretical positions open to us (Moi, 1989).

Thus – now, as well as in 1979 – the greatest danger may lie in diverting attention away from the continuing pervasiveness of current power-relations. Notwithstanding my own rather crude conceptualisation of power and my argument in this book for a more complex understanding of how power 'works', in the social and political context of the production and reception of my Headway Report, an assertive report was probably precisely what was needed. In the face of very powerful voices for low cost alternatives in pre-school provision (couched in the ubiquitous language of 'community development') the last thing that was needed was an equivocal, uncertain text.

It does not do to be too coy about the authority conferred on us by our institutional positions (in this case, as a university-based academic). Better by far to learn to wield what power remains to us more 'strategically, collectively and effectively' (Stabile, 1997, p 407) – a plea for the need for collective action rather than for individual academics speaking out as 'public intellectuals'.

With due acknowledgement of its limitations, my evaluation report on Headway was an attempt to define and articulate from a specifically Marxist-feminist standpoint certain needs and interests of women in Lochend. Its often blunt tone and its rhetorical claim to be a true analysis appear to me now to be a very vulnerable, exposed position to take up. This is especially so at present when so much academic writing (feminist included), in its excessive self-referential sophistication, comes over as a form of self-protective narcissism, refusing to make any truth claims at all in the mistaken belief, perhaps, that if we give up the search for 'the truth' (a straw 'man' if ever there was one) we can't claim any truth value for our analyses. *Headway*, for all its evasions of the self-in-the-enquiry, its uncompromising stance and its blindspots, at least runs the risk of being wrong. And, viewed from the standpoint of the current political climate and continuing attempts to reconstruct a political culture on the basis of individualism and self-help (a key focus of my own social critique of Headway) – with a sprinking of 'communitarianism' – I don't think I got it entirely wrong.

Critical thinking may well contain an inbuilt work ethic – a puritanical attempt to form a fixed purpose and act on it, establishing within ourselves the psychological equivalent of a dictator, as Lovibond comments. But we may romanticise uncertainty, fragmentation and doubt by seeing them as forces for change when they are really manifestation of post-political apathy. The former may be the real threat to prevailing power structures (Lovibond, 1994).

A bridge into my second case study: Counselling by stealth

I have said that what I have learned from this exercise – my return to Headway – is that I should not stand outside of what I write. In fact, my experience of the Women's Movement and of the informal women's education which it spawned should have taught me this. In discussion of my Headway account I maintained that ambiguities and challenges (to my own rather deterministic Marxist-feminist framework as well as to the project's) did to a small degree come through in my report – almost despite myself (although the friend mentioned above claims that my anger and emotional investments were easy to discern in the research quoted and she could hear the 'resistant voices' very strongly – they did not just 'peep through') I don't think it is stretching a point too much to suggest that two voices can be discerned in my original report: one, critical and deconstructive, arising out of my critical social science perspective, the other, more creative and constructive, arising, I believe, out of my own West of Scotland class based experience and my experience of the Women's Movement. Seen in this way, involvement in the women's movement and in the kind of informal feminist women's education which arose out of it (as well as my own class background) were valuable experiences which should have taught me not to remain outside of what I said in my Headway report. Academic training and the academic mode of production, on the other hand, go against this (see Smith, 1987; Stanley and Wise, 1990).

It was this experience of informal women's education as it arose out of – and continued to take as its reference point – a political movement which, I now think, created some tensions in the 'critical social science' model of research which I tried to apply to Headway. For that experience was not just 'critical' or narrowly rational; it did not rely on expert social scientific knowledge to provide the 'real' meaning of experience; and it emphasised emotional as much as intellectual understanding.

I think this experience operated at a subliminal level in my Headway research, disturbing the rational, critical social scientific account I saw myself as engaged in. These experiences which pre-dated and extended beyond my period at Headway have been pivotal, I think, in my own learning, but as a kind of unconscious learning, as much of process and style as of content. As the philosopher Elizabeth Minnich points out, learning takes place on many levels: it does not just affect what we consciously know; it establishes habits of thought and is part of the constant process of identity formation and definition. For this reason, to change the curriculum is not just to change what we think about. It is to change who we are (Minnich, 1989). However, it was to be some time before that self, which 'knew' about issues of complex subjectivity at first hand and appreciated the power of experiential knowledge and the emotional component of learning, came to the fore in her professional work, including her research.

In the next chapter I take up this particular aspect of the split between theory and practice which, I suggest, is a feature of my personal biography. In the research which figures in my second case study and which forms the substance of the next chapter it will become clear that here, unlike Headway, I *was* at pains to put myself 'in the frame' of my account and to engage my research subjects as 'co-subjects' in the research process. However, as will become apparent, yet another tension between my theory and practice emerged.

6 Counselling by stealth

Introduction

My second case study is based on research which I did with tutors teaching women's education (New Opportunities for Women or NOW courses) in a District of the WEA in the North of England. I chose the topic, 'Counselling for a Change' as the subject of my dissertation which was submitted as part of the assessed work for my MA(Ed)(Guidance and Counselling) which I was undertaking at Durham University from 1989 to 1990. The title was a play on the title of an edited selection of readings in the radical tradition of adult education by Jane Thompson: *Adult Education for a Change* (1980a). I chose the topic because of my interest in women's education and worries about its current tendencies.

In 1984, three years after completing the Headway research, I was already voicing my unease about the direction in which women's studies/women's education seemed to be going in the WEA (see Chapter 3) throughout the UK. In a Keynote speech, 'Women's education – the ways forward' which was given to an all-women conference organised by the WEA at Durham University, I took up the theme of 'experiential' and informal, community-based adult education for women as 'selling them short' (see the end of Chapter 3). By the time I gave this talk I had been in the WEA for about two years and was a member of its national Women's Educational Advisory Committee (WEAC). The talk was polemical and it assumed an audience of women committed to feminism in one form or another. Its sub-text (or hidden agenda) was my assumption that many of the women present – even most – would not identify with socialist feminism but with either 'liberal' or 'radical' feminism. The paper was written from a socialist-feminist perspective.

The talk considers a strategy for the protection and development of adult women's education/women's studies at a time of mass unemployemnt. After a quick run through of the 'three strands of feminism – liberal feminism, radical feminism and socialist feminism' – which, I say in my talk, have been influential on the content and processes of women's studies in Britain, particularly in adult education, and after gently chiding 'respectable' liberal feminists for their 'compensatory' goals, I proceed to focus in on what I regard as 'the central challenge of women's studies: its critique of knowledge-making or production itself'. The central message of my talk is that this challenge of women's studies/women's education as practised in the WEA and elsewhere is compromised by three things: its marginality; its 'bias against theory'; and its concentration on the similarities rather than the differences between women. I want to quote from that talk as a bridge into my second case study. The extract below begins at this central section of the talk:

Women's education – the ways forward

Limits

If we are looking at the potential of Women's Studies to challenge the status quo (and as an alternative model in adult education) then there are at least three features which I think are of special relevance and which must be explored in mapping out ways forward. These are:

1   *its marginality*
2   *its bias (sometimes) against theory*
3   *its concentration so far on the similarities between women.*

I concentrate on these because I believe all of them threaten the radical potential of Women's Studies: all can be seen to have conservative implications.

Marginality

Take again the structural position of Women's Studies in Britain compared with America. In America Women's Studies developed mainly in the universities and colleges with very few developments in non-formal and informal learning in the community. The hot issue now in America is whether Women's Studies should pursue a strategy of integration with mainstream higher education or separation / autonomy from it.

Integrationists see the main task ahead as the transformation of the mainstream curriculum (of the universities) and Women's Studies as separate is regarded as essentially transitional to this. In America there is a lot of bridging work going on between Women's Studies departments and general curricular change – through, eg in-service programmes. Women's Studies has been carried openly into a challenge to all received bodies of knowledge in the university.

Many are cynical about such efforts, seeing in them the route of co-option and reasoning that if we really believe that radical social change is necessary to change the position of women in society we can't really expect our ideas to be accepted in the mainstream – especially universities which are very firmly embedded in the present social structure. They would suggest (a) Women's Studies must retain its status as an outsider to some extent and (b) that there should be more involvement of Women's Studies in the community on the ground that if it is confined to universities and colleges it cannot touch the lives of the majority of women.

The issue of marginality is thus different in Britain from America – fears of co-option have always been much stronger in Europe and in Britain in particular and here Women's Studies has developed much more outside universities.

As a consequence it is poorly resourced compared to America. But there are benefits: women have been able to exploit adult education's rhetoric of student control, flexibility, personal growth and so on to win resources for Women's Studies. It is also a much more diverse thing here and it has become the home of some of the most innovative methods and best tutors in the adult education field. This is being increasingly acknowledged.

Because much of it takes place in local neighbourhoods, discussing issues of real concern to women themselves – housing, health, welfare rights, children, sexuality – counselling and educational aspects of this work are often indistinguishable. It calls for very special skills.

So the specific form its marginality takes in Britain is both a strength and a weakness of Women's Studies here. It is a strength because it is less elitist, touching the lives of a lot of ordinary women. But because it takes place in the least well-resourced part of the education system it suffers from the features of that system: many of its courses are short-term and one-off, offering few opportunities for sustained as well as well-resourced education work.

The setting up of Women's Education Centres run by women themselves is a recent hopeful development although they also have to operate on an insecure funding basis. And 'self-help' as a positive principle and way of organising/controlling resources is easily translated by funders into a moral imperative/principle of thrift. Such centres do have the potential for offering various sorts of educational opportunities under one roof and of bringing women together for purposes other than childcare and other domestic responsibilities.

But there still remains a huge gap between women's education 'in the community' – the only sort that working class women are liable to get – and third level institutions where the real power and resources lie.

So far we have largely failed to make the right sort of links between community and institutional education – links which might lessen the extreme marginality of working class women themselves and affect the institutions at the same time. 'Access' courses are not the answer – although they may be part of it. Properly resourced and staffed alternative routes may be another part of it. But for many women, moving on from a 2-hour weekly discussion session to something much more substantial and sustained – like the Southampton University full day a week/30 week Second Chance Course for women – can seem a huge commitment to self and one which many women will find very difficult to make.

Bias against theory

The second aspect of Women's Studies which I have singled out for particular attention is actually shared with a fair amount of adult education which purports to pursue a 'student-centred' approach to learning. This is a tendency towards a certain bias against theory or, at least, a reluctance to seriously engage with it. (In America, by contrast, the tendency may be towards an over academic approach). Sometimes the passionate (and absolutely right) upholding of women's experience as valid is coupled with an equally passionate hostility to theory and its production. It is almost as if theory somehow involved a 'masculinisation', of subjective experience and of what are seen as exclusive capacities of women – feeling and intuition. This feature of some Women's Studies involves a retreat into a form of romantic conservatism which is absolutely no help to the majority of women – in that it leaves everything as it is, ignoring the fact that all the feeling, intuiting and caring done by women didn't come naturally to them; that women care arises out of specific social arrangements which don't have to be as they are.

Starting from where people are is an excellent starting point but a lousy finishing point! It can too often leave them there. We must devise a pedagogy and research methodology that encourages learning which is related to people's lived experiences and feelings and which develops critical thinking – so that new thoughts and new ideas can be generated.

For working class women the emphasis on their own experience is an excellent antidote to the various forms of cultural imperialism to which they have been subjected. But that hunger for more disciplined study of a more academic, 'meaty' kind which is often expressed in women's groups shouldn't be interpreted as indicating some form of 'false consciousness', a too-easy acceptance of traditional/conventional ideas about education and knowledge. Maybe instead it should be read as signalling a desire to be involved in hard critical, thinking work, a right many have been denied. And after all, existing theory, as well as experience, is part of the raw material of knowledge production.

To despise theory because of worries about elitism suggests an uncritical and reactionary acceptance of a society in which access to higher education and to critical thought is denied to most people. Political engagement to change these arrangements is required – not the retreat from the difficulties of political struggle which is implied by this anti-theory stance.

An extremely relativistic view of knowledge often goes along with this stance. I can't go into this issue here, except to say first, not all theories are right, not all points of view are equally valid. There can be grounds for accepting one theory or belief in preference to another. At the same time, we must acknowledge that all knowledge, all beliefs are socially produced, hence not absolute. Second, constructing a rational case is the first step towards real understanding of the social world. Jane Austen speaks of the 'horror of mean understanding' – living in a circumscribed world constantly in the presence of over-developed opinions and under-developed understanding. It is easy to sympathise with Mary Evans, writing in Feminist Review No. 10 when she says that to say women 'should get in touch with their own feelings' and 'reclaim their own subjectivity' is to follow a path which leads to the most closed and unproductive of dead ends. Up to a point it has been important for women. Beyond that it's blinkered, less than helpful and conservative in its implications. To adopt a phrase of Kant's: 'Concepts without intuitions are empty. (But) Intuitions without concepts are blind'.

Similarities between women

The third characteristic of Women's Studies which limits its capacity for challenge is its concentration so far on the similarities between women. At the start
of Women Studies and separate education for women in the early 1970s it was
important to concentrate on the similarities between women – both for
sisterhood/solidarity and also for securing resources. Although by now a cliché,
it is nevertheless true that this sameness had tended to be a young, white, middle class one. It has been suggested recently that the time has come to 'concentrate increasingly on the differences between us as women which have divided
us under patriarchy and which cannot be allowed to continue to divide us as
feminists' – particularly divisions based on class, race and sexual identity.
Women's Studies courses have not reflected sufficiently the material conditions
and cultural inheritance of working class, black and lesbian women. This criticism may be less true in the case of working class women although even here
there is little room for complacency. The point is well made by Keith Jackson
when he says that until working class people take up education in their own
terms with the help of professionals it will remain a lost cause. Being the object
of analysis by people very different from oneself is not a comfortable experience.

'Education in people's own terms' is helped by recent developments in oral
history I think – recording the lived experiences of women as domestic and
industrial workers and as trade unionists – and in writers' workshops. Helping
make ordinary women's voices heard is a crucial task for Women's Studies.

In Glasgow and other areas of the West of Scotland a lot of exchanging of
stories goes on in groups, some terrible; many elicit outrage, compassion, laugh-
ter and feelings of solidarity. In another context this has been called testifying:
the tutors' role is to help make the process conscious and the content significant
by looking with the women for generalisations so as to start building up this
testimony in order to make sense of women's experiences, some of which are
rooted in class oppression. This is part of theory construction.

The struggle we're engaged in has to do with both the production of knowledge and its distribution. We need to find ways of getting past the 'gatekeepers'
of knowledge especially in the media, TV, magazines, popular journals, etc. We
need to understand better how they work in order to make our work more
widely accessible and, we hope, accepted.

It's a real threat to prevailing orthodoxies, suggests Jane Thompson, when
people who have traditionally been non-participants in adult education see a
direct relation between learning, action and their lives and when adult education lives up to its claim to 'relevance' and 'responsiveness' to 'needs'.

I have argued that our first priority must be to defend the gains already
made. But, to summarise some of the directions I'd like to see Women's Studies
taking in the future:

- It should be brought in from the margins in the sense of being properly
  resourced, funded and staffed but without losing its ability to challenge

the complacencies of the mainstream. Links must be built between community and institutional education – with both being transformed in the process.

- *It must lose (in some of its forms) its bias against theory, recognising that the validity of women's experience is enhanced, not undermined, by a critical, theoretical appraisal of these experiences. The converse is also true.*
- *And, third, we must be aware that our common cause as women is of limited value if it is not combined with an awareness of what our differences contribute to our lives and values.*

Given all of that we might have a really 'popular education' which in Richard Johnson's words means:

> *'Starting from the problems, experiences and social position of excluded majorities, from the position of the working people, women and black people. It means working up their lived experiences until they fashion a real alternative.'*

(extracted from Barr, 1984)

Commentary

My conference speech pre-figured what was to become a central theme of my work when I was at the WEA (and beyond) – a critique (by practical, organisational and discursive means) of what has been called 'therapeutic feminism' and its influence on adult women's education. When I was an evaluator of Headway, my feminism was firmly inscribed within an equality agenda and that agenda's then androgynous vision. I was reacting mainly against conservative and what I regarded as essentialist definitions of femininity and of being a woman as well as against restrictive notions of motherhood which, I believed, held women back (1).

At the time of writing the Headway report I was aware of that new strand within feminism – dubbed later as 'difference' or 'cultural' feminism – which, in its celebration of traditional female qualities and activities seemed to me to be every bit as 'essentialist' and politically conservative in its implications as the anti-feminist conservatism which in the early 1970s we all united against – and which was pivotal in my Headway critique. When I wrote my conference speech, counselling/therapeutic approaches to women's adult education, it seemed to me, were beginning to dominate work in the WEA. A counselling 'discourse' (although this is not how I would have put it then) was beginning to dominate 'progressive' debate in education generally and, more specifically, in adult education. This was to become the central motif of the research which I did as part of work submitted towards a Masters Degree in Education at Durham University, 1989–90.

It was not until the research which figures in my third case study that I really questioned my own attachment to theory with a big T and to have doubts about the 'romantic conservatism' depiction of more 'celebratory' and personal/psychologically-based forms of women's education which had figured in my speech. However, a major theme of this book is that research has to be located socially and historically; the same is true of feminism or feminisms; different forms of feminism, different feminist theories cannot be evaluated in the abstract; whether they are politically progressive or regressive depends on context. 'Everything is dangerous', Foucault reminds us: no theory can place itself beyond danger; and every new context requires that we 'assess the main danger'. This cannot be done in abstraction from actual practical – including political – activity. However, this insight escaped me when I came to do my next piece of research.

The Durham speech pre-figured a number of themes which were to be central to my future practice and, more specifically, to my future research. Centrally, these pivoted on the political conservatism which I saw attached to certain forms of (feminist) women's education and on the need for feminist women's education to give attention to issues of curriculum and knowledge development, going beyond personal experience towards critical thinking and the creation of new knowledge. By another quirk of fate, Durham was to be the place of the research which features in my second case study.

The rise of the counsellors

My reasons for doing the MA(Ed) in Guidance and Counselling, which required taking one year's unpaid leave from my WEA post, were complex. An official reason was that given the growing interest in counselling skills within adult education practice and in view of the kind of work in deprived areas which was expected of WEA tutors, by doing such a course I could pass on its benefits to my staff. The student-centredness and 'experiential learning' emphasis of educational programmes did sometimes bring up difficult emotional situations, particularly when working with women's groups in Areas for Priority Treatment (APTs).

I worried about tutors dabbling in 'therapeutic' work in which they had little experience or knowledge and I believed damage could be done if they saw counselling as part of their job. I also wanted an opportunity to read psychological literature (the course was run by two psychologists) because I felt rusty in the field. My last real thought on the matter was derived from Wittgenstein with whose philsophy I was possibly still in thrall. Psychology, believed Wittgenstein, can tell us nothing about ourselves. In psychology, he said, there are experimental methods and conceptual confusion.

My 'critical' agenda for doing the course included my belief that counselling had become increasingly institutionalised in 1980s Britain – in health and social services, in education (including adult education) as well as in explicit guidance and counselling services of various sorts, including private counsellors – and yet it was still a largely unexplored profession and set of processes. Several studies suggested that during the 1980s the number of women, especially, who had used the services of professional counsellors and therapists had increased dramatically. I believed that the growing faith in counsellors coincided with a waning of belief in politics and in social movements as forces for change and that it was part of the current trend to seek private, personal solutions to what were actually public, political problems.

In the 1970s sociologists were so thick on the ground that jokes abounded concerning sociologists and light bulbs. It seemed to me that the switch in the 1980s to the ubiquitous counsellor was a mark of a quite profound philosophical shift and change in popular consciousness which went beyond the popularity of counsellors *per se* (How many counsellors does it take to change a light bulb? It depends if the light bulb wants to change.). I recall sitting in my WEA office being told the difference between closed and open questions (a key distinction on beginners counselling skills courses) by a photocopier salesman fresh from a training course on salesmanship; and management training events which I attended at the time seemed indistinguishable from counselling skills training. I think I was anxious, too, that the educational point of tutors' work was becoming subordinated to a counselling role and that relationships based on solidarity and friendship were in danger of being replaced by professionalized notions of counselling.

At the same time, several of my friends, who in the 1970s organised politically for social change in their work and voluntary activities, seemed to be turning increasingly to therapy and counselling. Many were feminists who in the 1970s believed personal happiness involved social change; they fought for equal pay, improved childcare provision and more meaningful relationships beyond coupledom – including more human public services. I wanted to understand the current interest and faith in counselling because it seemed to me to indicate an important change in people's view of themselves and in their attitude to the possibilities for personal and social change (see Coward, 1989).

My interest in counselling was, then, broadly philosophical, since one of the practical functions of philosophy, I think, is to make us more aware of the 'mythological universe' within which we live – that body of assumptions and beliefs which develop from existential concerns, is culturally inherited and seldom questioned because mostly unconscious.

I confessed the nature of my interest at my admission interview for the MA(Ed), adding that I also had more personal reasons and, quite simply, needed time out. It was, then, with an attitude of scepticism that I embarked on the course. I had by then read Foucault's views on the modern predilection for 'confession' and was very taken with the idea that the modern spread of counselling in many institutional settings – social work, education, vocational guidance, general medicine – signified a new strategy of social control, a means of achieving discipline through self-discipline (see also Fairclough, 1989).

I thought that what was occurring within women's education in the WEA was part of a new, more general 'episteme' which was emerging on a wider societal level: a loss of faith in politics as a means of effecting change which, partaking in an ideology of intimacy and of the personal, transmuted political categories into psychological ones (see Coward, 1989 on this notion of an epistemic shift). I believed that the earlier, more political forms of women's education which took place in the WEA in the 1970s and early 1980s in close alliance with the Women's Movement were giving way to something much softer and less challenging. In a word, too much group counselling, confidence raising and assertiveness training – too little social, cultural and political education.

On a more personal level I also felt I had scores to settle with psychological ways of looking at the world and believed that immersion in its ways of thinking for a period would provide me with invaluable inside knowledge for critique or (I was open to the possibility) personal insight and greater appreciation of its ways. My feelings about counselling/therapy were certainly equivocal and ambivalent. I think I wanted to understand this ambivalence because it seemed to mirror other ambivalencies in myself, ambivalencies which have always made decisions difficult.

While researching this present book, I came across some lines from Sylvia Plath's *The Bell Jar* which I had written down shortly before embarking on the counselling course. Likening figs to choices, Plath writes:

> I wanted each and every one of them but choosing one meant losing all the rest, and as I sat there, unable to decide, the figs began to wrinkle and go black, and one by one, they plopped to the ground at my feet.

Things fade; alternatives exclude. Two close friends had recently died from cancer, one of whom I nursed as part of a support group of friends; my mother, too, whom I had also cared for, died soon after – also from cancer. I had developed a mysterious, excruciatingly painful arthritis. These experiences, coupled with the energy-sapping nature of the constant battle for funds in my job with the WEA, had left me physically and emotionally ragged, as well as self-questioning; they had also given me experience and inside knowledge of the workings of various alternative therapeutic approaches to health, including counselling.

People who have chronic illnesses like cancer and rheumatoid arthritis (my original diagnosis) are vulnerable to much quackery. Psychological explanations of such illnesses often go hand in glove with a kind of morality of health: illness becomes a failure (of personality, will power, personal lifestyle, inhibition or whatever) and health becomes a virtue – a further moral burden to add to an already desperate situation. In my distress and desire not to become dependent on heavy duty drugs, I sought out therapy, tried various diets.

Helpful colleagues and friends gave me vouchers for aromatherapy sessions and urged upon me books with titles like *You Can Heal Your Own Life* by Louise M. Hay. There seemed to be a spate of pop psychology and self-help books around at the time. (Maybe I just hadn't noticed before.) In Hay's book I read that arthritic patients are 'domineering but shy . . . and express their feelings in aggressive acts'. And in her helpful A–Z, from 'Abdominal Pains' to 'Wisdom Tooth Impacted' I learned that my arthritis was due to my 'deep-seated criticism of authority'. I might just have bought that account of my illness if I had not learned from a blood test that I had been bitten by a nasty little deer tick which carried Lyme Disease, an illness which mirrors the symptoms of arthritis and which, if not treated with antibiotics early on, can become chronic, even life-threatening.

Nevertheless, I was open-minded enough to believe there just might be something in the course for me. Given my mixed motives for doing the course, it is not surprising that, once inside it, I often felt like an outsider. Indeed, I sometimes took up the stance of observer, refusing the intimacies of our 'sensitivity group' for instance – a phenomenon not at all unusual on such courses. Indeed, such a stance was one which course leaders seemed adept at rationalising in terms of their own favoured frameworks for understanding group dynamics; from my point of view my refusal to engage was a quite passionate detachment.

Counselling in women's education

I chose my dissertation topic – the relationship between counselling and women's education in the WEA District in which the university was located – because I wanted to develop some of the strands of my previous theoretical and practical work; and I took my cue from Jane Thompson, bearer of the banner of radical and socialist-feminist inspired women's education in the 'really useful knowledge' tradition of adult education. At the time I came to do this research, Thompson was writing disapprovingly about a preoccupation with counselling and 'therapeutic feminism' within the WEA's women's studies programme. Thus, as a member of the Taking Liberties Collective, she criticised 'the lurch towards counselling and therapy models in women's education', which emphasise 'personal development through the interaction between the teacher/counsellor and student/client', for being both middle class and politically dangerous for women:

> Like psychotherapy from which all of these developments in women's education have their origins they also encourage their own brand of 'whitecoated expert'.
>
> (Taking Liberties Collective, 1989, p 158)

> Based on Kleinian (neo-Freudian?) and object relations theory and the work of Carl Rogers (haven't we had enough of all this?), this psycho-analytic approach to women's studies has very little to say about patriarchy . . . and even less to say to the majority of working class and black women for whom counselling (behaviour modification?) is not quite the radical solution to our poverty and oppression that we are looking for.
>
> (pp 129–30)

In preference to this 'unthreatening' version of women's education, the Taking Liberties Collective embraced women's education as political education explicitly linked to women's liberation.

A founding member of the NOW courses had acknowledged a few years previously that: 'This gradual shift of emphasis [towards more group counselling sessions concerned with personal growth] has raised the question of whether we are performing education or therapy' (Tallantyre, 1985, p 12). I decided to explore further the issues which already concerned me in my 1984 Durham conference keynote speech and that to do this I would seek the help of past and present tutors on the NOW courses. The aim was to discuss with them the relationship between counselling and education – and, to a limited extent, between personal and social change – in their own work. Eight tutors agreed to be involved.

The research

In the introduction to my dissertation, 'Counselling for a Change', I give an account of the research undertaken and methods used. In contrast with my Headway Report, I locate myself firmly 'in the frame'. I reproduce below an extract from this introduction so as to illustrate this (then) new self-consciousness and concern for 'reflexivity'. It is mainly written in the past tense because it was a *post facto* account of the research. Again, an ellipsis represents sections missed out of the original text.

Counselling for a change

Introduction

Knowing that the facts don't speak for themselves and being sensitive to how 'words weave the texture of our lives' (Mair, 1989, p 64) I wanted to understand the tutors' own frames of reference, to portray in their own words and in their own terms how they conceived of what they were involved in. I sought to 'make sense of' the tutors' 'making sense' of their experience as tutors on the NOW courses (Usher and Bryant, 1989, p 160).

I saw this in terms of getting at the formal and informal theories, values and beliefs lying behind their work and at the seldom surfaced 'practical knowledge' which is embedded in practice. Such knowledge according to Aristotle is unlike theoretical or technical knowledge since it is not knowledge about anything but is knowledge of how to act in an informed and committed way in the world, in this case as informed and committed tutors in women's education. It was through conversation, not structured interviews, that I pursued this . . .

In the process I resolved to adopt a principle of uncertainty, to be wary of truth and not search for final answers. In appropriately contradictory manner, therefore, I found myself both attracted and repelled by Miller Mair's Between Psychology and Psychotherapy (1989) in its plea for a 'poetics' of experience to set alongside any scientific approach to the understanding of human experience . . .

Agreeing up to a point with Mair's contention that in the pursuit of understanding ourselves or others 'intimate knowledge is likely to teach us more than distant knowledge . . . personal knowledge likely to change us more than impersonal knowledge' (Mair, 1989, p 2) . . .

I enjoyed the 'anything goes' approach warmly recommended by other diarists like Tristine Rainer and grabbed at the liberation contained in such promises as: 'Ambiguity is one of the primary qualities of honest writing. It is also a quality of a deeply felt life . . . Out of the contradictions and ambiguity a larger truth seems to emerge' (Rainer, 1989, p 40) . . .

Rowan regards 'making sense' as a key phase of the research cycle – reflecting on experience, 'negotiating meaning', research as a continuous reconstitution of knowledge rather than as seeking knowledge of the previously unknown. This kind of process is essentially open-ended and never-ending and is itself educational in that it effects change through the effort to understand (Usher and Bryant, 1989, pp 160ff). Implicit in this way of doing research is a view of the relationship between theory and practice whereby dialogue is seen as deepening understanding and opening up the possibility of new experience and so changes in practice (Usher and Bryant, 1989, pp 192ff).

I have no wish to produce a research report as 'sanitized text', with my hunches, assumptions, false starts, informal theories and reflections as well as prejudices excluded. In saying this I am in agreement with Rowan when he argues for multiple research cycles instead of the 'one big bang' type of research project . . .

Instead of talking about 'pilot work' and trying to get rid of this as quickly as possible to get on to the real thing, we should, suggests Rowan, talk of 'early cycles' of research which should be written up and made available for inspection. This is because it is in the early stages that we reveal our presuppositions most fully or, to use Usher and Bryant's phrase, it is here that our work is least 'sanitized' (Usher and Bryant, 1989, p 193) . . .

We can never surface all of our presuppositions, of course, and we must take the point expressed by Doris Lessing when she says: 'We do not know what our prejudices are. We are lucky if some friend from outside our own culture considers it worthwhile to tell us what they are' (Lessing, 1990).

However, the important things to say about myself in this context include the following:

I would describe myself as a feminist and a socialist . . .

I believe that education should not divorce feeling from thought, the affective from the cognitive. I warm to Mair's term, 'feeling thoughts' (1989, p 200) . . .

I also believe in the intimate connectedness of the personal and the political and with C. Wright Mills that only when the 'sociological imagination' is both personal and political can it 'make a difference to the quality of human life in our time':

> Know that the problems of the social sciences . . . must include
> both troubles and issues, biography and history and the range of
> their intimate relations. Within that range the life of the individual
> and the making of societies occur.
>
> (Mills, 1959, p 226)

Bad faith?

I find this almost impossible to read now without wanting to throw up. I think I was aware at the time of writing the above introduction to my dissertation that I was writing against the grain (of myself) in much of it. It embarrasses me now to read it. It feels like a pose adopted for a particular audience, that is, for the counsellors who were 'facilitating' the course but who were also my assessors. There was, in fact, a lack of fit between my know how about how to play the game (in order to meet discipline-specific examiners' expectations) and my considered theoretical views. I am not sure that this was a calculation on my part so much as an almost unconscious wish to please. But the introduction to my dissertation strikes me now, at least to a degree, as an exercise in bad faith. The pose I adopt in it was actually out of kilter with my real considered views at the time. This was especially so in relation to a claim in the introduction to be adopting the stance of 'new paradigm' research, as dubbed by Reason and Rowan (1981), and the favoured methodological approach of the course. Reason and Rowan construe 'new paradigm research' as involving a move from a 'male' (hard) towards a 'female' (soft) methodological approach: 'A feminine science . . . is not afraid of the good, the speculative, the vague or the unique; indeed it openly courts them, openly confronts them, and makes positive virtues of them . . . a Feeling [sic] science'. Interestingly, I do not refer to *this* aspect of 'new paradigm' research in my dissertation introduction. I had already scornfully rejected its notion of a 'feminine science' in an essay for the course. And I did so on the grounds that its image of femininity was a fantasy product of theories already assimilated to masculinity; as such it was totally unhelpful to those of us trying to do *feminist* research.

Another paradox exists in the disjunction between the voice of the introduction and the bulk of the dissertation. In the introduction I (very self-consciously) disavow any desire to produce a research report as 'sanitized text', with my hunches, assumptions, false starts, informal theories and reflections as well as prejudices excluded. I therefore provided a brief credo before launching into my research report. Yet, despite these posturings towards 'intimacy', 'ambiguity' and 'uncertainty' the actual product of the research is anything but ambiguous and uncertain. There is, in other words a lack of fit between the introduction to my dissertation, with its praise of ambiguity and incompleteness – its explicit repudiation of the aim of producing a sanitized text – and the main body of the work, with its implicit desire for coherence and closure. In other words, despite appearing as myself in the main body of the text in a number of conversations, and despite a research process which was, indeed, very open-ended and conversational, my supposed open-ended agenda concerning practical knowledge turned into what has been called a 'flight to theory' where different theories vie, abstractly, with one another (Stronach, 1989).

The voice of my introduction to 'Counselling for a Change', in its praise of intimacy, uncertainty and ambiguity and in its statement of personal values, certainly suggests a decisive break with the stance adopted in Headway. And indeed my actual research practice did to a significant degree meet 'new paradigm' criteria of good practice as I enunciated these in my dissertation introduction. That is to say, it was relatively open ended, collaborative and educational in the sense intended by Reason and Rowan and Usher and Bryant. My research practice with the tutors was educational in the sense required by new paradigm research. It was concerned with practical reasoning: my effort was to engage with the tutors' 'know-how', rather than their 'knowing that'. I wanted to know about the informal and formal theories which were implicit in their practice – specifically as these related to the interface between education and counselling/therapy. I was interested, that is, in their practical reason rather than their theoretical reason or knowledge *per se*. Our discussions therefore centred on their educational practice – what they actually did on NOW courses – and the knowledge contained in this practice in terms of which they made sense of what they did. And, because I consciously aspired to reflexive research practice, we also discussed the process of enquiry which I was engaged in. In fact my discussions with individual tutors figured in their own team meetings, thereby, reportedly, influencing their educational practice; and, reciprocally, their comments on what I was doing and how I was doing it had effects on my subsequent research interviews.

But in the research product – the main text of my dissertation – what I do is use quotations from tutors to illustrate different rationales for women's education and particular practices in it – rationales which I had already set up. In effect, I fit the tutors' views into my prepared, pre-packaged categories and dichotomies which pivoted on a division between, on the one hand, 'therapeutic feminism' (two versions: liberal/'person-centred'/Rogerian and 'radical'/psychoanalytic/Chodorowian) and on the other hand, 'socialist-feminism'. I then judge these in terms of a political framework – that is, as leading, on the one hand, to 'conservative', socially reproductive and reinforcing educational practices and, on the other, to 'radical', challenging ones. The categorisation of theoretical feminism within which my account fits is, then, broadly, the political categorisation of 1970s feminism – that is, liberal, radical, socialist/Marxist. It is around this same categorisation that a number of other sociological analyses of women's education have been organised (eg Blundell, 1992; Middleton, 1984).

Liberal, radical and socialist feminists

Thus, according to the liberal feminist discourse on women's education the aim is equal access to existing provision for women; women-only provision is construed as a step towards this – increasing confidence, encouraging individuals' 'self-actualisation' through the 'facilitative' group process methods derived from Carl Rogers; the emphasis here is on catching up, compensating for past disadvantage. I illustrate the influence of this liberal and person-centred discourse on NOW courses (having outlined this rationale in my text) through the words of several of the tutors, but primarily through one in particular:

> *For learning to take place you have to create an atmosphere with the same basic principles necessary to create a good counselling relationship. Positive regard, being non-crititical, showing respect for everybody. . . . Ultimately, what's important to me is understanding me. The understanding of all of the other things is for the understanding and therefore development of self.*
>
> *[BW]*

According to radical and socialist/Marxist discourses, on the other hand, women are not just disadvantaged but oppressed and this oppression is intrinsic to social structure; part of this oppression is their subordination within a knowledge system which is patriarchally constructed, that is, out of male experience, taken to be *human* experience. For this reason, neither radical nor socialist/Marxist feminists are content with an equal opportunity agenda for education, that is, attaining access to existing educational provision.

Radical feminists see women as having distinctive contributions to make in all areas of life and work; for them educational objectives should centre on nurturing and developing women in their own right (see Parsons, 1993). This means providing women-only courses and fostering the development of women-centred knowledge and, in sum, fostering women's uniqueness. In my research study I illustrate the influence on NOW courses of this discourse and its association, there, with psychotherapeutic assumptions, mainly through the words of one tutor (2):

> *The tutor's role is to be the container of everything, the outer boundary holder. At the beginning the tutor will have to be prepared to hold an awful lot of dependency needs for the individuals and the group as a whole. But if the group is working well and going through the usual stages groups go through, then, increasingly, members of the group will nurture one another, meet each other's dependency needs.*
>
> *[EA]*

At this point in the text I appear as myself, saying 'I'd be enraged if I thought my tutor saw it like that', to which the rejoinder from this tutor, also recorded, is that I wouldn't be, unless I was 'in flight'.

Marxist/socialist feminists are less happy with separate provision and criticise the emphasis on subjective experience, concentrating instead on the social and political structures which cause the experiences. They criticise radical feminists for failing to give due recognition to class and other differences between women which affect their experience (hence, eg Jane Thompson's criticism of WEA women's studies courses for being thoroughly middle class) and for not acknowledging sufficiently how adult education's ideology and curriculum, more generally, reinforce women's traditional role. The socialist feminist discourse stresses the need to transcend the individualist 'needs-meeting' ideology of adult education (see below and Keddie, 1980) and, rather than promoting separatism in the curriculum, it seeks to promote the transformation of the whole adult education curriculum (because of its underlying gender assumptions), acknowledging too the limitations of education as a means of social change. The importance of the development of knowledge beyond the confines of self is stressed (Parsons, 1993). This viewpoint is illustrated in my dissertation by means of quotations like the following:

> *I've got difficulties with person-centredness . . . I've seen several person-centred groups kind of revelling in it all. I think in what we've got, which is after all a fairly limited educational course, I want to bring in other things, like the experience of women who aren't in the group, encourage critical thinking, analysis and action, so it isn't just about validation. I want to open people's*

minds to what's happening to others. I'm aware of women's need
to develop themselves but we have to see it in terms of politics and
history.

[JO]

In my text, the conversations with tutors are organised around a theoretical discussion about 'counselling by stealth' in women's education and the need for an explicitly radical agenda for adult education generally, as well as women's education in particular. This critique draws on the idea, voiced by another critic of the WEA, that in recent years 'progressive discussion' among adult educators had 'privileged process over content and pedagogy over knowledge in its elevation of personal growth'. In short

> *it has again followed the line of least resistance, of the least risky*
> *form of innovation. The real challenge . . . is to find an appropriate*
> *curriculum for the coming years, to define what forms, fields and*
> *types of knowledge are needed by the social movements with*
> *which the WEA must form its strategic alliance of the future. It is*
> *not to be expected that the knowledge will simply replicate inher-*
> *ited academic disciplines; that definition of liberal education can be*
> *readily abandoned. But to opt for a simplistic celebration of spon-*
> *taneous consciousness is simply the pooling of ignorance. In the*
> *face of the forces ranged against us, it will not do.*
> *(Field, 1987, p 18)*

I end my dissertation with a clarion call to adult educators:

> *We have learned about process and the importance of listening and*
> *the benefits of networking from the marriage of feminism and*
> *humanism. And these must be spread throughout adult education.*
> *But now we have to grapple with issues of the curriculum, with*
> *what is the 'really useful knowledge' which will act as a vehicle for*
> *cultural and social change; with alliances with women's organisa-*
> *tions to act as counter-developments in educational policy and*
> *practice; and, crucially, I believe, with issues of class, race and sex-*
> *ual identity. I still agree with what I wrote in 1984 and delivered*
> *in a talk here, 'that the validity of women's experience is enhanced,*
> *not undermined by a critical, theoretical appraisal of these experi-*
> *ences' and that 'we must be aware that our common cause as*
> *women is of limited value if it is not combined with an awareness*
> *of what our differences contribute to our lives and values.'*

Theory and practice

In sum, rather than allowing beliefs, experiences and opinions to express them-selves as such (as the introduction to my dissertation enjoins) I actually set out to prove something. And what I wanted to 'prove' was precisely how certain discourses contribute towards reproducing or challenging the status quo regard-ing gender relations. In taking for granted my own categories of analysis, I interpret and organise, trim and edit, pinch and set my account around a number of boxes, set up as exclusive alternatives with nothing left over. My favoured 'social and political-education' definition of emancipatory education for women which comes at the end actually flows out of (is, indeed already contained in) my initial political and critical social science-inflected categorisation – with which I began. There is, then, a circularity and startling disjunction between the 'voice' in the introduction, with its stress on ambiguity, uncertainty and contingency ('no sanitized texts') and the main body of the text which finally emerges.

As a result, too, I also missed an opportunity to use the research as a space for discussing possible *new* subjectivities for adult educators, that is, self-concepts which might actually cut across and escape my own restrictive categories and polarities, (eg between therapeutic *or* political adult educators; between social/cultural reproduction *or* challenge). Such a project might have been more creative. In the next chapter which continues my second case study I pick up on this theme and in a discussion of women's education and feminist pedagogy which arises out of this chapter I try to move beyond the rigidities and simplicities implicit in my 'Counselling for a Change' research dissertation.

7 Feminist pedagogy and knowledge

The social context of inquiry

In this chapter I continue my second case study, concentrating on the view of women's education which I promoted within 'Counselling for a Change' and critiquing that view from the point of view of recent developments in feminist theory (including philosophy) and feminist pedagogy. I then locate the discussion within wider debates concerning popular/radical adult education practice.

First, I want to take up a theme which was introduced earlier – the need to evaluate texts contextually, that is, in relation to the institutional and discursive context in which they are produced rather than abstractly. And I want to suggest that it was precisely the social and cultural context in which I produced my 'Counselling for a Change' account that gave it its (political) meaning. At the time I wrote my account I believed that a crucially important distinction was being eroded among adult education practitioners and theorists, including those who saw themselves as progressive. This is the distinction between adult education as a complex socio-political process and learning as a psychological process.

At the time that I was writing up my NOW research for my dissertation, 'adult education' as a field of study, as it was conventionally understood, and as it was practised was, I believed, becoming conflated with and reduced to psychological theories and practices of 'facilitating adult learning' and 'meeting individual adult learning needs'. Notions of andragogy (the theory of how adults learn: see Knowles, 1978) had saturated the field and were, it seemed to me, becoming part of many adult educators' taken-for-granted worldview and self-legitimation. This, I think, is reflected in the continuing dearth of any significant literature on the political economy of adult education, a neglect which is part of a wider theoretical and political problem (1).

Anthony Giddens has argued that the nature of modern institutions is bound up with trust in abstract systems, especially trust in expert systems (1990, p 83). This feature of modernity, that is, the shift towards professionalism and certified expertise, poses, I think, particular problems for adult educators, who are not privy to any body of specialised knowledge on which to base a claim for special status (Keddie, 1980). But a claim to special status on the basis of expertise as *facilitators of adult learning* rather than on the basis of special knowledge seems to fit the bill. It also provides a kind of professional legitimation which rather neatly meshes with *current* policies of individualizing adult and continuing education through processes of open learning and new 'virtual' institutions like the University for Industry (see Barr and Birke, 1995).

In addition, the increased prevalence of a kind of therapeutic consciousness within progressive adult education was, I believed, an indication of a shift of emphasis from social to individual transformation. It represented, from my point of view, a shift away from adult education's radical purposes and concerns for generating and promoting 'really useful knowledge' for specific social groups and movements, towards an individual needs-meeting agenda which was thoroughly conservative in its implications and particularly unhelpful to women.

Furthermore, when I came to do my dissertation, it seemed to me that a shift towards 'cultural difference feminism' was well entrenched within feminist theory, that 'a feminist version of the eternal female haunt[ed] the dominant voice of British American feminism' (Segal, 1987). And I sympathised with Michele Barrett (1987) in her claim that such views, which actually exaggerate the differences between men and women, appealed to feminists who wish to celebrate essential differences between men and women, believing that femininity is the better identity, masculinity the source of brutality and insensitivity (conceived as universal characteristics because women mother worldwide).

What I objected to in this cultural feminism was its 'essentialism', that it seemed to take for granted certain culturally specific women's activities and attributes and, by valorising these – wanting to preserve rather than change gender differences – it diverted attention away from male practices and roles in favour of denigrating 'masculinity'. In sum, cultural essentialism, it seemed to me, was no better than biological essentialism. And it was mistaken, because it failed to account for the many women, including myself, who did not easily fit into their role as women but experienced many contradictions and conflicts within their feminine/female identity. It could not, that is, account for what Jacqueline Rose speaks of as 'the resistance to identity which lies at the heart of psychic life' (Rose, 1983, p 9) and which was so central to my own experience. That experience told me that the notion of a unitary, coherent identity as a woman was simply wrong and that on the contrary our subjectivity is highly complex and contradictory. It told me, too, that in some families, including my own, fathers are caring and nurturing, mothers distant and powerful; daughters may bond with fathers, mothers with sons; and class as well as race, I knew, from personal experience and reading novels and theoretical accounts, made a difference.

In other words, my main interest – and one reason, as I see it now, that I felt I was writing against the grain (of myself) in my dissertation introduction – was in a social cultural phenomenon, and in understanding this in sociological/political terms. This was, as I saw it, the colonisation of women's adult education in the WEA (and, indeed, of progressive adult education more generally) by a counselling discourse and set of practices. Viewed in this light, my account was a form of social critique, perhaps, even, a form of resistance. I wanted to suggest that those among us who are interested in adult education which might contribute to progressive social change – for women, specifically –

should resist assimilation into dominant ways of representing ourselves to our-selves – as, that is, 'facilitators' of adult learning, meeters of 'adult learning "needs" ', 'counsellors/therapists', 'human resource developers', to name but a few. And we should resist, too, the different versions of 'therapeutic feminism' which were infiltrating women's education because they did not sufficiently challenge this individual needs-meeting ideology of adult education.

But there was something else going on too. In the the academic context in which I produced my text, there was another growing orthodoxy: a 'postmodernist' critique of realism generally and a celebration of 'ambiguity', 'heterogeneity' and 'difference'. It could well be that despite what I said in my introduction to the dissertation (and further evidence pehaps that we are not transparent to ourselves – and not, indeed, undivided, unitary beings) my stronger inclination re-asserted itself in the body of the text, that is, to critique all claims of authority *and* all attacks on it, including those that had so quickly (and so, perhaps, suspiciously) become very powerful indeed within the acad-emy (see Minnich, 1989, p 155).

In sum, the context in which I was writing privileged psychological dis-courses in adult education generally and in women's education specifically; within feminism, too, cultural or 'difference' feminism was on the ascendancy, setting the terms of much of the debate in the late 1970s and 1980s; and, furthermore, new academic trends and fashions were gaining ground. Once again, in the particular context of its production and reception, writing an assertive text may be precisely the kind of intervention that was needed at the time. (More unkindly to myself, my incipient tendency towards what Feyerabend calls 'ratiofascism' was still in the ascendant, still dominant, however uncon-sciously; see Feyerabend, 1987).

Abstract knowledge

The problem with my account was that it was not contextualised but theorised in abstraction. Moreover, in proposing my view of women's education as, basi-cally, social and political education and in railing against the borrowing by adult education (specifically women's adult education) of notions from psy-chology (humanist/person-centred or object relations) on the grounds that it thereby adopts its problematic features, I was less fastidious about scrutinising my own sociological/political framework for its problematic features. And, in viewing and assessing these discourses through the lens of my sociologically derived discourse, judging them in terms of its criteria, I may have missed the point/failed to see some things which could not be captured by its categories. However, I did not provide this contextualisation in my account. Had I done so I might have been forced to notice that in the late 1980s, after 10 years of liberal feminist advice (still the dominant feminist voice in adult education) to join the male world, it was perhaps a helpful corrective to hear cultural (radi-cal) feminism argue the superiority of the virtues and values of a women's world!

In fact I now think that judging cultural 'difference' feminism in terms of its adequacy as a social/political theory largely misses the point and mistakes its value. It should be judged, perhaps, less in terms of its adequacy as a social/political theory (which is how I evaluated it) and more in terms of its psychological and aesthetic appeal. As such, that is, as the product of an aesthetic and psychological (rather than political) conception of liberation, it is less concerned with political, strategic means of ending the oppression of women than with expressing a vision of a different sort of world based on a different set of values and priorities from those of the present (Felski, 1989, p 149). As such, it has an important place in any feminism whose appeal is to be wider than the narrow confines of the academy or politics as conventionally understood. (We just need to be wary of mystified notions of femininity and uncritical celebrations of irrationalism which can lurk within this aesthetic and can lead to very conservative cultural and political practices indeed.)

A huge strength of feminism is that it is not just an academic discourse but inspires a social, cultural and educational movement. The point I want to make here is that a consideration of the political value of any form of feminism ('therapeutic feminism' included) cannot be decided in the abstract but only in the context of considering the relations among real women, concrete educational processes and wider social processes. Viewed in terms of this larger context and accepting that adult education should cut across all boundaries I would now reject my former puritanism *vis à vis* what is or is not beyond the pale. Indeed, recent commentaries emphasise the diversity which now exists within feminist theory and the influence of different feminisms (and not just academic feminist theory) within education. Gaby Weiner has enunciated some of these in her recent book (Weiner, 1994). This suggests that my classificatory scheme for my 'Counselling for a Change' dissertation was somewhat simplistic – even at the time. Some critics have also pointed to the difficulties in practice of identifying clear differences in perspective and strategy between different feminists working in education (Acker, 1986). Had I been more scrupulous in my dissertation I would have had plenty of evidence to make this point.

The 'man' of reason

I believe, too, that my dismissal of the preoccupation with subjective experience in much women's education was ill-judged. I was under the influence of male critics like Sennet who saw in the contemporary concern with subjectivity a degeneration of the public sphere into an unseemly obsession with private and personal affairs. From the point of view of women's lives and history, however, the implications of such a concern may be the exact opposite – precisely because women's lives have been largely defined, historically, by their location within the private sphere. It was for this reason of course that 'private', personal experience was often the starting point for critical reflection within the women's movement.

More importantly, perhaps, the open discusssion of such experiences and of their wider implications exemplified a shift of the problematic of 'femininity' *from* the private *to* the public realm (Felski, 1989, p 115). Following through on the implications of this is something that some feminist educators working in the theory and practice of women's studies have still failed to do. For it is in education that we learn what is acceptable knowledge. Here, in the main, things seen as private, subjective, emotional are denigrated largely *because* seen as feminine (2).

Some feminist philosophers have argued that the limits of reason have been fixed to exclude certain qualities which are then assigned to women (Gatens, 1991; Lloyd, 1984). Their claim is that 'femininity' is constituted partly by this exclusion:

> Rational knowledge has been construed as a transcending, trans-
> formation or control of natural forces and 'the feminine' has been
> associated with what rational knowledge transcends, dominates or
> leaves behind.
>
> (Lloyd, 1984, p 2)

This notion of reason as a method of thinking which sheds the non-intellectual and contextual and which requires rigorous training is very culturally specific. Yet it functions in our education system as a 'mystified concept', that is to say, as if it were entirely obvious and the only way of being rational (Minnich, 1989). Although it is not known if men and women differ cognitively the assumption that they do has had far-reaching consequences; it shapes in subtle and profound ways our lived experience. A telling example of how this works out in practice is provided in Valerie Walkerdine's research on secondary school maths teaching. Walkerdine recounts a striking tale of how girls who are actually doing well at maths are still seen by their teachers as not really 'having what it takes'. Boys, on the other hand, who are actually doing poorly, are still credited as 'having potential, just being lazy'.

According to Walkerdine, girls end up in a double-bind; no matter what methods they adopt in their pursuit of mathematical knowledge, none appears correct:

> If they are successful, their teachers consider that they produce this
> success in the wrong way: by being conscientious . . . and hard-
> working. Successful boys were credited with natural talent and
> flexibility, the ability to work hard and take risks. Further, teach-
> ers tend to think that boys fit the role of 'proper learner' – active,
> challenging, rule-breaking.
>
> (Walkerdine and the Girls and Mathematics Unit, 1989, p 155)

It is hardly surprising that when boys at school are asked why they are not doing well, they say it's because they don't work hard enough. When girls are asked the same question, they say they aren't clever enough (Grant, 1994).

While deterring many women from more abstract theoretical work, such dominant and gendered notions of what is and who can have 'real intelligence' and rationality may also serve to obscure other ways of being rational if these do not fit dominant ideals and social arrangements. If recognised and given shape in practical social arrangements and pedagogical practices, on the other hand, these other rationalities could serve as a challenge to dominant systems of thought which exclude so many (3).

Acknowledging other ways of knowing is a central message and focus of a rare piece of research carried out by Wendy Luttrell (Luttrell, 1989) on the relationship between working class women and knowledge. It is rare, because most of the feminist literature on the theme of women and knowledge has been carried out at an abstract, philosophical, level, with no reference to actual, historically situated women, or, if it is empirically based – like the much-quoted Belenky *et al.* (1986) study of *Women's Ways of Knowing* – it has paid little attention to important differences between women, differences based in their location within a society divided along race, class and gender lines, for instance. Luttrell's study of black and white working class women attending adult basic education programmes suggests that women's perceptions of knowledge are shaped by complex gender, racial and class relations of power.

All of the women interviewed by Wendy Luttrell distinguish between 'common sense' and 'schoolwise' intelligence, that is, between knowledge produced through experience and knowledge produced in textbooks by experts. They share similar ideas about their common sense abilities to care for others and regard common sense as a way of judging truth on the basis of what trusted people have seen or experienced and know to be true. The claim to have common sense knowledge, suggests Luttrell, recognises and validates working class solutions to problems despite the power of scientific knowledge: for example, relying on friends who know the ropes, seeking advice from people who can be trusted, not because they are professional experts but because they share the same problems.

It has been pointed out that how to share and develop the collective knowledge which results from caring for others is a problem when such experiential knowledge is dismissed as purely subjective. Yet knowledge born of practice, as in midwifery and nutrition, is often more securely founded than the proposals from an often 'arbitrary science' (Rose, 1994).

However, in Luttrell's study there were also differences between women. She suggests, for example, that although both black and white women claim common sense knowledge, they are distanced from their intellectual capacities in somewhat different ways. But, for both, the ideology of intelligence acts as a filter through which these women sometimes deny the actual experience and knowledge they have in everyday life.

In her study, white working class women, when asked about people they know who are intelligent, refer exclusively to men. That is, they see some aspects of common sense as real intelligence but only those ways of knowing associated with men's skilled, manual work and abilities. They ignore the range of their own self-taught activities such as helping children with their homework, and their own common sense abilities, which involve activities in the family or community, they similarly dismiss as trivial, as acquired naturally or intuitively, unlike the men's craft knowledge, which is more obviously acquired through public, collective experience. The black women interviewed by Luttrell also locate their common sense knowledge in a number of caretaking and domestic skills performed for others. Like the white working class women they refer to their common sense as 'intuitive' and as stemming from feelings; similarly, they most often focus on the common sense it requires to raise children. Luttrell (1989, p 40) comments:

> The [black and white] women's classification of their knowledge as
> 'affective', not 'cognitive'; as 'intuitive', not 'learned'; or as 'feel-
> ings', not 'thoughts' all reflect an acceptance of dominant concep-
> tions of knowledge and ultimately diminish women's power.

The important point is that the learning process involved in acquiring common
sense knowledge – based on the caring and relational aspects of the women's
lives – remains invisible; this 'intuitive' knowledge, suggests Luttrell, is individualized and personal, not collective or public. It is associated with feelings and
intuition as opposed to thinking and learning, experienced as affective, not
cognitive.

Indeed, Luttrell suggests that it is because women are not allowed, ideolog-
ically, to be the sources or agents of rational, legitimated knowledge that the
women she interviewed associate the (common sense) knowledge they do claim
to have with feelings and intuitions. Both classifications ('common sense' and
'intuition') place women in less powerful positions relative to men (both black
and white) and to white middle class professionals (male and female). And they
do so, she suggests,

> not simply because women are . . . seduced into believing in the
> ideological split between feelings and rationality . . . but because
> the real nature of women's knowledge and power is hidden from
> view and excluded from thought.
>
> (Luttrell, 1989, p 40)

However, black and white women do not experience their exclusion in the
same way. 'Race' influences how the women claim knowledge as well as how
they experience exclusion from what counts as knowledge. This is reflected in
how the black women, unlike the white women, do claim their own common
sense or 'motherwit' as real intelligence, perceived as being based, in part, on
the ability to work hard and get the material things they and their children
need, with or without a man's support. They also regard their ability to deal
with racism as another form of real intelligence which they share with black
men against the ignorance of whites. I see this as relating to Patricia Hill Collins'
distinction between knowledge and wisdom, and the use of experience as divid-
ing them. Knowledge without wisdom is adequate for the powerful, says Collins,
but wisdom is essential to the survival of the subordinate (Collins, 1990,
p 208).

Luttrell suggests that it may be because black women's work as women is
also manifestly the work of black survival that it is not as easily trivialised as
white women's. Also, black working class women are not distanced from their
knowledge in the same way that white working class women are: the daily
reminder of their collective identity as working class blacks, Luttrell suggests,
mitigates the daily reminder of their individual identity as women.

Nevertheless, the black women's claim to 'real intelligence' cannot be translated easily into perceptions of academic skill or competence, for the fact remains
that some modes of knowing and rationality have come to stand as pinnacles of
what is regarded as real knowledge. Knowledge arising out of the ability to
work with people, with emotions and with a range of modes of thinking is

devalued as subjective knowledge. Knowledge which arises from an ability to deal with tightly defined abstract systems is valued highly as 'objective' (4).

A richer education: The limits of critical reason

Feminists working in education claim that a central challenge of an education for all women is to confront these divisions, and to acknowledge their power. If women are to claim rather than simply receive an education – an act that 'can literally mean the difference between life and death' (Rich, 1979, p 232) we have to 'make visible what has been rendered invisible' – women's work, knowledge and power. This requires, in turn, not the abandonment of rationality as somehow inherently masculine, but re-envisaging it in less exclusive ways and in ways, specifically, which do not construe emotions and intellect as distinct and separate faculties. According to some commentators, a narrow view of what is rational has created educational systems that can make many of us feel inadequate because 'our ways of thinking, of making sense, are not met, recognised, given external form, clarified and then returned to us refined and strengthened' (Minnich, 1989, p 111). Recent feminist writing stresses that we need to find the 'suppressed voices' to change and enrich education.

I now believe that the social/political education project as defining women's education which was implicit in my dissertation was too limited and narrowly rationalistic, neglecting issues of complex subjectivity, downplaying the emotional component of learning, relying on 'seeing the light' through a purely rational understanding of causes and structures and giving too much power to the tutor to define its terms (Lusted, 1986). It may be that, in my concern to critique politically 'soft' constructions of the work of (feminist) adult education practice, and my espousal of a more 'critical' pedagogy, I failed to notice the tendency in my own thinking and writing towards a notion of the adult educator as 'transformative pedagogue' and 'master (or mistress) of truth' which subsequent feminist writing has tried to dispel.

My Durham dissertation ended with an exhortation to those working in women's education not to dismiss the 'theoretical appraisal' of women's experiences, echoing my Durham keynote speech in its insistence that to 'despise theory' is self-defeating. In this I was in fact implicitly wedded to a narrow notion of theory; I accorded far too much respect to the theory produced by academic feminists like Mary Evans who were most concerned not to jeopardise the fragile position of women's studies in the academy by undermining the status of the women's studies teacher or the rigour of what is taught. I had not incorporated into my writing that 'juicy' notion of rigour which attached to the informal educational work of the women's movement. Nor did I acknowledge that the writings on pedagogy which derived from that academic world contradicted the kind of project afoot in women's studies/women's education in an adult education context. For the trouble with the knowledge written and produced by people like Evans (and myself at the time) is that it is likely to denigrate – deem as not-knowledge – in an academic context the other knowledges of students. In such a context 'expert knowledge' always wins. I mistook theory for Theory. And yet, as Walters and Manicom insist,

> The process of bringing to light aspects of experience, reflecting
> upon and making sense of them, finding concepts and drawing
> connections, pulling out and exposing the assumptions – this is
> theorizing . . .
>
> (Walters and Manicom, 1996, p 11)

The trouble with my 'political education' construction of women's education, even though it foregrounded *feminist* knowledge, was that it came very close to 'banking' education, depositing one's worldview on others – a process hardly likely to be empowering to the receivers. Indeed, the 'really useful knowledge' tradition in British adult education on which I drew in my dissertation has been criticised on the grounds that, all too often, the adult educator working in that tradition believes she/he holds the key; in other words, she *knows* what this really useful knowledge is (see Lusted, 1989). In essence, it is social and political knowledge of a specific sort – and not just in the sense that all knowledge can be said to be political.

Furthermore, in my anxiety to place questions of knowledge-production centre-stage in feminist education I wrote as if 'we' had cracked issues of pedagogy and process. And this was far from being the case.

Feminist pedagogy

A 'critique of rationalism' (best understood, I think, as a critique of narrow notions of rationality, as excluding emotions and verging on what I've called elsewhere in this book 'ratiofascism') finds expression in the range of ideas which come under the heading of 'feminist pedagogy' which is now a kaleidoscopic mix of liberal, socialist, radical, cultural and postmodernist feminisms (see Aird, 1985; Pritchard Hughes, 1995; Lather, 1991; Weiler, 1991; Ellsworth, 1989; Berlak, 1989; hooks, 1994; Thompson, 1983). Feminist pedagogy has arisen partly out of so-called 'critical' pedagogy and criticisms of it for ignoring gender (Ellsworth, 1989; Weiler, 1991). Most theoretical discussion of it derives from women's studies in colleges and universities in North America and Western Europe, that is, from the formal sector. This is an indication of the unfortunate gap (referred to in Chapter 3) which has grown up between good grassroots women's education and academic feminists 'who tend to belittle the impact of the former because they feel it is not sufficiently grounded in academic theory' (McGivney, 1997, pers. com.).

A complex notion of feminist pedagogy can be derived from this still emerging body of work, much of which accords a central place to feeling as a source of knowledge – including oppositional knowledge – of the world. It is notable in this respect that of two of adult education's frequently cited 'founding fathers', Dewey and Habermas, Dewey was friendly to emotions as potential sources of insight, Habermas, following Kant, positively hostile to them as sources of delusion (Nussbaum, 1994). Weiler (1991) has pointed out the awkward contradiction in treating emotion and experience as sources of knowledge while recognising, too, that they are socially constructed. But she accepts Audre

Lorde's view that because we have the capacity for self-reflection and self-critique we are never wholly socially determined and can challenge our *habitual ways of feeling* as well as thinking. Lorde retains belief in the power of deeper feeling to challenge dominant stereotypes and notions of truth and as a guide to action. She questions the depth of critical understanding of the forces that shape our lives that can be achieved using only the rational and abstract methods of analysis: 'For the master's tools will never dismantle the master's house. They may allow us to beat him at his own game but they will never enable us to bring about genuine change' (Audre Lorde, *Sister Outsider*).

We have the capacity to challenge our own ways of feeling and emotion – as well as knowing – through collective enquiry, insists Lorde. This notion, of the importance of paying attention to gut feelings as a potential source of insight, is not part of critical pedagogy's frame of reference. But tied to a recognition of *positionality*, that is, of one's location within a social network of relationships and 'axes of power', to use Nancy Fraser's very useful notion (Fraser, 1989), it was central to the women's movement's more educational work. And as I have already argued (Chapter 3), it was central to the informal educational programmes which arose out of it in British adult education. Jane Thompson has spoken of the role of anger in women's education in a startling piece of prose:

> Growth through anger, focused with precision, can be a powerful
> source of energy, serving process and change. Anger expressed
> and translated into action in the service of women's visions and
> women's futures can be a liberating and strengthening act of clar-
> ification, for it is in the painful process of this translation, that
> we identify who are our genuine allies and who are our enemies.
>
> (Thompson, 1983, p 54)

Women and silence

Some of those writing in feminist pedagogy argue that women are badly served by traditional models of education which overvalue assertive debate and objective truth and undervalue knowledge arrived at through connection and personal experience (Belenky *et al.*, 1986; Weil, 1988). Research on women's experiences in traditional learning situations have been suggestive about how more collaborative methods of learning can be undermined by the silencing of women in discussion. For example, Magda Lewis and Roger Simon (female student and male teacher) have written an interesting paper on the ways in which female students were silenced in a graduate seminar in which they participated:

> men were allowed to speak at length – and did. Their speaking
> was seldom if ever interrupted. When a woman and a man began
> speaking at the same time, the woman always deferred to the man.
> Women's speaking was often re-interpreted by the men through
> phrases such as 'what she really means . . .'. More than just a few
> times the actual talk of women was attributed in a later discussion

by a man to a man. Women's ideas – sometimes re-worded, sometimes not – were appropriated by men and then passed off as their
own. Whenever a woman was able to cut through the oppressive
discourse, the final attempt at silencing took the form of aggressive
yelling. It became clear to us that the reversal of this dynamic
would have been totally unacceptable to those who held the power
of legitimation.

(quoted in Knights, 1995)

Magda Lewis stresses that for women there has to be more than 'offering women
spaces within which to speak' or simply including women in the curriculum.
Such a strategy does not reach deeply enough into the sources and political
potential of women's silence, suggests Lewis. A common feature of our experience as women – an experience which binds us together across divisions of
class, race, age – is that we are all subject to 'those social forces and power
relations that would keep us from naming the world from our own experience'
(Lewis, 1993, p 75). Thus, according to Lewis, we need new pedagogical skills
which will 'enable us to create curricula out of the invisible and silent' (p 194).
This includes learning how to see women's silence not as deficiency, absence or
lack but as a political act with subversive potential, indicating, sometimes, active
resistance rather than passive compliance. This point is graphically illustrated
in the film, *A Question of Silence* (Gorris, 1981). In the film, several women
(who are completely unconnected with one another) kill a male boutique owner
– without a word being spoken between them.

Feminist popular adult education

The kind of theoretical debate around feminist pedagogy which has been outlined above derives mainly from women's studies courses in formal higher education institutions of North America and Western Europe. Feminist popular
adult education on the other hand supports the struggles of women in oppressed
communities (Walters and Manicom, 1996). Taking the view that adult educators cannot ignore the wider social and political context of their work, feminist
popular educators focus on the gendered aspects of the restructuring process
which has been underway within capitalism in recent years worldwide. The
main site for feminist popular education is no longer social movements as it
was in the 1970s, but mainly NGOs (non-governmental organisations), voluntary organisations involved in building civic society; and 'women and development' projects in various parts of the world, mainly, but not exclusively in the
so-called Third World (5). Walters and Manicom (1996, p 7) characterise feminist popular education in the following way:

> It is a participatory, democratic, non-hierarchical pedagogy which
> encourages creative thinking that breaks through embedded for-
> mats of learning. It valorises local knowledge, working collectively
> towards producing knowledge, the principle of starting from where
> people are situated, and working to develop a broader understand-
> ing of structures and how these can be transformed. It strives to

> foster both personal and social empowerment . . . [it] must . . . engage with the ways in which the social categories of race, ethnicity, culture, age, social class, sexuality and physical ability are implicated in constructions of gender.

Walters and Manicom stress that the pedagogical cannot be separated from the political, unless popular education is to be reduced to a series of games and techniques. Indeed similar techniques to those developed within a popular education context have been incorporated within the private, corporate classroom; and the language of 'empowerment', 'working with diversity' and 'training for equality' has been similarly appropriated (6). They emphasise that while experiential knowledge is privileged over 'expert' knowledge in popular education, theorising is integral to it. They suggest, too, that the recent attention within feminist theory to the contested nature of experience (as, that is, never 'pure' and unmediated but always shaped by language) poses a number of strategic issues and tensions for feminist popular education.

These 'strategic issues' pivot on the tension between celebrating women's daily concerns on the one hand and challenging the gender relations that limit and confine on the other; and the tension between eliciting the huge wealth of collective understanding and perception ('subjugated knowledges') and validating this as a source of truth, on the one hand, and imparting knowledge from outside their own sphere (books, theories and so on) on the other. There is indeed a tension within the covers of the book between those readings which see women's experiences as a source of truth and others which see them only as a good starting point for the production of knowledge – a tension which, I think, is echoed in different versions of 'standpoint' approaches to knowledge (see, this book, Chapter 9). Such tensions are not new; in the 1970s, too, as activists and teachers, feminists (myself included) wrestled with the issue of direct experience, seeing it as both strength and weakness – not unlike (though less theoretically fine-tuned than) the recent essay by Joan Scott on this topic, written from a post-structuralist standpoint (Scott, 1992; Segal, 1997).

Other themes which are focused on in the book include the pedagogical importance of attending to feelings and emotions, – ignored, it is claimed, in much gender-blind popular education – as well as to pleasure and fun. The essay by Denise Nadeau, in particular, argues for the incorporation of exercises like 'sculpturing' and other sorts of bodywork in education (Nadeau, 1996, pp 40–60). This is to recognise that we do, indeed, learn with our bodies as much as with our minds (see Chapter 2). And it echoes what others have maintained recently in connection with more mainstream adult education – that the place of desire and play needs to be foregrounded much more – alongside, or even instead of, the search for enlightenment (Field, 1994; Usher et al., 1997). The potential for empowerment through learning about pleasure is not something given much attention in any part of our education system, however.

Re-forming radical adult education

Taking a view 'from below' leads to a research and education agenda where the emphasis is on bringing to light the actual experiences of people in the throes of economic restructuring and cultural change and in posing problems and questions 'against the grain'. David Alexander (1994) insists that the subjugated histories and knowledge of the people on the downside of current changes are not minority views, but, on the contrary, are the 'suppressed knowledge of the majority who know that the present globalised growth and development project is cruel, rapacious and morally indefensible' (p 20). These histories, he believes, form the 'language of hope and possibility' and adult education has to re-claim them, building a curriculum around them in an effort to develop the really useful knowledge required for a more sane world. Who speaks may indeed be more important than what is said because asking questions against the grain, posing questions which normally don't get asked isn't likely to happen from among those who benefit most from present social, political and economic arrangements.

I have referred to Sally Westwood's view that the individualising tendencies on all fronts present opportunities for adult education, for it to become, that is, 'a space for alternative traditions where other discourses can be maintained and where a diversity of cultures can thrive' (Westwood, 1989, p 9). This suggests a limited vision of adult education and its transformative potential: rather than seeing ourselves as masters of truth and transformative intellectuals (as some are tempted to do) we might accord ourselves a humbler role – akin to underlabourers, creators and seekers out of spaces where people themselves can act and speak on their own behalf – spaces of enunciation for the development of new possibilities of knowledge. Such a project concerns the 'struggles over how to hear and be heard' which Chapter 1 identified; it is based on the claim that it is not individuals who develop knowledge but groups and communities and it recognises that although knowledge cannot be *reduced* to power, 'positionality' influences what counts as knowledge at specific times and places. That is to say, *who knows* matters because one's position(s) within networks of power largely determines who gets to 'name the world'.

This is the central organising idea of my third case study, to which I turn in the next chapter. It is precisely because knowledge is socially created that some kinds of knowing have more power and legitimation in our culture. Science communities, though not the only epistemological communities (Nelson, 1990, 1993) are the ones granted and exercising most cognitive authority (Addelson, 1983).

Summary

Before moving on to my third case study I offer a brief summary of this chapter. In line with the project of the book, I have concentrated on the social, cultural and political context in which I produced my research on women's education, arguing that research has to be viewed in the light of the historical context of its production and reception. I critiqued my own failure to contextualise my account at the time, a failure which, I suggest, lay behind my overly abstract criticism of some women's education and connected with my overly rationalist position on feminist women's education.

Acknowledging important insights from recent writings in feminist pedagogy which emphasise making spaces for excluded voices in curriculum development I broadened out the discussion to consider what this might mean in the present social and historical context of adult and continuing education. I suggest that now (as then) a priority must be for adult educators to develop an understanding of how their own work relates to that wider context and to take a stand in relation to it. For radical adult educators this could mean devoting their energies to educational strategies geared to increasing the engagement of currently excluded social groups in the development of curricula and knowledge – curricular and knowledge development, which starts from and is located in experiences and understandings derived 'from below'.

Final case study

Moving on to my third case study which deals with a neglected area of the adult education curriculum – science – I pursue the notion of the promise of adult education as lying both in its traditions of critique and as lying in a more creative project of working up from knowledge from below in order to challenge the mainstream. Here the discussion will focus more directly on the notion (introduced in Chapter 2) of 'healing the breach' or transcending the divide between ways of knowing which in our culture are separated off from one another: knowledge from below and knowledge from above; cerebral and emotional understanding, scientific and common sense knowledge, academic and experiential knowledge. Finally I return to what was identified in Chapter 1 as the central problematic of the book – healing the breach between words and things.

It was in a transformed context of adult education that I was to do the final piece of research which features in this book – a context dominated by fast track degrees, Access courses, vocational education and a continuing inadequate response of progressive adult education. Shortly before embarking on this research I had written a short article in the WEA's *Reportback* journal criticising women's education in the WEA for ignoring the social and political context of its practice:

> Meanwhile it is 'enterprise' training/education which is pulling in the resources – including, it must be said, many of the ideas, techniques (and sometimes tutors) formed within the WEA and allied education organisations. Wrenched from their original emancipatory interest, those ideas and methods – still cloaked in the rhetoric of progressive education – are being re-packaged and served back in the name of 'enterprise' to serve the interests of a straightforwardly individualistic market economy.
>
> (Barr, 1991, p 21)

In the article I call on the WEA and others to return to one of the original objectives of women's studies/women's education, that of re-defining the content of knowledge and what is to count as knowledge and I suggest that the challenge for the WEA is to: 'grapple with issues of the curriculum, with what is the "really useful knowledge" which is needed by those social groups and movements with which we share a common cause' (p 21). Issues of curriculum are central to my third and final case study.

8 Really useful knowledge?

In this chapter I introduce my third case study which concerns women's relationship to science and scientific knowledge. After a brief autobiographical note, I contextualise the research study which figures here in relation to two of the central themes which helped give focus to the research: feminist arguments concerning the need to democratise science and science education and the potential role of adult education – more specifically, women's education – in such a project. I then outline the methodological approach adopted in the research. The remainder of the chapter consists of extracts from an account of this research, which I carried out at Warwick University during the phase in my life as an adult educator/researcher referred to in Chapter 2 as affording me an opportunity to engage with feminist theory's new 'epistemological turn'.

Autobiographical note

Between 1991 and 1992 I was Senior Research Associate at Warwick University's Centre for Continuing Education Research, employed mainly to work on a project with Lynda Birke on women's perceptions of science. The MA (Ed) in Counselling had given me a chance to reflect on my future; work on my dissertation for that course had convinced me that a major thrust of adult and continuing education research over the next few years should be related to curriculum development – to what is provided and how. The Warwick post as researcher in a major study relating women and scientific knowledge seemed an excellent opportunity to pursue a number of my interests, in an area of the curriculum badly neglected by adult education, an area, too, in which women are grossly underrepresented (except in the biological sciences). In addition, women's education/women's studies, like the rest of adult educational practice, had largely ignored science.

The research post also gave me a chance to immerse myself in recent feminist theoretical writing. I commented in Chapter 2 that what I found here was disquieting – a new feminist methodologism – an abstract rejection of making any generalisations about women on *a priori* grounds. 'Difference' had become central to feminist theory – differences between women – and there was a marked lack of confidence in the category 'woman' *per se*. Journal articles and books were preoccupied with 'essentialism' and with self-chastisement for feminism's own essentialising tendencies. This was bound up with the poststructuralist critique of humanism, a precursor, some were arguing, of a shift in philosophical paradigms termed 'postmodernism'.

Some feminists were utilising poststructuralist insights (especially those derived from Foucault) in an unobjectionable way, to make feminist theory and practice more sophisticated while still maintaining that women share a common interest in some sense. Others who embraced postmodernism appeared to have abandoned all hope of understanding the structural causes of women's oppression. It seemed to me that postmodernism's refusal of any 'universalist' analytic tools like class and gender and its consequent inability to conceptualise power as other than de-centred and between individuals actually pulled the rug from under feminism – indeed, from any movement which seeks the emancipation of broad social groups. Its epistemology and politics were anathema to me. It seemed to me that feminism's capacity for self-critique (one of its great strengths) when aligned with postmodernism, amounted to shooting itself in the foot.

On the other hand, postructuralist-influenced feminism's critique of crude efforts to explain oppression simplistically, replacing these with an understanding of our lives as structured by a number of forces which are discursively as well as materially real, seemed to me to be on target. So too were its criticisms of women's studies for allowing too much discursive space to white, middle class, western, heterosexual, able-bodied women (a point I made in my Durham keynote speech). Such efforts were at least directed at achieving a better, more complex understanding of how power actually operates, and, as a result, could point to better means of resistance. This does not mean abandoning belief in people's ability to engage with and change the world; on the contrary, it is directed at achieving an understanding of how the discourses and social structures within which we live and experience our lives operate and so how to change them. In relation to my Headway reappraisal, this critique has been useful, I believe. Nevertheless, as I indicated earlier, many feminists already had a quite complex understanding of power and how it works from their collective practices in the 1970s (1). I have already indicated, however, that I did not integrate this understanding fully in my Headway study (I 'knew' it but didn't know it).

The research project:
Women's perceptions of science

The research which figures in my final case study was based primarily on interviews with women involved in community groups and/or local adult education courses. Lynda Birke and I wanted to explore how women standing largely outside formal educational structures perceive (physical) science and scientific knowledge.The social and historical context in which we pursued our research – a context in which the development of opportunities for specifically adult learning and training was on most government agendas – presented new opportunities for adult educational programmes geared to developing really useful knowledge around science. The question was 'Whose knowledge?'. I was particularly interested in how these women's views on science might relate to feminist critiques of science which had been underway for over a decade. These formed part of a developing feminist epistemology which focused not only on a critique of traditional (or patriarchal) systems of knowledge and ways of thinking about knowledge but also attempted to create an alternative (see eg, Alcoff and Potter, 1993).

Feminist epistemology and critiques of science

Helen Longino's characterisation of epistemology as 'the theory of what practices produce knowledge' (Longino, 1993, p 103) signals a rejection of the very problematic of traditional epistemology and the division of labour between the sociology/history of knowledge/science and epistemology. Traditionally, epistemology has regarded knowledge as a product to be justified, not as a dynamic social process to be understood and evaluated (Addelson, 1983, p 269). And it narrowly defines what is to count as knowledge, defining it in terms of the methodology used to identify it – 'detached', 'value-free' – thereby relegating experiential and practical knowledge to the merely subjective. Maths and science are thus deemed the most valuable and real knowledge because seen as the least subjective.

Feminist epistemologists, among others, stress how knowledge is socially constructed, rather than discovered and that science itself is a set of social practices guided by notions of what's real. They have sought to substitute different practices, including not limiting what is deemed to be 'knowledge' to that which is produced by legitimated experts and they have insisted that what gets developed as knowledge is linked to social structures in which women are subordinated.

When I came to do the 'women's perceptions of science' research, postmodernist feminists were busying themselves disputing the possibility of *any* authentic knowledge. Other feminists, however, were *engaging* with scientific knowledge, continuing a critique which had been underway for about 15 years. This agenda had by then shifted from a concern to expose sexist practice and content in specific sciences (typically, biology) to a broader concern with scientific knowledge: how do we come to know what we know? It had indeed moved, in Hilary Rose's words, to 'a robust attempt to re-vision a defensible feminist concept of objectivity' (Rose, 1994, p 93). And this agenda was firmly located in a struggle to create something better.

Philosopher Sandra Harding, addressing the need to democratise science, asserts that we are all inside science, even those who appear to be outside its practice – women, racial minorities, inhabitants of the least privileged parts of the globe. Because they are in practice outside, suggests Harding, people in these groups could bring to science their diverse experiences and standpoints and in so doing benefit science (Harding, 1991). Harding believes there is a political and epistemological imperative for science and scientists to seek out criticisms of their practices and (often unconsciously held) assumptions and values from the perspectives of the lives of the least advantaged groups in society. Such 'outsider' perspectives are required, believes Harding, if science is to achieve what she calls 'strong objectivity', not merely 'weak objectivity' (Harding, 1986, 1991, 1993). This requirement, as she points out, demands 'affirmative action' as a *scientific goal*, not just as a moral imperative. And it requires discarding the God's eye view of science for good: 'Social communities, not either individuals or "no-one at all" should be conceptualised as the "knowers" of scientific knowledge claims' (Harding, 1993, p 18).

This enjoins us to see science for what it is: 'the name we give to a set of practices and a body of knowledge delineated by a community, not simply defined by the exigencies of logical proof and experimental verification' (Keller, 1985, p 4). It is also a clarion call for the recognition of a multiplicity of 'epistemological communities' as the agents of scientific knowledge (Nelson, 1990, 1993).

The important point here is that the knowing which we do as individuals depends on some 'we' – some group or community – which constructs and shares knowledge and standards of evidence. 'Communities, not individuals, are the primary epistemological agents' is how Lyn Nelson sums up this point. Paulo Freire expresses essentially the same point when he speaks of consciousness as a social activity and insists that to know implies a dialogical situation. I can only know what some 'we' can know or learn (Freire, 1972, 1983). But the people who have dominated in the epistemological communities of science have been, on the whole, privileged, white men.

The absence of science in women's studies

It is central to feminist arguments in and around science that there exists the possibility of developing science more democratically, as a mass phenomenon, not simply as a democratic duty but as a way of making science better because it would then include the voices and knowledges of a wider range of people (Nelson, 1990; Harding, 1991). And it is central to recent feminist philosophy of science that gender provides a division in experience deep enough to make a difference to the direction of research and the content of scientific theorising. Yet, apart from groups focusing on health, women's education groups and women's studies have largely ignored science. There remains a strong tendency in academic women's studies, too, to simply see science as heavily patriarchal rather than to analyse it in detail and deconstruct its conceptual frameworks. One result is that science is largely absent from women's studies teaching and research. Our research was premised on the belief that this was a dangerous move for feminists, since to ignore science is to place ourselves outside of the cognitive authority and power that is science. It is also irresponsible, as Donna Haraway has eloquently emphasised:

> To ignore, to fail to engage in the social process of making science,
> and to attend only to the use and abuse of the results of scientific
> work is irresponsible. I believe it is even less responsible in present
> historical conditions to pursue anti-scientific tales about nature

that idealize women, nurturing, or some other entity argued to be free of male war-tainted pollution. Scientific stories have too much power as public myth to effect meaning in our lives . . .

(Haraway, 1991a, p 107)

Haraway's plea is above all for 'responsible knowledge', for learning to take responsibility for the social position from which we speak.

Women's perceptions of science: The research

It was from such a perspective – and the potential role of adult education or, more specifically, of women's education in the process of democratising science – that Lynda and I approached the research. In the current climate of accreditation there was, arguably, more space for science than in the past. But in a context of credit transfer, accelerated degrees and institutional adjustment to market forces, narrowly vocational courses had become predominant; what little provision there was around science in adult and continuing education fitted closely to the Government's enterprising agenda. Yet I believed that, just as adult education had proved to be a receptive space for the development of women's studies in Britain, so, too, it could be a very suitable place for the open, democratic, critical and creative science education urged by Sandra Harding and others.

Having outlined briefly some of the background ideas to our research on women's perceptions of science I shall now outline the methodology adopted, after which I devote the remainder of the chapter to reproducing extracts from the research account.

The research began with a pilot study, based on interviews with 15 women who had attended a basic adult education course for women called 'Inside Science' (Birke, 1992). These women ranged in age from 22 to 60; all were white (all the women who had attended that particular course were white), and most were working class.

The main part of the research, however, consisted of three phases. We sought to sample from a range of women who were engaged in some form of adult education, either formally in a course, or informally through membership of community groups. Most of these were in the West Midlands town, Coventry. The economy of this town has depended to a large extent on the automobile industry, combined with light industry. It is fairly diverse ethnically, with substantial groups of Afro-Caribbean people, and of Asians (both Hindus and Muslims, as well as some from China and southeast Asia). Other women we interviewed were participating in a residential college for women, or in a rural health group in Derbyshire.

We began by approaching these various groups and asking women to fill out a questionnaire: 110 women did so. The questions were deliberately open-ended, because we wanted to find out what kinds of images of science sprang to mind. We asked them, for example, to finish a sentence, 'My image of science is . . .'.

This was followed by semi-structured in-depth interviews with 40 women drawn from the 110 who had completed questionnaires. For this stage of the research we concentrated on women from a narrower range of courses and groups, selecting one science-based women's course; an institution offering various science-related Access courses such as Access to Nursing; a residential women's college; a community-based rural health group; two black women's community groups and a literary and cultural studies course. Having selected these groups on the basis of the kind of spread they gave us, we then sought volunteers from these groups for interview.

The ages of the women ranged from 23 to 66, with a median age of 42. Of the 40 women who volunteered to be interviewed, 8 were black, 2 were Asian, and 30 were white. Social class analysis is notoriously slippery where women are concerned. According to father's occupation (and using Goldthorpe *et al.*'s 1987 model of the British class structure), just over half of the women were 'working class' (semi-skilled and unskilled manual – occupational class vii); the remaining fathers had mainly lower professional and administrative 'middle class' occupations (occupational class ii). According to the women's own occupational position (current or last job) the picture changes, with a large majority falling more or less equally into routine non-manual positions, mainly clerical/shop assistants, or semi-skilled manual ones. A minority were in lower professional and admininistrative jobs – mainly nursing or school teaching. Part-time and sporadic employment and taking jobs at a lower level on returning to work after having children were features of many of the women's working lives

Our prior analysis of the questionnaires helped give focus to and influenced the terms of the interviews which consisted in extended conversations about the meaning of science and scientific knowledge to the women involved. At the beginning of each interview we stressed that our interest was in how the women felt about and perceived science, scientists and scientific knowledge and that there were no right and wrong answers. Interviews, which were semi-structured (more like conversations with some, but question and answer with others who were more comfortable with this format) covered the same ground as the questionnaires, but in greater depth and with additional discussion topics/questions. Additional topics covered included important learning experiences; preferred ways of understanding various phenomena eg childbirth; and perceptions of alternative health. Interviews lasted from one hour to two hours. They were tape-recorded and, immediately afterwards, listened to and roughly transcribed by the interviewer (either Lynda Birke or myself). Notes were taken on the emotional atmosphere and other non-discursive aspects of the interviews and interviews were later transcribed in full by a professional transcriber.

In the third phase, we approached three ongoing groups for discussion in focus groups. One of these was a specifically black group; one consisted of women studying at a residential college; one was a rural health group. This involved us feeding back some of what we had found out – or rather, our interpretations of the material – and discussing it with the women concerned. This 'member check' became for each of the groups an occasion for further reflection with one another and with us. We regarded this as an important part of the research process. We also asked them to comment on and discuss some specially written 'media accounts' featuring science (a composite made up from several sources). At a later date, an additional group of Muslim women was constituted to explore issues around Islam and science. We did so mainly because the way in which we selected people for interview, that is, on the basis of a sampling of groups and, thereafter, volunteers, actually served to screen out Asian women. Since they form a substantial part of the local population we decided to seek to rectify this skewing to some degree at least.

We approached groups, different constituencies of women in different contexts, in an effort not to individualize women or de-contextualise the research too much. This involved us in fairly labour-intensive work to recruit volunteers for interviews. In some cases, this could have been easily achieved via tutors or group leaders, but we always attended class and group meetings to explain what we were about. Black women's groups in any case made it clear that they would have insisted on us meeting them as a group to discusss the nature and possible usefulness of the research – even if we had not thought it a good idea to do so! As soon as they were convinced that the research was worthwhile they were happy to participate (see Cannon, Higginbotham and Leung, 1988): consistent with the views about science which they expressed, the pursuit of knowledge (ours in this case) which would not serve some really useful purpose, was anathema to them. This did not mean it had to be seen as having a direct pay-off for them, however.

That social relations of class, gender and race are relevant to the production of knowledge – that they are epistemological factors – was a founding premise of the research. Our own experience as researchers and as adult educators, as well as our reading of feminist theory and the social studies of science, convinced us that this is so. It is obvious that our position as white, university-based female researchers had a bearing on the kind of conversations we had with the women and so on the final product of the research.

Below, I reproduce two extracts from the research: 'Product 1' is an extract from our analysis of the interview material which concentrates on differences in perceptions of science held by women in different adult education groups. 'Product 2' concerns – mainly – similarities which existed across groups.

Differences

There were clearly differences in our interviews which reflected varied life histories, related for example to age, class and ethnicity. One noteworthy difference, however, was that between women from different groups or institutions. Some were attending particular courses, others taking part in community groups. As we interviewed several women from the same group or course we noticed consistent themes emerging from within each social group; there was a marked tendency for women from the same group to answer in similar ways. For example, in one institution, one renowned for its emphasis on experiential learning and for its women-centred approach, half of those interviewed shared a distrust of experts, a view that science should 'come out of the closet' and a refusal of the notion of 'scientific facts'. Such refusal typically construed scientific facts as 'right or wrong, black or white'.

The first extract from the research report which I have chosen to reproduce below concentrates on the differences between that institution – Hillcroft
– and another women-only group studying science with feminist tutors – a
Women and Science course. The aim of this part of our analysis – which com-
prised a number of case studies of different courses and groups – was to highlight how narratives as ways of understanding the world are developed in
different contexts. In looking at the different groups we were interested in how
they might produce different 'epistemological communities' in their discourses
around science. This matters, we thought, because knowledge construction and
validation are co-operative, constructive endeavours; they are not the result of
the activities of isolated individuals (see Nelson, 1993; Assiter, 1996). It mattered to us as feminists because of the feminist insistence on the collective nature
of feminist knowing and recognition of the strong relationship between that
knowledge and changing social and political relations (Nelson, 1993, p 150). I
quote verbatim from the draft report of the research. Ellipses indicate cuts.

Product 1

Hillcroft

*Our first case study centres on Hillcroft College, a residential college for women
lying south of London. Residential adult education is central to the distinct
tradition of adult education in Britain, and Hillcroft, as the only residential
college for women, is a microcosm of changes in that tradition. Its changing
emphases also reflect (and contribute towards) changes within feminist thinking about women's education. A marked shift to Access courses to higher education (courses designed for adult entrants who lack traditional entry
qualifications for university study) in recent years has not compromised its
renowned emphases on a women-centred approach and experiential learning.
Weight is placed on developing women's confidence in their abilities as learners, starting from and drawing on their own life experiences and strengths and
stressing the emotional as well as cognitive dimensions of learning. Science is
not on the curriculum although staff would like it to be included, regarding
learning about science, its relevance to society and environment, as integral to
learning in science.*

*In the Hillcroft interviews there is a stress on personal knowledge and on
what Belenky et al (1986) call 'connected knowing'. With connected knowing,
truth which is grounded in firsthand experience and validated through shared
experience, is most valued (Belenky, p 118). Empathic understanding is its key
feature. What has been called a 'counselling discourse' permeates the interviews
(see Fairclough, 1989; Kitzinger and Perkins, 1993) and a notion of 'blocking
out' science and scientific knowledge is peculiar to some of them.*

*For example, one woman, voicing the attraction felt by all interviewees to
Hillcroft's caring approach to its students, says, 'It's opening things up, helping
me explore myself'. Another student who finds it difficult to speak in large
groups comments on her philosophy course: 'I have the same difficulty with
philosophy as I'd have with science, I think. I can't get into the argumentative*

mode required'. (Analogously, Michele Le Doeuff has suggested on the basis of her own experience as a philosopher in a largely male world that if you are a woman and a philosopher, quite simply, it helps to be a bit bad-tempered; see Le Doeuff, 1991.)

Similarly, a woman, who, in her questionnaire return, expressed an oddly self-conscious view of science as 'a subject I'd rather stay away from. Science means not me. Science means asking why?', continues the theme in her interview:

> *Other than the psychological side of things I'm quite ignorant of anything 'scientific'. But I'm quite proud of that. Not quite glad that I'm ignorant, but it doesn't bother me at all. My brain has just shut off from it completely.*

This comment, a mixture of defensiveness and pride, sums up well the kind of resistance to science – as blocking it out – shared by half of those interviewed. At the same time it suggests that it is 'connected knowing' which she feels she possesses.

When asked to recount their most significant learning experience all refer to experiential learning which is personal or relational eg giving birth, watching a child grow, understanding anger and forgiveness for the first time, being a drug addict and waking up to cherry blossom, identifying with nature, a leaf, even: 'just touching a tree and feeling vibes through my body. Feeling at one with nature'.

There is awareness of and distaste expressed for what Freire calls 'banking' education (Freire, 1972); a view that science education epitomises this: 'It's having so much contained in your head of that kind of knowledge'; and a strong preference for Hillcroft's experiential approach to education.

Anger at the oppressiveness of an educational system that leaves you in the dark is apparent in one woman's comment about science at school: 'Personally, I can't relate to the whole idea now. I found that teachers never explained what the hell was going on. Sticking things in test tubes . . . I never understood the purpose of what I was doing'.

Scepticism about expert scientific knowledge and methods for acquiring it comes out in the following extract from discussion with the focus group. In these groups students were asked to read a number of mock press reports on scientific issues (including one on arthritis research) and to comment on them. The extract also illustrates an aspect of what has been called the 'condition of modernity' (Giddens, 1990; see also Beck, 1992): the lack of control or sense of powerlessness which many people feel, in a world increasingly dominated by technical and scientific experts. Expert information, as well as re-cycled knowledge (eg via the media and friends), is often inconsistent, and yet, in order to act, we must believe in something. This extract is taken from the middle of our discussion . . .

Interviewer:	*Listening to you, it sounds like you're pretty sceptical about what you read in the newspapers.*
Student A:	*The trouble is you read something one day and a few weeks*

later something that contradicts it, so you've got to be sceptical.

Interviewer: So if you needed to find out something say to do with your health what would you do?

Student B: Read books.

Student C: If I had arthritis diagnosed I'd not rely on written evidence. I'd talk to other sufferers because I'm sceptical about anything I read.

Student D: But you've got to believe somebody.

Interviewer: I think C is suggesting you can't always rely on expert opinion.

Student D: I've a horrible tendency to believe them even if I don't like them or what's said. If it's got a touch of the scientific I'll believe it.

Interviewer: So it's about who says it?

Student A: There was an article about the need to eat more meat in . . . and when you looked closely it was research paid for by the Meat Council. So you need to look at who is funding the scientists.

Student D: But it makes me feel inadequate and who am I to say this is rubbish when I don't know enough about it?

Student E: I worked in a psychiatric unit and every year students have to do the same test on rats to prove the same thing. Computer data could have been used but no-one said why do this? The students were just as moronic as the professors. And they killed these rats by bashing their heads against the table.

Student B: Maybe it's to do with learning from experience? . . .

The interventionist, controlling power of science is a dominant discourse in the Hillcroft interviews. One student remarks: 'Nature is as Nature is and it's just constantly changing all the time but they (scientists) are just trying to speed up the process. Science tries to control and change things. It has created a lot of monsters and without science we wont be able to undo the monsters'. Another woman, troubled by recent media coverage of research on 'homosexual brains', and worried about the inaccessibility of expert knowledge, expresses the double meaning of manipulation when she says, 'That's what's frightening about not understanding science. You think, how the hell can they do that? And you've just got to accept it. It could mean tampering with genes. It could be a load of rubbish and we could really be led up the garden path on some issues and that's really frightening.'

We live increasingly, as Beck (1992) has recently pointed out, in a 'risk society' that presents particular challenges to adult education. The women we interviewed at Hillcroft and from other groups are well aware of the ecological risks to which they and their children are exposed – through nuclear hazards, genetic engineering, food additives . . .

Adult education has devoted much attention in recent years to the issue of experiential learning; at Hillcroft and in women's education more generally . . . It is regarded as an important aspect, perhaps the most important *aspect, of an education which can be empowering. But there is a danger that, in focusing on experiential learning, educators ignore the fact that many of the risks to which people are exposed are beyond daily experience; we cannot know through experience, for instance, how the ozone layer has developed a hole. In their ambivalence towards experts and the authority of science, the women are articulating just that sense of science as outside our daily lives.*

An empowering science education for them would, at the very least, have to make connections between this lived experience and structures and processes not available within it. In defining science and argumentative modes of reasoning as 'not me', in valuing personal and connected ways of knowing over the kind of knowledge they see science as representing, they may deny their own capacity for knowledge which goes beyond the familiar. Yet, in their disdain for 'proven' scientific facts and preference for knowledge they feel they 'own', and in their dismay at the interventionist, controlling power of modern science, the women are also articulating a sense of the poverty of a scientific 'rationality' which, in its narrow instrumentalism, subordinates other human needs to the goals of 'efficiency' and profit (see Grimshaw, 1986). It is central to our argument that probing such resistance to knowledge, paying explicit attention to it rather than ignoring or trying to 'correct' it, is a way of creating new conditions for knowledge; of extending the boundaries of possible knowledge at any given moment and in any given social and cultural context (Nelson, 1993).

Women and Science course

Our second case study focuses on a group of women on a science course taught in Coventry for women only. The Women and Science course (WS) has been running for four years. Initiated by a group of feminist scientists, it takes place in local schools in Coventry, an industrial town near Birmingham with a high unemployment rate and a large Asian population. The course, which has crèche facilities available, runs for a morning a week over six terms ... WS is one of the few examples of a broadly based science course for adults with no clearly defined vocational purpose and a rare example of a course based on science taught specifically to women by women (indeed, by feminists). It provides a useful and rare case study to explore our theme of epistemological communities outside science.

The course developed from a precursor, called Inside Science, run at a local primary school. The WS course was intended to be a much deeper and broader introduction to science, aimed at reducing women's fears of it and helping them to recognise what they already knew.

A case study of the pilot course, 'Inside Science', involved interviewing 15 women who had attended all or part of an IS course. Our later study of different adult education groups included interviews with six women who were at an early stage in their Women and Science course, somewhere towards the end of their first term. Similarities clearly emerge from both sets of interviews. Almost half specifically allude to the fact that the course was for women only, some noting that at school they had seen science (except biology) as a boy's subject;

others feel less intimidated, 'more equal' without men, a finding which accords with other studies of women returning to study.

In the time honoured adult education tradition the course starts from what the women already know and builds from there. It also focuses right at the beginning on how other kinds of knowledge have been excluded – women's, for example, or the contribution of Islam to modern science and technology. This can be empowering, particularly when the subject matter is science. One woman who thinks it important that women are teaching the course explains:

> *The majority of men are rigid. I get the feeling that what we've done, you know, about nuclear energy, would have been very stereo-typed. I do find a lot of men don't expect women to know and if you ask a question it's taken as questioning their ability to put over information . . .*

Another puts the point nicely: 'They [the teachers] get at you from the inside. They bring out to the surface what you know'.

All of the women interviewed have clear perceptions of women's exclusion from science, beginning with school science. Those who had done some science at school refer to their sense of fear of things scientific. One, for example, speaks of having a 'panic attack' in the middle of the session on atoms and molecules and 'feeling how I'd felt at school – lost, almost' . . . One way of expressing this fear is to define science as whatever you don't understand: one woman feels like this about medicine: 'I don't know enough about it, so it must be science!' . . .

Women claimed that prior to their adult education course they had had a perception of science as highly abstract. It also had its esoteric aparatus: as one woman remarks, 'Science is about life but before Inside Science I'd have said it's about labs, bunsen burners, test tubes, that sort of thing. Now I feel it's something that affects us all' . . . Another woman, who sees 'real science, the most scientific' as 'delving very deep, going really very deep into a subject, to the most basic, right down as far as you can possible go . . . the hidden bit of things you don't see' thinks 'the less familiar the words, the more scientific' . . .

While the interviews reveal a distinction between science and commonsense, they also reveal that one way in which the women's perceptions have been changed by the course is to admit more of the everyday aspects into the category of what counts as science. The arcane world of the laboratory bench is replaced with 'the world around us'. This dominant motif of the interviews is almost revelatory: scientific knowledge is not separate from everyday life. I do have scientific knowledge in my common sense! For example, 'Before it was test tubes and mad scientists; at school physics was above my head. Here, it's areas that affect you. I didn't realise that pollution came under science . . . and everyday things like cooking. I just think that everything is scientific now' . . . Again, 'I used to think things like chemistry, things I don't really understand, and science labs, experiments [that you] didn't understand, experiments that didn't really work. I didn't really think of science as to do with the

world around us' . . . *The women on this course share a sense of science perme-
ating everyday life, as not set apart from their own experiences; they share, too,
a sense that what they already know, as 'commonsense' matters.*

*Many of the women relegate some of the material discussed on the course
to the category 'commonsense' – and so not science. What is labelled as
commonsense are things that 'you could discover for yourself', as against the
'very deep . . . things you can't see' . . . The contrast between commonsense as
'things we know' and science as things we do not is summed up clearly by one
woman:*

> *Well atoms and electrons, radiation, nuclear power – probably
> lasers [are all scientific]. It depends how you are actually looking
> at them. They all need science, but like the road building, energy,
> it's more commonsense . . . I suppose it's because we think we
> know a bit about those. Well, the rest, if you know nothing about
> it, it's totally scientific. I think it's something that's completely out-
> side of your sphere, if you like . . . it's like going to the
> moon . . . it's totally scientific.*

*But what is significant from the point of view of 'empowerment' is that it is
precisely in these areas of 'commonsense' that they can identify things they
already know. Nutrition, reproduction and pollution are mentioned by several.
One comments:*

> *I think a lot of the [topics] you knew something which you didn't
> think you did . . . like the nutrition, a lot of the aspects that M
> covered you had a basic knowledge of that. And reproduction and
> I suppose radiation, things you'd picked up as general knowledge,
> that stimulated me really. It's stored at the back of the brain and
> you get a bit of stimulation and you think, oh yes, I know that.
> You had a basic awareness at least.*

*And one woman . . . when asked to say how she would describe scientific know-
ledge says: 'Mm, hard one, I mean what is knowledge? From my own experience I can know something without knowing I know something about it . . . a
sort of inner knowledge and it's like bringing it into focus. [Scientific knowledge, commonsense knowledge] are the same, just a difference of degree.' This
comes close to the philosopher Quine's notion of knowledge as 'seamless' and
'all of a piece', the theorising some of us do as scientists being no different in
kind from what we do as laypersons or even philosophers. For Quine, science
in the broadest sense consists of almost all our efforts to organise our experiences. It is virtually without boundaries. Science in the narrow sense is just
refined or 'self-conscious common sense' (see Nelson, 1990, p 109).*

*We could say, then, that a notion of science as refined common sense is
beginning to appear in these women's discourse around science. It is, indeed,
fostered by the course. Such an attitude towards science certainly creates opportunities for new learning in and about science; it may also foster (may even be a
condition of) the production of self-critical scientific knowledge . . . [The] prevailing common sense of science is that it is detached – that values and politics*

*are irrelevant to the knowledge produced in it; this 'lie' both maintains sci-
ence's authority and insulates it from critical discussion of the 'common sense'
values, social and political experiences (including those concerning gender)
which find their way into scientific research.*

*Given the authority of science in our society, the need for self-reflection on
the role of such 'common sense' elements is compelling. But such self-reflection,
at bottom, has to be done by communities – and not just scientific ones.
Wrestling with them is a matter for the larger community and should not be
left to the few who are committed to the view that science has nothing to do
with values and politics (see Nelson, 1990). By challenging the notion of science as something apart and separate from women's own common sense knowledge, courses like WS open up a space for such scrutiny, while not absolving
women's own knowledge from similar scrutiny. In so doing they create new
conditions for the construction of knowledge and, potentially, enlarge, for all
of us, what it is possible to know in any given historical, social and cultural
context.*

*We have produced the above case studies to illustrate how consistent themes
tended to emerge from within each of the different social groups. Such differences between groups and institutions, we believe, have important implications
for adult education practice . . . What these differences tap into could simply be
the sharing of ideas about the research before we arrived, to create some consensus and common discourse. In itself, this illustrates an aspect of experiential
learning which is not adequately addressed in the literature on adult education:
the group itself as an important part of learning. We believe, however, that
these differences reflect more than just a few pre-interview discussions.*

*Perceptions of science are socially constructed. What interests us as adult
educators is how the various adult education contexts and institutions may
have affected the women's views of science, either directly, through a women-
only science course, for example, or indirectly, through involvement in a non-
science based course or institutional culture influencing their view of knowledge
and themselves as knowers. In other words, it may be that experience of adult
education (or some forms of it) counteracts dominant ideologies of knowledge
in significant ways – ideologies which often undermine women's confidence,
collective identities and claims to knowledge – and in ways which may be very
relevant to science education for women. Indeed, we believe that the views
expressed by the women in our research study reflect not only perceptions of
science in Western culture, but also the ways in which particular standpoints
and ways of knowing can emerge out of engagement in particular communities.*

*It seems unlikely that women's perceptions of science and scientific know-
ledge can be easily separated from their perceptions of knowledge more generally, or from their perceptions of themselves as 'knowers'. It is probable,
therefore, that their experience of adult education – even if science is not a part
of it – could have a significant bearing on their perceptions of science and
scientific knowledge. Relatedly, the 'dialogical' emphasis of adult education
and on sharing ideas and experiences may encourage individual and collective
thoughtfulness and critical reflection which, coupled with the importance of the*

group and its dynamics in learning, may be more significant in the present context than the specific content or emphasis of any particular course, community group or institution . . .

Adrienne Rich [believes] . . . that the first lesson in any education for a woman that can be liberating is that she is capable of intelligent thought. Our reading of the evidence suggests that most of the women we interviewed had learned this first lesson (they are, after all, women who have made a decision to seek education). Many do respect their own minds and ways of knowing. The important point is that although, for example, most of the women see themselves (realistically) as passive consumers of science, many do not see themselves as passive knowers per se. . . .

Our findings contrast with the mainly college women who were interviewed by Belenky et al. in their study of women's ways of knowing, many of whom had not yet learned to see themselves as capable of intelligent thought. It also contrasts with Kim Thomas's findings regarding young women's experiences of higher education. She found that exposure to higher education actually increases the underconfidence of many women instead of challenging it (Thomas, 1990). The ability of the women we interviewed to see themselves as active knowers could, then, be a testament to adult education for women; it could also reflect the importance of arriving at the initial decision to return to structured learning, as itself enabling women to construct themselves and their futures.

Similarities

I now want to give my second extract, 'Product 2' which concentrates on some similarities (as well as some differences) across the different groups. A theme of the study was women's shared experience of discursive marginality: they have on the whole been excluded systematically from theory-formation and from 'naming the world' from their own experience (see Lerner, 1993). This, we thought, is likely to shape women's perceptions of science in fundamental ways.

The processes by which women are excluded from scientific knowledge are complex and women do not experience exclusion in the same way. Nor are processes of exclusion peculiar to women. However, we found that the language used to express their exclusion was often gendered – invoking science as 'a man's world' – for example, or it related to women's continuing role as primary caregiver in the family. Thus, anxieties about future technologies were often expressed in terms of what might happen to the children while others referred to the involvement of science in domestic work and others still to the position of women in the labour market. Given women's relationship to the family and to the labour market it may be that women's relationship to science is in some ways different. Indeed it has been suggested by feminists that women's lives – in particular, their role in caring for others and in subsistence production in the global economy – provide a space for questioning some dominant social priorities. These are some of the themes explored in the extract given below.

Product 2

Getting through a day is like a science for some women

(Bell)

The story the women tell us is . . . of contradiction and exclusion. At the same time it is one of commonality through difference and it serves as a reminder that women seldom slip easily into their roles as women, whether they be black or white, middle class or working class, young or old. The women's voices quoted here suggest some common ground; they also make visible differences between women rooted in different social experiences . . .

In the women's talk about science, some linking themes emerge. Perhaps the strongest is the impressions that the women give to us – in their body language, their pauses, their silences. 'Science' seems to evoke powerful memories, for many, of school science – experienced as deeply alienating, or at best as irrelevant. Some of these memories are simply painful recollections of experiencing school as an alienating place, where one was rarely accepted. But, insofar as part of the painful memory for some women had to do with the feeling that they could not 'get the right answer', then the apparent certainties of school science teaching produce a special kind of discomfort. Indeed, one woman began to weep as she recollected what school science lessons were like; she explained that the very situation she was in – answering questions – combined with the specific nature of what she had to recall (science) brought it all back to her.

Racism also powerfully structures experiences and recollections of school days. For Gita, an Asian woman, the problems were partly to do with institutionalised racism, partly to do with language. She had always felt an outsider at school, neither black nor white, not quite Asian but having Asian roots; always having to deny her background, even to the extent of 'never [leaving] my clothes around at home' in case they smelled of curry.

Language, however, was a significant problem both for Gita and for her mother who had had an unnecessary hysterectomy because of language difficulties. Gita was subjected to IQ tests which were culturally biased:

> *they were asking me things about farming and vocabulary which I never come across . . . because to me that was [a] different language . . . I mean even mixing with white kids my English was totally different to theirs, mine was an inner city sort of broken English . . . where I've been brought up with two languages . . . there's a blockage, I wouldn't say I'm Asian, I was white, I was treated like white with the [other] girls and I was fighting for my identity so that's my way of surviving.*

The language problem hindered her science studies too:

> *because they were using words and the kids were used to it, and also they had the books and the knowledge they developed quicker, and I didn't, so that was the blockage . . . .*

If Gita sees her primary problem to have been language, for many others it is the inherent difficulty of science. This theme is summed up eloquently in the quotation [above]. Primarily, that quote is intended to mean that women's daily existence is often very difficult, a perpetual struggle. Science here means the epitome of something hard. It also symbolises the need to plan carefully, as well as the sheer drudgery of everyday work: for several women, science means boredom, a plodding approach to solving problems.

Some women explicitly express being excluded from science and scientific knowledge, demonstrating awareness of powerful institutional, cultural and educational processes which continue to exclude women. The young black woman, Bell, explains: 'I feel so excluded from it. Science at school is made so impersonal and girls are told they don't have the capacity for it. That's a load of rubbish. And people don't know black people's contribution to science. As a black woman I don't want my children growing up to think black people have played no role in shaping today's world.' In voicing a conscious awareness of exclusion this woman is also voicing resistance.

More common, however, is an implicit reference to exclusion through a number of recurrent tensions. These may perpetuate women excluding them-selves from science and scientific knowledge in reinforcing ways. While the women we interviewed see science in many contradictory ways, two particular tensions stand out. One is that when they label knowledge as scientific it usu-ally means something they do not understand: what they understand, by con-trast, is likely to be labelled common sense. The second tension can be summed up in the aphorism: 'Science is in everything, but it has nothing to do with me'. Taken together, these themes serve as a stark reminder of the extent of wom-en's exclusion from scientific knowledge . . .

Science affects everything in our lives: 'We can't get away from it', asserts Edna, including many daily activities in the category: hoovering, using electric-ity (except cookery which is 'sheer pleasure'). Yet for her scientific knowledge is: 'all the things I don't know the answers to, things that don't seem to have answers and I don't want to know.' For her, 'Scientists and food have become the new religion. We've replaced faith in God with an obsession with health and living long' . . .

Many women clearly expressed their feeling of being excluded from sci-ence. Thus, although Barbara acknowledges that she has some scientific know-ledge from her daily life, she comments: 'But I don't home in on it. It's the hidden part of you. I see talking about science as a man's world and you're not taken seriously if you talk about these things.' The exclusion here recognises the gendered construction of scientific knowledge which feminists have often pointed out (Keller, 1985) . . . We pursue the theme of silence as an epistemo-logical strategy [below]. Sometimes it is associated with fear – an emotion which may be vividly expressed in interviews: 'With science it's a fear of not knowing, a deep inner fear of not being able to do it. I panic. With science I never questioned it because I was so afraid. It can still bring tears to my eyes. I'm still fearful of being put in a situation, even this one, of being given a puzzle to work out' [Denise] . . .

Constrasting images of science as certainty and science as contingency also appear; 'there aren't any right answers to anything' may coexist as a belief alongside a view of science as facts (right versus wrong). Recognition of the changing, contingent nature of science makes no difference to the sense of exclusion that women feel, because the self is not part of the negotiation of 'the facts'; that is the prerogative of experts. Research into how different social groups understand science has shown that people are often quite well aware of its contingencies and uncertainties (Wynne, 1992). Collins (1985) makes a plea for science teaching to include the social science of science, observing that the model of science as certain and of scientists as authoritative tends to be reproduced within normal science teaching. Rather, he suggests, in science papers, 'certainty increases because the details of the social process that went into the creation of certainty become invisible' (p 160). What the science paper leaves out is experiment as 'a piece of ordinary life', as process. Science teaching and scholarly science papers are a fraud, he believes, at odds with actual practice. And once those data find their way into textbooks they become cast as absolute certainty, all contingency written out (Latour, 1987). The model of science put forward allows lay citizens only two responses to science, either awe at its authority, or rejection 'the incomprehending antiscience reaction' (Collins, 1985, p 161) . . .

'Science has created a lot of monsters and without science we wont be able to undo the monsters', says Monica. For her, science is about controlling nature, yet 'Nature is as Nature is'. This echoes what some radical science critics have maintained: that nature cannot be controlled – only 'artificial nature', itself a creation of science: 'What modern science may be capable of achieving is correctional hypotheses for earlier erroneous ones . . . A great deal of science, then, is circular science' (Nandy, 1988). Edna, despite her desire to claim pleasurable activities as outside science, claims to admire scientists 'more than all others'. For her, experiments are 'using knowledge to prove a point'. Moreover, 'people are overpowered by it, baffled by it, take it on trust and later its theories are disproved.' For her, then, science is both certainty ('proving a point') and contingency. Perhaps it is little wonder that she thinks that reading science must be boring . . .

[The] notion of scientific knowledge as something passively acquired by the few, very intelligent among us could be graphically expressed: thus, asks Chris, 'How can they hold all that knowledge in their heads?' The individualized expert and his knowledge stand opposed in her question to the more obviously collective practices of knowledge creation with which she is engaged as part of an explicitly feminist teaching programme. There are two points of contrast here. The first is that, in relation to scientific knowledge itself, women typically portray themselves as (at best) passive consumers/receivers of knowledge, who might perhaps acquire odd bits of scientific information (reminiscent of the 'passive knowing' that Belenky et al. described). The second is to contrast the expert and his possession of elite knowledge with knowledge that women (sometimes explicitly) feel they 'own' and which 'I'd rather have than all that science stuff' (Chris). One woman, for example, says, 'I can only grasp an idea if I can put myself into it' (Rita) . . .

Referring to the 'science is everywhere versus nothing to do with me' polarity, Chris goes on to say:

> *I don't feel it personally . . . I know it but don't feel it . . . that science is everywhere. I pigeonhole it and see it as separate and that's how I divide it from common sense and women's intuition. . . .*

In these accounts, what scientists do is perceived as boring, tedious, mathematical. While those with some connection with science tend to see what scientists do in terms of 'the scientific method' (testing hypotheses, for example), others tend to see experiments as 'luck, a matter of trial and error' – though this does not appear to affect their trust or lack of trust in scientists . . .

Some of [these] themes . . . are not surprising: it is widely known, for example, that women feel excluded from science. But what we want to emphasise here is that these themes are rooted in oppositions – between science and commonsense, between owned and alienated knowledge, between science as everywhere but 'nothing to do with me' . . .

In their account of women's different 'ways of knowing', Belenky et al. (1986) distinguish several approaches to the acquisition of knowledge, ranging from the silent knower, through to the knower who actively constructs knowledge. Several of these are identifiable in the interviews, sometimes in the same person. The point here is that although many women have no difficulty in seeing themselves as active knowers and constructors of meaning this perception seldom extends to the realm of the 'scientific'. Nonetheless, it would be a mistake to see the women we interviewed as necessarily or merely passive in their relationship to scientific knowledge. Science, for example, is held by some women to be the antithesis of 'real knowledge' which they can intuit or arrive at through their own processes of analysis. This is more meaningful to them than the kind of knowledge which science represents to them . . . There is more to it, then, than becoming merely passive in the face of scientific knowledge and expertise. Sometimes, they actively put something in its place.

Thus, in saying 'I can know without knowing' (Jenny); in describing 'heart' knowledge as 'survival' or 'whole' knowledge (Gita); in insisting that 'everyone has a natural intuition about what goes on in the world around them' and on the need for science to acknowledge the 'nebulous' in things (Selma) and the limitedness of science (Edna) – there is a challenge to the dichotomy of feeling and rationality, in the way that some feminist critics of science have argued (see Sayers, 1983; Rose, 1994). It is, moreover, a challenge in which the prevailing image of science as master narrative is contrasted to an understanding of science as socially and politically constructed (see Barr and Birke, 1994).

In some interviews, metaphors of connection, of listening, of conversation even, replace those of detachment, observation, control, as more appropriate ways of seeking knowledge of the natural world: thus, Tania claims that feeling at one with nature was one of the most satisfying and important discoveries she made, yet she makes no connection between this and science as the study of nature. Similarly, Chris, speaking of natural health remedies, says, 'It's like the earth providing its own answers rather than scientists sitting over their test tubes. I find this comforting'. Even students on the feminist-inspired women and science course produce such metaphors. Thus Jenny believes we should 'listen to your body, let it tell you what it needs'.

Perhaps what is being invoked here is that the modern scientific way of finding out about the natural world is, after all, a recent cultural phenomenon (Keller, 1992): Carlo Ginzburg's work on historical epistemology (1980, pp 5–36) documents an alternative scientific paradigm with ancient roots. This 'conjectural' tradition is, he argues, rooted in the everyday and the sensual, but not irrational, and is peculiarly the perspective of those who are not in a position of power in a given society. Often such knowledge is dismissed as trivial or unscientific. 'Womanly intuition' is an obvious example – a tricky word which has been denigrated for its association with 'mere' feeling and with irrationalism but which is more accurately seen as 'another way of describing the instantaneous running through of the thought process . . . [and as] . . . neither more nor less than the organ of conjectural knowledge' (Ginzburg, 1980, pp 28–29). What comes over from some of our interviews is an urgency to apply this central idea to knowledge of the natural world – to acknowledge that natural reality is opaque, that any project to 'know' it completely is fantasy, to control it, self-defeating (as feminist critics have often argued). Such discourses fly in the face of Western culture, of scientific certainty that can yield control over nature . . .

Our research reveals widespread anxiety about science 'going too far' and beyond its understanding . . . Yet there is little evidence in the questionnaires or the interviews of any simple turning away from science. A much more insistent voice is for a reformed science. It is thus not only exclusion that is expressed but also anger and disillusionment at the kind of science we now have. Although often expressed in somewhat essentialist terms, for example, in terms of the need to integrate right and left brain, 'male' and 'female' ways of thinking, dissatisfaction with the abstract, controlling power of modern science is made clear . . .

A note on methodology

The approach we took to analysing the research data was influenced by the writings of Dorothy Smith (see 1979, 1987) and by her idea of feminist research as involving the researcher being located on the 'same critical plane' as the women being researched. In practice, what this meant was that we did not see our job as involving interpreting the women's testimony in terms of any fixed feminist, sociological, or any other given categories or theoretical project. At the same time, our understandings and interpretations were clearly deeply influenced by our theoretical beliefs and by our experiences as feminist women; they were also emotionally invested and contextually located (see Stanley and Wise, 1990, p 39).

In the research process and our writing up of the research our aim was to move between different standpoints and contexts – between accounts of individual women and different groups and between what was said to us and our own comments (influenced by our own reading of feminist and other theory and our own experiences) – in an effort, not to arrive at some privileged account, but to produce a text, which, in doing justice to the women's own testimony, 'exceed[ed] our own understandings' (Lather, 1994, p 7). Our strategy in ana-lysing the interviews, questionnaires and group discussions was to seek a bal-ance between identifying persistent themes across the interviews, charting differences between different groups and treating each woman's narrative as a complete text.

We attempted to make the research as interactive and 'power-sensitive' (Haraway, 1989) as possible – as I hope the above extracts demonstrate – notwithstanding the constraints of time and the 'academic mode of production' within which the research was located (see Stanley, 1990). In the end, of course, we had the pen; it was our job to give form to and interpret the data and the women involved had the right to expect us to do our job (2). That, after all, was the name of the game.

In the next chapter I discuss this research in relation to the central organ-ising themes of the book before trying to pull all of the strands together in the final chapter.

9 Adult education and really useful knowledge

Introduction

In Chapter 2 I indicated that my concern as a teacher and researcher in adult education had come to be defined in terms of 'healing the breach' between ways of knowing and forms of knowledge which in our culture are separated off from one another, specifically, between knowledge developed 'from above', in 'the academy'; and knowledge developed 'from below', rooted in everyday life. I think that the research approach adopted in the women's perceptions of science study reflects most closely that current personal agenda. In this chapter I want to locate this research in relation to that current personal agenda and to draw out some implications for feminist research and adult education. First, I outline the notion of 'science' which we adopted in the research.

Science as culture

Our research adopted a notion of science as a set of material and cultural practices which embodies a particular way of knowing the world. This way of knowing grew up in the context of European expansion and the development of capitalism; it grew up, too, as a worldview which was thoroughly grounded in gender and race (Harding, 1993; Merchant, 1982; Schiebinger, 1989). Science has come to be seen as representing some ultimate truth, its methods and language, its alleged reliance on the detached, value free pursuit of truth being seen by those inside science and outside it as allowing it a privileged access to nature. In this, the practice of science has involved the denial of other ways of knowing the world. Scientists typically ignore the expertise of those deemed to be non-scientists and of communities whose knowledge is not generated by those recognised as scientists. In this way, the local knowledge of, say, the medically useful plants of the Amazon, has been largely ignored.

The gap between the scientific expert and members of the public who are believed to be ignorant or uninterested in science is a relatively recent phenomenon. During earlier centuries, some historians of science have argued, there was more general interest in science as another form of human knowledge. Scientific knowledge in Europe in the eighteenth and nineteenth centuries was disseminated in a number of ways including the activities of the mechanics institutes and literary and philosophical societies. Scientific instruments were even part of the general culture, so that the *London Magazine* of 1828 could report that 'in every town, nay almost in every village there are learned persons running to and fro with electric machines, galvanic troughs, retorts, crucibles and geologists' hammers' (Layton *et al.*, 1986, p 32). Some historians of science have suggested that what mattered was 'science for specific social purposes', that is, what do we (some group, profession, trade) need to know for such and such a purpose?

This approach to knowledge, rooted in need-to-know and experience, is quite different from the approach embedded in science education today, which is usually removed from everyday life and is rooted in a need-to-know related to technological control over nature. By the turn of the twentieth century science conceived as an apolitical, universal, empirical and uniquely objective form of knowledge unlike any other, and pursued by professional experts, came to dominate (Stepan and Gilman, 1993). And schools (particularly in England and Wales) came to adopt a science curriculum marked by abstraction, decontextualised and apparently disconnected from social values of the wider society.

Linda Shepherd (1993) cites two articles about science education, written in 1938, which admonish scientists to denounce emotions and to learn to 'think coldly' (Shepherd, p 51). And Karen Barad, writing about how students of physics learn to accept this view of science, comments:

> The scientific method is hailed triumphant. It is as if we are to believe that the scientific method serves as a giant distillation column, removing all biases, allowing patient practitioners to collect the pure distillate of truth. There is no agent in this view of theory construction: Knower and known are distinct – nature has spoken.
>
> (Barad, 1995, p 66)

What Barad and other feminist authors highlight is that the 'object of knowledge' of science is never pure, unadulterated nature. It is social and cultural. It is always nature under some description, for example, nature as a teleological system or nature as a mechanical system or nature as a complex interactive system (Knorr-Cetina, 1983; Longino, 1993; Harding, 1993). Such ways of seeing reality and the metaphors which unconsciously influence scientific work are shaped by the values and concerns of the wider cultures within which they are developed. Modern science privileges the application of mathematical hypotheses to nature, the use of controlled experiments and a mechanical model of reality (Needham, 1993, p 31); while not all scientists adopt this model it is the dominant one lying behind and guiding advancing technology.

The metaphors of science

Donna Haraway, scientist turned historian of science, has produced sustained critiques of some of the main metaphors which guide scientific enquiry, documenting how gender-influenced ones abound, for example, in the extensive use of military metaphors in contemporary immunology (Haraway, 1991a). She and others have pointed out connections between sexist and racist traces to be found in sciences, particularly primatology, the study of apes and monkeys (see Haraway, 1989; Stepan and Gilman, 1993). Haraway does not believe that we can avoid metaphorical thinking in science or elsewhere, only that we should be conscious of how they shape the way we see the world. They can be empowering; they can also be dangerous. She advocates the adoption of different metaphors from those which are widely shared in modern science, believing we would do better to think of the world – as the 'object of knowledge' of science – as an actor or agent; to see accounts of the world, not as 'discoveries' but as 'conversations', and to accept that 'we are not in charge of the world' (Haraway, 1991b, pp 198ff). Evelyn Fox Keller, too, has commented on how metaphors of engagement and identification can assist our understanding of the world, revealing how notions like 'ensouling' and 'a feeling for the organism' guided the work of geneticist, Barbara McClintock (Keller, 1983). Strikingly similar metaphors were present in our interviews with women in our research study (Chapter 8).

This body of work implies that the reconstruction of scientific knowledge is inseparable from the reconstruction of ourselves. It implies, too, that in educating scientists, the education of the 'emotions' may be as important as the education of 'mind'. The emotions we experience reflect the forms of life in which we participate. The reasoning of science is informed by 'passion' as well as 'reason', is how Janet Sayers puts it (Sayers, 1983). And in our divided world this means it is informed by the passions, interests and values of privileged, white men. Even well-intentioned elites need to become aware of how their own practices and desires (for example, to be in control) and even their very self-understandings (for example, as hero or saviour) may actually work against democracy. Issues of emotional understanding and emotional development are seldom addressed in any of the literature which addresses procedures for democratizing the processes of inquiry, in science or elsewhere (see Alcoff, 1995).

One lesson from women's studies/women's education is, as I have already suggested, that to change the curriculum is not just to change what we think about. It is to change who we are (see Minnich, 1989). A corollary of this mutual interdependence of the 'who' and 'what' of knowledge is that a different science – along lines envisaged by feminists, for example, – cannot await a different society. A different science and a different society will come about together – or not at all (Nelson, 1990, p 316).

Knowledge from above, knowledge from below

It is significant, I think, that the emphasis on abstraction in science education took place alongside a move to de-radicalise the self-education practised in many working class communities in Britain in the late nineteenth century and to replace it with provided education. More recent examples of such science-related self-education have suffered a similar fate. Women's self-help groups, environmental groups and third world science movements provide examples of how lay people have produced really useful knowledge around science (Braidotti *et al.* 1994; Shiva, 1988). Yet there is now a tendency for such campaigning groups to have become themselves professionalized, using expert scientific knowledge – created in the epistemological communities of science – rather than forms of knowledge created by and for lay people, groups and movements. In the case of women's health groups, for example, Wellwomen clinics have been developed, replacing self-help groups. This change is double-edged. It has allowed more women access to better health care but what has happened here is analogous to what has happened to the battered women's movement in the United States, where the women involved have been translated into 'cases' and 'clients' of services, the need for financial independence has become the problem of 'low self-esteem', and consciousness-raising has been replaced with therapy (Tuana, 1992). In this way politicised understandings have become translated into objects of state intervention and spaces for challenging, oppositional knowledge of the world have been reduced.

Work in the philosophy and social studies of science has come to focus increasingly on the ways in which knowledge is socially constructed – in natural science, as it is elsewhere. There are, it is argued, no theory-free facts; knowledge is always created. There is always a slack between theories and the evidence supporting them (that is, scientific theories are 'underdetermined': see Knorr-Cetina and Mulkay, 1983, pp 4–5). Whatever pretensions science may have to be the pursuit of 'the truth' or of scientists merely discovering the laws of nature, even scientific knowledge is created by human beings, located in specific social and historical contexts. This being so, the social factors which shape the direction of scientific knowledge deserve further examination (Addelson, 1983). Yet the belief persists – among scientists as well as the rest of us – that science's special methods and special language, its espousal of the detached, value-free pursuit of truth, allow it a privileged access to nature. To listen to scientists on the radio during British National Science Week – the media's annual effort to popularise science – does nothing to dispel this perception. Broadcast talks gave the impression that the speakers believed not only in 'the truth' but also that it is only scientists who can 'name nature'.

Our research on women's perceptions of science rested on the belief that there exists the possibility of developing science more democratically, as a mass phenomenon – and not simply as a democratic duty but as a way of making science better. The development of science and its application to social problems is more likely to be advanced in proportion to its democratic inclusiveness, that is, to the closer it gets to the articulation and examination of all possible views (Nelson, 1990, p 170). Our research aimed to 'bring the margins to the centre' – that is, marginalized ways of knowing and aspects of identity (gender, ethnicity, class, race) which have been largely excluded from science and other public arenas and institutions – such that in the process 'they are themselves transformed and transforming' (Bordo, 1993, p 42).

I now want to locate the women's perceptions of science research within such a project – a project which is more 'bottom-up' than 'top-down'.

From critique to constructing knowledge

In Chapter 7, in the context of a discussion of Wendy Luttrell's research on working class women's relationship to knowledge, I suggested that education for women must render visible, in order to draw on, women's own resources and strengths. This was the standpoint from which we carried out the perceptions of science research. In listening to women talking about their views of science we listened, too, for the gaps and silences. Our own experience as women, as feminists, as learners and as teachers told us that women's silence is not always an indication simply of an absence of words or a lack; viewed in its political, historical and more immediate context (like that of being interviewed by university based women researchers) women's silence can be a powerfully subversive practice.

Furthermore, in looking at science and scientific knowledge from the standpoint of women 'outside' science we were not suggesting that there is any typical 'woman's point of view' on science. Difference must be centred within feminist analyses, and not just between them and the dominant culture, says Sandra Harding, summing up a recent broad shift within feminist thinking and a central organising idea of our own research. In addition, we were interested in exploring how such differing perspectives might contribute towards the creation of better, not just more democratic, science. In taking this approach, we were influenced by a shift of emphasis in the epistemological debate within feminism – from a critical to a more creative project.

A central question in this project is to ask, what difference would it make if women – their lives and experiences – were central to the creation of knowledge, instead of marginal to it? This is, of course, a difficult question to pose without getting into hot water, without seeming to suppose that women are all the same. 'Difference' is now critical for feminist theorising: We are, clearly, not the same (see Braidotti, 1994; Harding, 1991; Spelman, 1988; Ligones and Spelman, 1983). If we focus on epistemological communities as the primary agents of knowledge (as we urge in this research) such attention to differences need not encourage an individualized, fragmented view of the world. We are not committed by it to the enunciation of countless, shifting standpoints and endless relativism. The differences which 'make a difference' and which are epistemologically significant are social and political, rather than merely individual (Bordo, 1990, 1993).

It is a central feature of our research approach that it is because groups and communities construct knowledge, share standards of evidence and so on that social and political identity are epistemological factors and that issues of 'race', class and cultural difference as well as gender are important in women as subjects of knowledge (Tuana, 1992). It was, after all, mainly black women, lesbians, working class women who insisted that the struggle for equality had to lie in the assertion of difference within feminism. And not just difference from (white, middle class, heterosexual women) but, rather, difference as marking a condition of possibility or potentiality. This is to see 'subjectivity' as constituted *positionally*, not, that is, in terms of internal attributes and qualities but in relation to a shifting context of economic, political and cultural conditions and ideologies. It requires seeing issues of race, gender, class, ethnicity and other 'axes of power' (Fraser, 1989) as equally constitutive of people's subjectivity as of their life chances. Feminism claims that women's position in this network lacks power; it critiques existing social arrangements and tries to change them. And, as Sheila Rowbotham maintains, feminism as a theory and practice of social transformation works (as does socialism) to realise the dream 'that all human beings can be *more* than present circumstances allow' (Rowbotham, 1983, p 353).

Discussing 'standpoint' approaches to knowledge, Sandra Harding maintains that a standpoint is not a perspective or a way of knowing. To count as a standpoint, says Harding, we have to insist on an objective location, women's lives, from which to start research.

This idea is central to our science research and relates to the central role of epistemological communities in the generation of knowledge. For, it is as a member of a group that one achieves a standpoint. A *feminist* standpoint is itself an achievement, emphasises Sandra Harding, born through political struggle in engagement with others involved in the same community of interest and concern and committed to the same emancipatory values (see also Assiter, 1996, Chapter 5). Moreover, it is women's lives and experiences in their diversity and difference – and in many ways in conflict with one another – which provide the standpoint of feminist standpoint approaches to knowledge

Many groups are transient – as is the case with the groups of women who formed the basis of our study – but their importance in the creation of 'situated knowledges' (Haraway, 1991a) should not be underestimated (1).

To repeat, the suggestion here is that science and science education need to include many 'others' if it is to be better, not just fairer, science. At present, though, the authority of science rests on the majority being excluded – or included only as underlabourers (2). And this needs to change. A premise of our research was that such change cannot be with a view to socialising many more into science's current common-sense of abstraction and objectivity. On the contrary it has to involve the recognition of what other groups and communities of knowers, with different experiences and ways of seeing, can contribute to the development of our knowledge of the world. This is conveyed in our research, for instance, through our presentation of Hillcroft College and the Women and Science course as spaces which foster new possibilities for the creation of knowledge – knowledge which transcends traditional boundaries between rationality and emotion on the one hand and between science and common sense on the other. Transcending boundaries is, indeed, a key theme.

Breaking down boundaries

Feminism too demands a dialogue and discourse among women worldwide which transcends academic and knowledge boundaries (Harding, 1992). A basic premise of feminist standpoint epistemology is that knowledge or knowledges should be useful to those who produce it – it should be 'really useful', not merely useful. Yet as I maintained in Chapter 3, a striking feature of the feminist epistemological debate surrounding science is that it has so far been conducted at a highly abstract level, among a small group of feminist women academics and scholars (and who are mainly white and North American) who constitute a tiny epistemological community. Lugones and Spelman have commented:

> Theory cannot be useful to anyone interested in resistance and
> change unless there is reason to believe that knowing what a the-
> ory means and believing it to be true have some connection to
> resistance and change.
>
> (Lugones and Spelman, 1983, p 579)

For feminists the purpose of 'doing epistemology' cannot be to satisfy curiosity
alone (or to be seen as clever; see Skeggs, 1997). It has to contribute to an
emancipatory goal. The litmus test of the recent debate about knowledge within
feminism must therefore be its effects on the struggle for 'really useful knowledge' occurring in a wider frame of reference than the academy. It is, moreover, implicit in that dialogue that there will be little progress towards the goal
of useful, empowering knowledge until feminist epistemological debates are
brought down to earth and practical spaces are opened up for democratic knowledge making and until many more voices are added to the conversation. To
repeat:

> If we wish to empower diverse voices, we would do better, I
> believe, to shift strategy [from methodological debate] . . . to the
> messier, more slippery, practical struggle to create institutions and
> communities that will not permit some groups of people to make
> determinations about reality for all.
>
> (Bordo, 1990, p 142)

It is in relation to this practical struggle that the 'women's perceptions of science' study has to be located. For it is informed by the belief that the question
of knowledge which so concerns feminists has to be taken out of the academy
in order to grapple with the thoughts, concerns and feelings of other knowers,
other epistemological communities. Such engagement is particularly crucial in
the case of science because of the authority it wields and because it relies on
exclusive, expert knowledge, created by communities of knowers which have
historically acted to exclude women (among others). It is also particularly important at this moment in adult education's history. For it is a moment when such
practical epistemological spaces for challenging thought as have been opened
up, through struggle, are in grave danger of being lost – from memory as well
as from the landscape of adult education.

In attempting to use our research in the service of carving out such a space,
it was in the belief that women and others who have been historically
marginalised by powerful knowledge and institutions would stand to benefit.
Their experiences could begin to count in the creation and legitimation of knowledge. And this could benefit science too (3). Moreover, the strategy adopted in
writing up the research was itself influenced by this project, in that it was more
reflexive than my previous research accounts, consciously constructed around
and moving between different standpoints and contexts – including our own
and our theories – while at the same time not denying the authority conferred
on us by our institutional positions.

Thus, in the science research we try to strike a balance between depicting
what is shared in the women's relationship to scientific knowledge and what
differences exist in relation to cultural background and age, for example, as

well as for reasons of personal biography. In emphasising the processes of exclusion and marginalisation which are involved we do not paint a picture of women as 'cultural dopes' but as agents in these processes (Bordo, 1993; Bourdieu, 1993; Giddens, 1990); we also seek to show resistance to dominant stereotypes and notions of knowledge without, however, romanticising the degree of cultural challenge that exists and hence diverting attention away from continuing patterns of power, exclusion, subordination and 'normalisation'.

I now want to draw out some of the implications of our research for the education of adults and for further, useful feminist research.

Gender, race and doing research

The first thing to note is the remarkable resonance between the women's voices in our research and feminist critiques of science. The second is the potential for the enrichment of these critiques by the inclusion of many more voices in the conversation. What I want to stress here is that if we are to extend the conversation to include many subjects – the dialogue among women worldwide which feminism demands – academic and knowledge boundaries must be transcended.

One such boundary is that between the kind of knowledge produced by academic feminists and women's everyday knowledge. If feminism is to achieve the worldwide dialogue about science – and other knowledge – which concerns us, the barriers which prevent some women from speaking for themselves need to be shifted. From this point of view it matters a great deal who has set the terms of the conversation in the first place. Women can only engage in a mutual dialogue, equally, if the cards are not already stacked against some, for example, by opaque and esoteric language and scholarly and culturally specific discourse (Lugones and Spelman, 1983).

Further, in our research, the kind of conversations we had with the women interviewees was conditioned in many subtle ways by our own social position as white women academics. In some cases, women made explicit reference to that difference. Monica, for instance, felt able to speak about racism and the interviewer's whiteness: 'there is no place yet for the black woman [in science] . . . you know, our white counterparts . . . perpetuated this myth about the black woman as matriarch . . . which is a powerful statement from [one] woman to another, you know I am telling you, you are white and I am black . . . and when you have got all that going on, when the [black] woman actually decides that she wants to put pen to paper and say, right, this is how I see something will go, she's going to be sent down each time before she can make a scientist, before she can make any strides forward, and it's not going to happen by men specifically, it's going to be done by other women'.

Similarly, the good humour and, even, gentle mocking, for example, by one black community leader who was 'flabbergasted' by our interest in the subject but yet thought it wonderful that we were concerned; the silences as well as the deep engagement with the issues – all of these were a measure, not only of women's perceptions of science and our abilities as researchers, but also of their perceptions of us and ours of them. It is important to acknowledge that our whiteness was a significant factor in setting the terms of the discussions. Whiteness, as Toni Morrison has stressed, is a concept assumed and deeply entrenched in Western literature and culture (Morrison, 1970).

A more challenging science education would not only have to pay attention to other ways of making science and to its own racism; it should also attend to the ways in which whiteness itself remains unproblematised in scientific (including social scientific) discourses. I did not question this taken-for-granted whiteness in my first two case studies. Yet the childcare project in Lochend was used and run solely by white women; similarly, the women's education discussed in my second case study was overwhelmingly white. Moreover, throughout the 1970s and 1980s, the issue of racism (and, more generally, of cultural diversity) was scarcely ever mentioned in adult education (research) journals.

If we genuinely believe that it is necessary for women worldwide to engage in and with feminist thinking about science and to develop theory (knowledge in and about science) jointly, how should this be arranged? And how can the insights gained from feminist scholarship inform and assist practical struggles around science? Or, indeed, around knowledge production more widely? The paradox is that while feminist theorists in the academy have produced very radical ideas about science (and other knowledge) they have done so within very traditional modes of scholarly discourse; on the other hand, feminists whose ideas about science have been less challenging to its dominant modes of thinking (even if only because they have turned away from it) have often been very radical in the ways in which they teach and organise their courses: this is particularly true in the case of feminists working in adult education – an academically marginal context, but one in which particularly fruitful attention has been given to issues of pedagogy and process as well as to content and curriculum. Ways need to be found to bring together these different groups of women so that their knowledge and skills can be combined in the promotion of the kind of dialogue envisaged above.

Building on experience

'Product 2' in Chapter 8 consisted of that part of our analysis of the interview material which concentrated on the tensions which seemed to permeate our research. These were presented as indicating something about women's shared social position in relation to scientific knowledge. The first clear pedagogical implication of this is that if you only teach the 'science curriculum' to women as it is this will do nothing but perpetuate what helped to create the tensions in the first place. The contradictions emerge out of women's marginalisation from the authority of scientific knowledge while they simultaneously recognise that 'science is everywhere'. A science curriculum (or any curriculum: see discussion of Luttrell's research on women involved in basic education programmes in Chapter 7 above) that ignores these tensions plays into the gendered and racialised structures which created the marginalisation in the first place. What is required is a greater openness to different ways of knowing as potential resources in the development of new knowledge of the natural world.

The links between masculinity and science were forged early in the history of modern science. Schiebinger (1989) has described how science and its institutions were, from the early seventeenth century, explicitly linked with gender; the Royal Society of London, for example, excluded women from its membership. By the end of the eighteenth century, she argues, a science stripped of metaphysics, poetry and rhetoric was being championed by philosophers and scientists; literature was banned from science as 'feminine' and Goethe's reputation as a poet was said to ruin his reputation as a scientist! Schiebinger's argument is that femininity has come to represent a set of values excluded from the practice of science as we know it. These excluded values may be part of a larger set of values typically attributed to a broader group of 'outsiders', for example, black people, who, like women, have been largely barred from the practices of modern science.

Recent scholarship on the legacy of imperialism and the workings of 'race' in modern science has re-evaluated the causes and conditions of development of Western science. This work bears out Schiebinger's claim (see, eg, Needham, 1993). For, while revealing the debt to independent science traditions of other societies like Africa, India and China, it also suggests that science has been too narrowly defined – precisely, to exclude and devalue other forms of scientific thinking, because they are not useful to dominant groups in the West (see also Harding, 1991, Chapter 7; Harding, 1993, 1994; Ginzburg, 1980).

Awareness of this feature of modern science and resistance to it is clearly expressed by some women in the study – by Bell, for instance, who felt excluded from science at school because it was 'made so impersonal' and because 'people don't know black people's contribution to science'.

The second implication is that if women are to claim knowledge rather than simply receive it, 'starting from where women are' may be the most useful standpoint in science education. This might mean, for example, encouraging them to label knowledge they already have as 'scientific' and, as such, subject to empirical check like any other scientific knowledge. This was the approach taken in the Women and Science course which featured in Chapter 8. It must also mean valuing the knowledge that they bring from their membership of their various communities. The women who had come to Britain from Africa, for instance, brought experience and knowledge of healing and of the natural world that should be valued, not seen as 'other'.

Broadening the meaning(s) of science and science education to encompass a wide range of people's experiences, as feminist critics have urged, is necessary if the perception that science is done by experts and 'has nothing to do with me' is not simply to be reinforced. Although we should have reservations about basing an education on 'women's ways of knowing' (as some colleges in North America are attempting to do), an equal education for women of all social groups (as for the men of unprivileged groups) cannot be the same as an education which has been developed in a culture based on the exclusion of some of these groups (Minnich, 1989).

Moves such as these would certainly broaden the meaning(s) of science and science education to encompass a wide range of people's experiences, as feminist critics have urged. Most importantly, to build on experience means moving away from the prevailing model of scientific knowledge as facts and certainty. Moreover, the 'women's perceptions of science' research suggests that narrow notions of reason and 'science' deny us rich possibilities, as does labelling as irrational anything to do with the emotions, experience or intuition. Part of the problem posed by science (and the distance of most of us from it) is to do precisely with that separation of feelings and reason. A challenge to the dichotomy of feeling and rationality which feminist critics of science have argued forms a major part of the discourse of many of the women we interviewed.

Through integrating experience, the notion of science as 'boundaryless' (Nelson, 1990, p 11), as 'all around us' becomes more tangible. As such, it becomes inseparable from common sense, politics, philosophy, history, language and metaphor and so less exclusive, more human and more 'ownable' by women (4). Indeed, Ruth Hubbard has observed that it is as political beings that women will change science – that is, as citizens (Hubbard, 1990). A creative/critical science education would, in consequence, involve working with women's groups in the community, drawing on their own agendas, whether to do with housing, health, roads or the environment, in an effort to develop more broadly based 'scientific communities'.

The kind of science education envisaged here is an aspect of citizenship education, of 'pedagogy through politics' rather than an educationalist pedagogy centred solely on the classroom (see Le Doeuff, 1991). Opportunities for adult learning rather than more narrowly, adult *education*, are to the forefront in such an approach. Central to it, too, is the notion of 'responsible knowing' and the fostering of a collectivist form of consciousness which addresses the question of the kind of future we want, while drawing on different critical analyses of science and society.

Global challenges

The 'women's perceptions of science' research underlined the central importance of the group and its dynamics in learning; for example, it stressed how important the group seems to be in developing frames of reference and in contributing to women's sense of themselves as epistemological agents. In many ways the critical role of the group in the construction of knowledge is undercut by current trends in adult and continuing education which emphasise structures for individualising students and learning – often in the name of increasing learner choice. As a result there is an increase in a person's isolation from other learners (Edwards, 1991a).

I think that our research also indicates the need for a critical/creative science education which draws on approaches to curriculum development which have been developed in women's adult education over the past twenty years or so. From this work we know some of the processes which encourage collective knowledge making. We know from it, too, that a purely intellectual approach to science is not enough, that what is needed is a large number of people in movement seeking change – a collective effort to develop really useful knowledge of the world in view of a future society.

Mechtild Hart's questions are important here. What would a population that is concerned about preserving the natural conditions of life have to know? What would it have to learn? And what skills, competencies and attitudes would allow for understanding and knowing nature in a non-controlling way? (Hart, 1992, p 203). Questions such as these, asked 'from below', urge the development of a kind of knowledge which, in referring to the future rather than the past, would not reproduce the 'science curriculum' but would transform it. Adult education can play a role in providing a space for such 'knowledge from below' . The women in our study could make a real contribution to such a project; and the further identification and exploration of epistemological communities which might take part in such a research/education project seems justified.

On a global level, there are some challenges to the status quo. The Dutch 'science shops' are one example. These act as brokers between community groups, seeking help to solve a particular problem (how to deal with local pollution, for instance) and university researchers. Closer to home, Easthall Tenants Group in Glasgow, working on dampness problems with scientists from the local university along with environmental architects, is another example. What is important about such initiatives is that the questions that guide research come from the community not the researchers. There are, too, 'people's science' movements in India and Africa.

Initiatives such as these are urgent. Not only are women (and many others) marginalised by the 'master narrative' of science, but it has been argued that we are moving towards new mechanisms of knowledge production (and not only in science) which could further increase the marginalisation of marginalised groups. Knowledge production is becoming institutionalised in yet new ways. Michael Gibbons and colleagues have argued that the production of knowledge is characterised by greater transdisciplinarity. It is produced in a wider arena, including government think tanks and commercial organisations and is critically dependent on global communications and electronics. This encourages scientists, among others, to be less interested in solving basic problems and more interested in the market. This sort of knowledge production is more distributed and open ended – but, left to the market, it is also likely to enhance global inequalities (Gibbons et al., 1994). Working class women, for instance, are unlikely to be participating in this emerging nexus of knowledge creation linked to markets – except as nimble fingers for the manufacture of electronics components in sweatshop factories of Asia.

The point which needs to be underlined, I think, is that nobody – no social group, gender, class, race or epistemological community like science – has a monopoly on defining or making knowledge. Further:

> The fact is, we are mixed in with one another in ways that most
> national systems of education have not dreamed of. To match
> knowledge in the Arts and Sciences with these integrative
> realities . . . is the intellectual and cultural challenge of moment.
>
> (Said, 1993, p 401)

What the 'perceptions of science' research sought to emphasise was that difference also needs space for the development of new possibilities of being and knowing – particularly differences of gender, race, class and (dis)ability. That is to say, we need to explore and develop a much richer range of lives and voices for the development of a really 'human' common education of the sort Said dreams of. Survival *is* about the connection between things, as Said maintains. We are mixed in with one another in ways which education systems have scarcely taken note of. But we are not all the same. Undoubtedly, the claim that we are can be a profoundly ethical one, calling on us to remember our human connectedness but it is dangerous when we misconstrue sameness: 'The brotherhood of man' is all too often precisely that – white man to boot.

Summary

In summarising the main points made in this chapter I shall refer back briefly to points made earlier in the book. I began the chapter by outlining the historically and culturally specific nature of modern science and the notion of science as culture which underlay our 'women's perceptions of science' research. I emphasised that the research approach which we adopted explicitly repudiated science's and scientists' special claims (the 'gifted heroes of our epoch') as sole arbiters of legitimated knowledge of the world (Miller and Driver, 1987). Further, by treating women as knowledgeable agents, I suggested, our research stance made central the following issue (which was evaded in both of my earlier studies): how to analyse the women's experiences and descriptions in ways which allowed these experiences to influence our categories of analysis. I have suggested that in the research which figured in my first and second case studies I privileged my own social scientific theories and categories; in the 'perceptions' study, in contrast, both in carrying it out and in writing it up, we tried to let the women's accounts shape and re-shape our own theories.

Radical heroes

To refer back to a theme introduced in Chapter 2, the way we conducted the study attempted to help 'heal the breach' between ways of knowing and forms of knowledge which are usually separated off in our culture: 'expert' knowledge and lay knowledge, academic and everyday knowledge. It was also informed by the belief, which was outlined in the opening chapters, that as feminist theorists, researchers and teachers we need to develop notions of theory and knowledge which do not exclude the majority from the outset. Thus, a major premise of this penultimate chapter has been that if we are to develop more inclusive practices of knowledge development we need to abandon once and for all the prevalent individualistic and heroic notion (and myth) of knowledge development which is enshrined in our education system. We need, in other words, to acknowledge the part played by social processes and collective change in the development of knowledge (Evans, 1995). This goes as much for adult education as a field of study as any other. In the adult education literature, certain figures – like Paulo Freire, Antonio Gramsci and Raymond Williams, for instance (but especially Freire) – have huge symbolic significance as 'radical heroes'. And, as Diana Coben points out, the trouble with the radical heroes story is that once individuals are fetishised, their ideas cease to be open and productive of new insights, challenge is disallowed and debate dies (Coben, 1998).

I have emphasised in this chapter the need to develop feminist research and educational approaches which seek to transcend various boundaries, both conceptual and material: between academic and everyday knowledge, reason and emotion, sciences and arts; and between feminists in the academy and feminists in adult education, feminists and other women. Adopting such an approach in the 'perceptions of science' study, revealed, for example, that feminist criticis of science and the women in our study seem to agree that the privileging of the rationality of highly abstract knowledge goes hand in hand with a failure to produce really useful knowledge – knowledge of a kind which enables an understanding of human experience (Evans, 1995).

Finally, a central theme of this chapter – and the book – has been that educators (feminist educators especially) need to leave the internal debates of the academy in order to articulate urgent problems with people other than academics. A premise of the book is indeed that it is the marginal, non-mainstream position of adult education which has been its particular strength and which, in its more radical forms, has enabled social movements and community groups to secure the services of intellectuals for their own ends and projects. In the final chapter I return to this theme, connecting it to a theme which has been briefly touched on in this chapter – the global changes underway in the knowledge industry and the threat and promise contained in such changes for democratic education and knowledge production. But I begin the final chapter with an attempt to summarise and pull together the main threads of the book.

10   Liberating knowledge

Introduction

In this final chapter I want to pull together the main strands of the book in relation to its themes concerning feminist research and adult education as a prelude to thinking towards future adult education practice and research.

In Chapter 1 I described the aims and strategies of the book in terms of 'finding ourselves in cases'. The idea proposed there was that in order to improve our own practices as adult educators we need increased self-understanding of our present and past practices – an understanding which cannot be achieved through individual self-analysis and navel-gazing but requires public discussion and dialogue.

I have used a variety of strategies in pursuit of this primary objective. I have organised the book around three 'cases' in which the research itself, and the subject of the research are viewed as historical events – part of what Foucault has called an apparatus: 'a thoroughly heterogeneous ensemble consisting of discourses, institutions, . . laws' (Foucault, quoted in Kuhn, 1990, p 6). I have viewed my cases, that is, as social practices and processes which contain possibilities for resistance and transformation as well as reproduction and continuity. A central argument of the book is that, in addition to critique of existing conditions, a task for the radical adult educator/researcher is to seek out the possibilities for change and renewal which are always present in such cases. We need better strategies for understanding how our work relates to wider power structures and ideologies and we need tactics for transforming that understanding into action.

In constructing my object of study in this way I sought to reconstruct the three pieces of research which figure in the book by placing myself 'in the frame' – the argument here being that reflexive social research should not efface the researcher/writer in the processes and products of research.

First case study

In the case of Headway I argued that my failure to make myself visible in the text resulted in various 'maskings' – of whose point of view was being represented at any one time (eg mine or some theorist's) as well as my own emotional investments. Thus, in my original Headway text, other theorists (critics of community development, for instance) entered 'from above', adding legitimacy to what I was saying. In my new 'situated' account, in contrast, other theorists' voices enter as other points of view, selected for particular purposes. Thus I contextualise the influence of the writings of community critics like Sennet and of Marxist-feminist writing on my Headway interpretation by viewing these in the context of debates current at the time and in relation to my own political activities in various left and feminist groups.

In my re-appraisal of my Headway research I argued that by interpreting the Headway project in terms of my (implicit) Marxist-feminist categories – and because of the excessive theoreticism of my favoured structural approach – I failed to see what escaped these categories, for example, women's caring work. I suggested, too, that my rather crude notion of power failed to capture the complexities involved, including various emotionally invested resistances and small transgressions by the women. As a result I effectively muted their capacity for critical engagement in the day-to-day workings of the project.

I indicated a number of paradoxes in my position, suggesting, for instance, that by adopting a neutral, disembodied, observer stance in the Headway account, this actually went against what I 'knew' – namely, value-free social science is an impossibility. Further, I 'knew' about the complexities of power and resistance from my political and collective practice in the women's movement. Yet this did not find its way on to the page. I suggested, too, that had I taken my own emotional response to Headway seriously rather than masked it (even to myself) this might have operated as a clue and a way in to the complex relations of power, resistance and accommodation which were actually operating in Headway.

Although I failed to chart these in my Headway account, nonetheless, some of these complexities did seep through, disturbing my cut and dried Marxist-feminist rendering of the women's experiences. I suggested, tentatively, that this more muted 'voice' derived from my own experiential learning (acquired from my own class background and from my involvement in the women's movement) – learning which did not privilege expert academic knowledge or prize intellectual over emotional understanding.

Second case study

In my second case study, which centred on my research on tutors teaching NOW courses in and around Durham, I reproduced an extract from the introduction to my account. Here, in contrast with my Headway account, I adopt a posture of openness and 'reflexivity', but in practice – as evidenced in the body of my account – I trim and edit what the tutors say around a rigid, tripartite classification of feminisms and again, I impose my favoured reading. In the process, as I suggest in my reappraisal, I downplay questions of subjectivity, pedagogy and process in women's education. In this evasion – just as with Headway, I suggest – I continued to be seduced by theory with a capital 'T'. This time it is theory produced by academic women's studies lecturers like Mary Evans whose main concern was actually to safeguard the prestige of women's studies in the university (which was not at all on my agenda) by not threatening the 'rigour' of what was taught through 'women-friendly' methods (see my earlier reference to a different kind of rigour which I learned, subliminally, I think, through involvement in the women's movement).

As a result, in the final part of my dissertation I leaned uncomfortably close to a 'banking' view of feminist education. Here, the tutor has the (feminist/political) knowledge, to be deposited in the women in the group, and the women's own experiential knowledge is downplayed, deemed not knowledge or interpreted only in terms of the tutor's categories. In returning to that conception of feminist women's education as political education, in my reappraisal, I outlined developments within feminist pedagogy and feminist popular education so as to draw out a model of feminist education in which co-learners and educators put in question the discourses and structures within which we live our lives so as to understand them better – in order to transform them. That is, the emphasis is on what has been called 'praxis' (Lather, 1991).

In all of this, emphasis is put on the role of the group in the production of knowledge. 'Views from below' or 'subjugated knowledges' are taken into account in the development of a curriculum which is organised around the idea of 'really useful knowledge'. A narrowly rational approach to learning, is rejected, the role of emotion in all learning is acknowledged and it is recognised that working for change requires desire for change (Berlak, 1989). And reflexivity is built in – an explicit acknowledgement that all knowledge is socially situated, socially constructed and mutable. However, as Donna Haraway argues, it is no good simply being reflexive. As feminists, we need to get beyond an awareness of the constructedness of knowledge to seeking knowledge which will help create a more just world.

In my first two case studies I emphasised that judging the usefulness of research texts for feminist purposes cannot be done in the abstract; it is a contextual matter, decidable only in practice, not in theory. Thus, in re-visiting my Headway and NOW research 'products', notwithstanding my current concerns about the limitations of these accounts, I also suggested that assertive texts – in the context of their production and reception – were actually what was needed in these cases, at the time. That is to say, a more 'open' text might have been weaker in its impact in the very places in which it might be used in the interests of women and other marginalized groups.

Thus, in the face of very powerful voices for low-cost, self-help alternatives, the impact of my Headway report on local authority decision-makers (through Strathclyde's Social Strategy Sub-Committee) might have been considerably lessened had I produced an uncertain text. Similarly, in the case of the NOW text, in the academic and adult education contexts of its production and reception at the time – in which there was, on the one hand, a growing 'postmodern' paradigm of knowledge and, on the other, a psychological/individualistic 'episteme' taking hold – an unequivocal text was probably more challenging and more useful for feminist ends than one which displayed the contingencies and values which went into its construction (see note 1).

Third case study

It was in my research on women's perceptions of science that I practised a more reflexive approach than hitherto: a more personal voice was allowed in and the study was more explicitly located politically, historically and culturally. It was carried out from an explicitly feminist standpoint and a commitment to 'responsible knowledge', that is, to research which takes responsibility for the standpoint from which it is pursued. Here, unlike the NOW study, I think, there is a fit between the stated aims and its execution. We did not try to fit what the women said into our pre-determined categories (in contrast with my NOW research). Rather, we showed how what they said resonated with other, more academic voices and made it clear that their own voices exceeded any efforts on our part to contain and categorise them.

Coming full circle

The book has argued that each of the studies (and what it is a study of) has to be situated within its specific social and cultural context – on the grounds that reflexive social or educational research which is aware of the conditions of its own production cannot restrict itself to merely putting the individual self 'in the frame'. My autobiographical sections (especially Chapters 2 and 3) were also written with this in mind. An implication of the need to contextualise any research is, as I have already said, that no research text can be evaluated in abstraction from the social context of it production and reception; and, since 'everything is dangerous', we must, in each specific historical and cultural context, re-assess 'the main danger'. I have suggested that, as I see it, one of the main dangers now for feminist theory and practice lies in the demands of 'professionalism' which cut it off from feminism's grass roots and which, in its highly abstract, self-absorbed, dense, postmodernist guise, reduces feminism's transformative possibilities, effectively excluding most concrete 'others' from the conversation (Bordo, 1993).

Despite its marginal status – maybe even because of it – adult education theorising, too, is becoming increasingly abstract and subject to academic fashions. Those who traditionally have power (and time) to write books and define what is to count as worthwhile knowledge (and Research Assessment Exercise protocols!) tend to assume that their audience is pretty much like themselves. And building on this assumption – of shared, but actually very culturally specific experience – keeps most others out of the discussion.

There is a growing and highly influential trend in Anglo-American adult education writing and theorising towards treating adult education as *discourse*. This trend takes its point of departure from an engagement with postmodernist preoccupations and attitudes – of scepticism, 'doubt' and irony. Yet in the highly self-conscious, abstract and excluding discourse adopted in such writing there is an odd lack of awareness of its own historical and social locatedness and a total failure to acknowledge its own complicity as follower of fashions and perpetrator of traditions in theory making which are very old indeed.

Underpinning my book is what has been called a 'storied epistemology', one which recognises the power of narratives in enhancing understanding – in this case, of how knowledge is constructed in different times and places. The book is a plea for engaged and engaging work which does not overvalue academic, formal, abstract argument and which acknowledges the force of the demand for educated *imaginations* and ways of knowing which 'objectivist' epistemologies are ill-equiped to provide.

In this, I have come, in a sense, full circle: it was that highly abstract, disembodied standpoint with which I began (from my philosophy days); and it is towards practical knowledge-making projects directed at developing 'really useful knowledge' that I have been moving. In this, I have stressed that a major concern must be to develop research strategies and pedagogical practices which do not impose our own pre-determined frameworks on people. On the contrary, by giving recognition to 'knowledge from below' and ways of thinking which do not necessarily fit narrow notions of rationality, such attention should, as I said in my introduction, help 'transcend the divide between ways of knowing and forms of knowledge which in our culture are separated off from one another'. I have indicated how my own practice fell short in terms of that criterion: over-privileging academic and abstract knowledge and under-valuing knowledge born of experience and emotional understanding (see Chapters 5 and 7 especially). Indeed, my reasons for this present study resonate with that anger of which Jane Thompson speaks (see Chapter 7). I can still feel echoes of an earlier anger when colleagues – otherwise kind, thoughtful and insightful men – fail to see the gendering of their favourite stories about adult education's past and present: a boys' own tale of brotherhood and heroes which through repetition (for example, in books, reading lists and research) shuts out the possibility of other more complicated (and collective) stories.

Knowledge is not the product of disembodied minds. We cannot, of course, know what difference it would have made to our intellectual heritage – to the philosophy, literature, history and science enshrined in our education systems if women had been central to it from the outset. But the question is worth asking: If women (and other 'others') *had* been included in defining the terms of valuable knowledge, would knowledge which arises out of the ability to work with others, with change, with the emotions, with a whole range of modes of thinking and feelings which are integral to lived daily experience, be devalued, as it is at present, as 'subjective' (Minnich, 1989)? It may well be that as Sandra Harding has suggested, learning how to see from below, that is, from the standpoint of the lives and experiences of the powerless, offers us a better bet for seeing things in a less distorted, less false way, than knowledge constructed from the standpoint of the powerful (Harding, 1992).

Changing feminism

In acknowledging the impact of feminist theory and practice on adult education we should recognise that the forms which feminism took in the 1970s and 1980s were culturally and historically specific, as I have stressed throughout the book; the same goes for the forms which feminism is taking in the 1990s.

Feminist theory has always posed questions about knowledge and power, antic-ipating postmodernist/poststructuralist critiques in crucial, and usually unac-knowledged, ways. I have indicated how my own feminism has developed and changed and how these changes relate to wider theoretical, political and per-sonal changes. I stressed at the beginnning of the book that my changing approach to feminist research and women's education should not be seen as moving towards the correct view or 'right answer'; rather, what I construe as an appropriate approach has tended to shift, in relation to these wider proc-esses and internal changes.

Yet throughout all of my work in sociology, the philosophy of the social sciences, women's studies and adult education I know that learning to be a feminist has embodied all of my learning. That this has not always been con-scious has been one of the themes of this book. For me, feminism has not been a defined set of beliefs so much as an orientation, both political and epistemo-logical; it has required, I believe, a continuous revising of my thinking and it has been accompanied by a desire (felt progressively more strongly as I have got older) to bring the intellectual and personal dimensions of my life more closely together. Such an orientation contrasts with the highly abstract 'view from nowhere' of my philosophy undergraduate days which I tried to ape well beyond its sell-by date.

The power of metaphor

I have stressed, too, the role of metaphor in shaping our perceptions of the world. Metaphors can have empowering potential and can help free us from ways of thinking which limit and restrict. I have already suggested that we might do well to cultivate that kind of thinking conveyed in Hannah Arendt's metaphor of the sea-diver, prising loose pearls from the sea bed. Such a form of thinking, though located in the past, is directed at the future: it requires a 'sea-change' (see Chapter 2). There *are* several pearls to be prised from our recent past of women's education as I have already suggested; and the 'percep-tions of science' research also provides reasons for optimism concerning adult education for women. But in looking back on a particular period of women's adult education, the point is not to urge a return to some past golden age of adult education. It never existed.

It has long been recognised that old traditions of radical adult education rooted in a male working class and based on the impulse to 'enlighten' accord-ing to the radical educator's definitions of reality simply will not do. Similarly, it is clear that there are now several women's movements with diverse aims and varying power. These movements, though virtually ignored by the media (and much adult education), have mobilised beyond the women's liberation groups of the 1970s. In so doing they have created new national and international networks which have become a focus for much new learning. Many women, particularly the poorest, faced with new and extreme circumstances, have *had* to learn fast and intensively. Some women's groups and networks have grown out of a basic need to survive in the face of 'flexibility' and the dominance of market forces. Their starting point may not have been a desire to be women in new and challenging ways – a key impulse of the women's movement of the 1970s. Yet they have found themselves 'doing and thinking the unimaginable' as Sheila Rowbotham observes (Rowbotham, 1997). This is true for many community-based women's groups in Scotland, Ireland and other parts of Britain. It is also true in Mexico, Peru, Brazil, Nicaragua and South Africa where many thousands of women, unable to care for their families, have mobilised around prices, basic social needs, schools and sanitation.

Where is adult education in all of this? International human rights movements, often in the form of NGOs, are now one of the main sites for popular adult education. Overwhelmingly, it is women who are involved here. In the present world there should certainly be plenty of space for popular education if what we mean by this is starting from the problems, experiences and social position of excluded majorities, working to develop the new knowledge which is needed to deal critically and creatively with our lives (Johnston, 1988). And as an intellectual and cultural project which has always recognised the social interests involved in the development and ownership of knowledge, adult education generally could be at the cutting edge of the far-reaching intellectual change which some commentators are heralding (see Gibbons et al., 1994; Scott, 1995).

Present social and cultural conditions in which traditional institutions (including universities) are being eroded may indeed favour a return of the old, creative space adult education once inhabited. However, adult educators will have to struggle with the dominant instrumental values which are oiling the wheels of the new forms of knowledge production and which, left to the market, will enhance, rather than diminish global inequalities (see Chapter 9). In recent years civic, spaces have been giving way more and more to market places/spaces.

Marjorie Mayo believes that adult education has been the focus of a great deal of Government attention recently precisely because it can be a means of promoting conformity and flexibility in a rapidly changing world. Nevertheless, as the kind of women's education depicted in this book has shown, it can also be a means by which people deal creatively and critically with the world in order to change it (Mayo, 1995). Adult education remains one of the few spaces left where the democratic control and development of knowledge can be pursued as an ideal of citizenship. In view of the dramatic changes underway in the sphere of work and civil society worldwide there is a greater need than ever for adult education geared specifically towards increasing such critical and creative engagement (Barr, 1996).

There are many people who yearn for a new culture of pluralism and of developed democracy which 'might transform people's sense of themselves as citizens rather than cogs in a huge and ruthless economic machine' (MacMillan, 1995). Assisting in the development of such a civic revival and in the creation of diverse 'spaces of enunciation' – to enlist Henri Lefebvre's evocative phrase – is an obvious task for adult and continuing education. It is obvious, that is, for an adult and continuing education whose creative and social purpose goals have not been entirely displaced by the ideological drift in favour of individual advancement. To be adequate to such a task, adult and continuing education will have to refuse to accommodate itself wholesale to the dominant agenda of credentialism. It will have to guard against metaphors of 'coming of age' in relation to the mainstream, and against being seduced into deafness to other voices by its aspirations to be in a position, at last, to embed continuing education principles and ideals in the mainstream (Barr, 1996).

There seems little doubt that new subject areas can develop better outside formal structures and institutional power divisions. Arguably, women's studies, for example, would not have got off the ground in the UK if adult continuing education in the WEA, local authorities and universities, hadn't provided the space for its germination and growth throughout the 1970s (see Barr and Birke, 1994). Its project was the complete transformation of existing curricular and institutional hierarchies, as well as radical change in pedagogical methods and in what counts as knowledge. In its coming of age in relation to the mainstream it has lost connection with its social and political grassroots and thereby much of its radical edge. A theme of this book has been that the marginality of adult education is part of its strength – a strength which gets lost in metaphors of 'coming of age'. In groping our way forward we should dispense with metaphors which betray an aspiration to be up among the big boys.

Liberating knowledge

The dual meaning of liberating knowledge is that on the one hand knowledge can be liberating; on the other hand what counts as knowledge is contestable as well as actually contested: sometimes, too, challenging and subversive ways of knowing and acting can be liberated through teaching, research and other educational work.

Tom Steele argues that adult education has traditionally invoked a mode of thinking which is imaginative and forward-looking (even utopian) as well as critical. It has embraced a collective project which concerns, crucially, what William Morris has called the education of desire (see Steele, 1995). I think the same is true of feminism. Through imagining how things might be otherwise adult education and feminism can stimulate the desire and will for a different way of living. From this vantage point we can begin to seek transformation of the present. I believe that feminism and adult education are more vital than ever in identifying and opening up spaces where such challenging and imaginative thinking (and desiring) can be formed.

It is a central strand of this book – one traced progressively through my three case studies – that such imaginative and practical projects need to be located in people's real lives, histories and concerns and that a key resource for their development rests in an alliance with that which has been silenced, repressed – or merely disdained – in our culture. This includes the 'subjugated knowledges' of those people on the downside of current social and economic changes; knowledge from below; emotional and practical knowledge; and what Gramsci has called 'good sense'. In a passionate indictment of the 'discourse of derision' of the 'underclass' as a group without culture, Lyn Tett has argued that: 'As long a people are voiceless, with their experiences interpreted on their behalf, by others, then their own meanings are rendered illegitimate' (1995, p 10). The point which has to be emphasised here is that the majority are not dupes of their circumstances; they understand only too well what is happening around them. That understanding and that resistance are resources for the future, as John Payne has suggested (Payne, 1995).

A major premise of this book is that questions of methodology underpin all theory making; another, related one is that there has to be a serious re-thinking of the relationship between 'expert' theory, experience and reality. Questions of who we hear, how we listen, to whom we regard ourselves as accountable, who we address or imagine as our audience, and how we address them (indeed, who we think 'we' are) are key methodological, epistemological and political issues (Skeggs, 1997; Bourdieu, 1993). These are also central questions for those engaged in adult education.

I have learned from adult educators like Paulo Freire that education can only be liberating where *everyone* has a stake in developing knowledge. And I have learned from the women's movement and my own life that striving for knowledge contained in books is limited if it is not connected to people's aspirations for knowledge about how to live in the world. It was that aspiration which took me into philosophy in the first place. Yet what I learned there was to become smart in book knowledge, to indulge in philosophy's overestimation of the power of thinking and its centrality to human life and to forget that original goal. I think that the personal journey depicted in this book represents a return to that original starting point, where, that is, I have begun to heal the breach between words and things.

Ideas do matter: This book urges those with the luxury of time for research and for creating theory in and around adult education to leave the internal debates of the academy in order to articulate urgent problems with people other than academics. A failure to transgress – by being far too deferential to academic, abstract knowledge, for example – all too frequently goes hand in hand with a failure to produce really useful knowledge, that is, knowledge which enables an understanding of human experience, enhances self-respect and helps people to deal critically and creatively with the world in order to change it (see note 2).

Notes

Chapter 1

1. A recent book suggests that this means that the *ontological* radicalism of thinkers like Michel Foucault concerning the nature of social reality is lost because his insights about bodies, force and power – insights about living and being – are collapsed into debates about meaning, discourse and knowledge itself (see Battersby, 1998).
2. Lynne Segal has criticised this strand in contemporary feminism for its historical distortions, particularly of 'seventies feminism' (Segal, 1997).
3. See, eg, Edwards, 1991a, 1991b, 1994, Edwards and Usher, 1994, Usher *et al.*, 1997 for analyses of adult and continuing education which utilise this model of power. These suggest that adult education is becoming a 'site of normalising practices', a site, that is, for producing people as modern 'subjects' with certain attitudes and skills which are functional to the contemporary socio-economic situation. Through the associated discipline and discourses of psychology especially, adult education helps 'bring forth' adults *as* adaptable, 'self-actualising', self-regulating, 'lifelong learners' with 'competencies'. External discipline is displaced with self-discipline, and 'confessional practices' of all sorts proliferate, for example, guidance and counselling, the accreditation of prior learning, learning contracts, records of achievement, self-evaluation (Usher and Edwards, 1995). Thus, through certain practices and techniques people's inner lives are brought into the realm of power, through 'educating' them to govern themselves. And power operates through seduction rather than repression.
4. Lorraine Johnson-Riordan (1994) brings the notion of adult education as discourse into focus in an article which discusses, among other things, the colonising effects of the discourse of HRD (Human Resource Development) on the contemporary Australian scene.
5. Books like *Testimony* (Felman and Laub, 1992) and *The Black Atlantic* (Gilroy, 1993) suggest the limits of purely rational debate and argument in struggles for liberation and being heard. Thus Gilroy presents two life stories – of Frederick Douglas and Margaret Garner (the latter fictionalised by Toni Morrison in *Beloved*) as illustration of this. He quotes from writings of the black intellectual, Frederick Douglas, once a slave. With heavy irony, Gilroy suggests that Douglas discovered an 'ideal speech situation' (Habermas, 1989) at the very moment in which he held his tormentor (his owner) by the throat:

'I held him so firmly by the throat that his blood flowed through my nails. "Are you going to resist, you soundrel?" said he. To which I replied a polite "Yes sir".'

The story of Margaret Garner, who chose to kill her children rather than they become slaves, can be read alongside Douglas's, says Gilroy, as part of a tradition of black autobiographical writing whose authority stems from its deliberately personal tone, 'in which autobiography becomes an act of simultaneous self-creation and emancipation . . . [and where] in the hands of slaves the particular can wear the mantle of truth and reason as well as the universal' (Gilroy, 1993, p 69).

6. Such spaces are variously called, in this book, 'rhetorical spaces', 'spaces of enunciation' and 'epistemological communities'.

Chapter 2

1. It is interesting that a contemporary book from the USA on the 'postmodern challenge to social science' invokes the same Kantian divide in suggesting that this challenge to social science will eventually divide each of its disciplines into two separate fields: one inspired by the natural sciences, the other derived from the humanities: one dedicated to discovering the causes of social phenomena, the other preoccupied with criticism and the exploration of language and meaning (Rosenau, 1992, p 180).

2. This notion of writing the self is taken from Laurel Richardson's book, *Fields of Play* (1996). She is much influenced by postmodernism. I find her ideas provocative and useful, notwithstanding the postmodernist trappings. Her boredom with standard sociological writing I share and I like the simple message contained in her observation that writing in standard ways does not prevent writing in other ways (p 93).

Chapter 3

1. A British feminist philosopher, Ann Seller found that her theories about gender equality, gleaned from Anglo-American traditions of theorising could hinder dialogue when she visited an Indian women's university:

'At best such theories provide a platform from which to view the problem. At worst they obstruct rather than facilitate dialogue. I was also beginning to recognise that the more abstract and theoretical our formulations, the more culturally specific they become. Intuitively, I had expected the opposite.'

(Seller, 1994, p 243)

Chapter 5

1. For example, it has been argued that the problem with this strategy in the *current* context of professionalised academic feminism is that rather than serving a clearly political goal of empowerment the 'strategic use of essentialism can turn into an alibi for proselytising *academic* essentialisms' (Spivak, 1993, p 4, my emphasis). I shall return to this point about context at various points in the book.

2. Moreover, I was tied in my analysis to a notion of the State as a monolithic entity in which power resided and I saw capitalism as 'needing' the Welfare State to uphold the traditional institution of the family. In the light of the thoroughgoing internationalisation of capital and labour which has occurred in recent years, as if in the blink of an eye, it seems clear that capitalism has no need of the British welfare state. Even in 1979, 'the family', so pivotal within that framework of analysis, seemed, in Lochend, to be much more like an improvisation than an institution (see Ehrenreich, 1992). The same could be said for the 'local state' in its various manifestations and sites and as represented in my report by the voices of various local politicians, local authority workers and project staff stating their views on the project. These voices were as often as not contradictory: 'Community identity . . . It's lack of community identity

that's the root cause of vandalism'; 'It's a way of avoiding childcare resources'; 'It's the spin-off that's important. People get to the point of questioning things through being involved'. These points, of course, indicate the need for a *better* understanding of capitalism and the state – not their abandonment as categories of analysis. And, indeed, it could be argued that the monolithic, centralized British State which I merely *assumed* in 1979 is more of a reality now than it was then. From Margaret Thatcher's much-repeated dictum that there is no such thing as society, through John Major's Citizens' Charter which completed the transformation of 'citizen' to 'consumer', the British State has become steadily more centralized and far less open to influence by relatively independent sources of power – like trades unions and adult education, for example (see Jackson, 1995 on this point).

3. A recent book by Beverley Skeggs exposes some of the processes through which working class women are disciplined to 'care', to derive pleasure from domestic work and to invest in respectability. In an excruciatingly painful account of her research with women undertaking 'caring' courses at an FE college – some of whom were already her friends – Skeggs shows how their desire to belong, to be normal, not to be judged are deeply rooted in structural organisation, in their social location as working class women. She also expresses her gratitude to them for providing her with knowledge that her own formal knowledge had closed off, observing, too, that the 'academic filtering process' of her own book is inadequate for conveying just how interesting and insightful, sharp and funny, complex and resilient the women were (Skeggs, 1997). This observation matches exactly my own experience of research.

Chapter 6

1. It was uninflected, that is, by later arguments in the 'equality–difference' debate within feminism which paralleled and were a response to the 'cultural difference' discourse which emerged from US feminists in the late 1970s and early 1980s (Chodorow 1978; Gilligan, 1982; Rich, 1979; see also Barrett, 1987 on the concept of 'difference' in feminist theory).

2. It may actually be better to categorise this tutor's views as a version of 'cultural difference feminism'. There are different versions of this which criss-cross in the literature in often confusing ways. This tutor combines elements of radical feminism with psychoanalytic object relations feminism: the main point here is that most versions of 'difference feminism' (which emerged towards the end of the 1970s mainly from the USA) believe there are extreme personality and skills differences between the genders, whether regarded as innate or socially derived. Non-biological schools of difference feminism include psychoanalytical feminism and some radical feminism: they see these differences as largely produced through the sexual division of labour, especially parenting practices which in our society are usually done by women; this creates in women a more relational sense of self than men, who are produced as more autonomous (see Chodorow, 1978 especially).

Feminist psychoanalytic theory suggests women need recourse to therapy to undo damages of being denied proper nurturance for self-autonomy in childhood. Radical feminism favours a collective process where women bond with other women to revalue feminine work and values. The tutor mentioned here combines both. Some radical feminists like Jane Thompson are also socialists and would positively dissociate themselves from psychoanalytically derived cultural feminism. The need for this note indicates the difficulties involved in trying to fit all feminisms within the divisions established in the early 1970s and developments within deconstructive feminist theory compound this (see also Weiner, 1994).

Chapter 7

1. Historically, there has been a tension between adult education's mission of servicing social movements committed to social justice goals and its role of servicing the economy and state. Over time the latter has become predominant and has led to increasing professionalisation and bureaucratisation. As a result, much adult education practice is instrumental and unaware of its social and economic location and effects. This failure to locate our educational practice within much wider social and economic processes is now critical as the processes of economic, cultural and workplace restructuring, are having an increasing effect on our work of adult educators (Foley and Morris, 1995). At a time of global change, most workers, including teachers, are being turned more and more into narrow technicians with 'competences'. Their work is being radically restructured precisely to exclude wider social, political and cultural understandings and engagements. In such a context, the danger is that adult and community educators become simply the deliverers of the prescriptions of politicians and business interests.
2. Christine Battersby cautions care here, noting that for privileged classes and races of males, 'femininity' is also valued: geniuses, that is, 'super males', are accorded intuition and emotionality, qualities in our society usually associated with the female sex (1998, p 21). Similarly, Rita Felski has also pointed out that qualities normally thought of as 'feminine' are read differently if embodied in a male person. An example she gives is Richard von Krafft-Ebing, the sexologist, who claimed that masochism could only be seen as a true perversion in men, for nature had given to women, 'an instinctive inclination to voluntary subordination' (1995, p 102).
3. This is not to argue that women and men do think differently in some essentialist way. But, on the whole, highly gendered societies are likely to produce men and women who do have somewhat different views of the world.
4. The point being made here is not that there is anything wrong with abstraction *per se*. The problem lies with what Minnich calls 'mystified' abstractions, for example, notions of 'rationality' which, by 'taking the one for the many' -- one way of being rational as the norm - 'mask the possibilities of approaching, at least, visions and concepts and commitments that could inspire us all' (Minnich, 1989, p 181).
5. Marjorie Mayo provides some post-war examples of what she calls 'education for transformation in the south' from India, Cuba, Tanzania and Nicaragua which contain some elements of what is described here as a popular education approach but which were usually intermixed with other interests and approaches (see Mayo, 1997, Chapter 3; see also McGivney and Murray, 1991; Steele and Taylor, 1995). Segal points out that an important continuing thread between feminism in the 1970s and 1990s is the continuing growth and vision of the international human rights movement, now often in the shape of NGOs, but that even there it has been easier for women to get their demands taken seriously by the United Nations if they have been gender-specific, for example, rape and violence, than when they have addressed illiteracy, poverty or employment rights (see Segal, 1997, p 14)
6. I have discussed this process of incorporation myself and quote from that discussion later in this chapter (Barr, 1991).

Chapter 8

1. 'Seventies' feminism has indeed been caricatured in much 'nineties' feminist theorising, which has produced distorting - and paradoxically sweeping and totalising - accounts of that period; see Segal, 1997.

2. Acker *et al.* have commented on the inappropriateness of 'just being equal' in the relationship between researcher and researched, particularly when the researchers are university-based. They suggest that in such a context attempts to create a more equal partnership can too easily become exploitation and use (see Acker *et al.*, 1983).

Chapter 9

1. There is no litmus test for identifying epistemological communities (Nelson, 1993, p 149) which are 'multiple, historically contingent, and dynamic . . . have fuzzy, often overlapping boundaries . . . evolve, dissolve and re-combine . . . and have a variety of 'purposes' which may include . . . but frequently do not include (as a priority) the production of knowledge' (p 125). I think that the identification and examination of epistemological communities provides a dynamic to standpoint epistemology and that fostering a concern with science among a multiplicity of such communities could contribute to a more democratic science. Also see Assiter (1996, Chapter 5), for a useful discussion of feminist epistemological communities.
2. As Hilary Rose observes, women are in fact over-represented in some parts of science – as they are in other parts of the highly segregated labour market which character-ises our domestic economy and the 'new international division of labour' (Rose, 1994, pp 102ff). They are present in huge numbers as the underlabourers of science (paralleling their 'primary tasks' in the home) but are absent, as elsewhere, from science's 'centres of power' (Cacoullis, quoted in Rose, 1994, p 102). Indeed, Rose argues that it is likely that the relationship between two systems of production – the production of things or commodities (for profit) and the production of people (for life) – holds the key to understanding why there are so few women in science and why the knowledge produced by science is so abstract and disembodied (see Rose, pp 22ff). See also Hart, 1992, especially pp 118ff, for a similar argument and an exam-ination of its implications for adult education.
3. In arguing for more inclusive notions of science so as to include the experiences and understandings of excluded others I am not of course arguing that such experiences and understandings in themselves provide reliable *grounds* for knowledge claims about the world. Our 'experience' often lies to us, not least because subordinated groups internalise what dominant groups believe about them. We can acknowledge the role experiences play in the creation of knowledge from the standpoint of oppressed lives without claiming experience grounds that knowledge. Harding insists that experience does not provide *grounds* for feminist knowledge claims; for this, experience has to be processed through reflection. Nor would I want such arguments to be taken as justifying curricular and educational approaches which, in an effort to validate women's lived experiences, short-change women by not moving outwards from the confines of their own lives. Nevertheless, if knowledge is to be created from the perspective of many women's lives – 'from below' – as feminist standpoint approaches propose, the public act of women naming their experiences in their terms is a fundamental prerequisite. Otherwise, they will not see themselves as the kind of people who can make knowledge (Harding, 1994, p 20)
4. The science/not science boundary needs to be challenged rather than taken for granted. This might be done, for example, by the inclusion by feminists working within scien-tific disciplines of literary analyses of scientific texts (something which is fairly com-mon outside scientific disciplines but rare among those who have a detailed knowledge of science from the inside). It is equally important for feminists working in the human-ities to attempt to engage with the sciences rather than reject science outright – a

'them' and 'us' approach which leaves the authority enjoyed by the sciences essentially unchallenged and, indeed, misunderstood.

Chapter 10

1. I am uncomfortably aware of the contradictoriness of my position here but just as we cannot judge how radical or conservative a text is *per se*, so too with this paradox. It can't be resolved abstractly. This is because it derives from the many real contradictions which attach to being a feminist in an un-feminist world. I am especially conscious now that in playing the game of textual analysis as in my first two case studies I may actually be playing into the hands of those 'nineties' feminists castigated by Lynne Segal recently for their distortions of 'seventies' feminism (Segal, 1997).

2. Although the book argues for more explicitly located research in adult education I am not arguing for the substitution of local for universal knowledge. All knowledge is historically, socially and culturally situated; it is only ever provisional. But that does not mean that generalisations are anathema or that we cannot judge between knowledge claims: some knowledge claims are better because 'less false', reasons can be adduced for such claims, signifying a step from a less good to a better understanding of the thing in question (see Taylor, 1995). When feminists pointed out that the supposedly universal categories of Enlightenment thought were not really universal but generalised from a tiny group of men's experiences they were not just saying that dominant theories were partial in the sense of being limited. They were claiming that they were partial in the sense of being distorted – that is to say, to a greater or lesser degree, false; and they provided good arguments for their claim. Moreover, what was demanded by their challenge was not merely a theoretical response but practical, institutional and intellectual change (see Strickland, 1994).

References

Acker, J, Barry, K, Esseveld, J (1983) Objectivity and truth: Problems in doing feminist research, *Women's Studies International Forum*, 6, 423–35.

Acker, S (1986) What feminists want in education, in A Hartnett and M Naish (eds) *Education and Society Today*, London, Falmer Press.

Addelson, K P (1983) The man of professional wisdom, in S Harding and M Hintikka (eds) *Discovering Reality: Feminist Perspectives on Epistemology, Metaphysics, Methodology and Philosophy of Science*, Dordrecht, D Reidel.

Agarwal, B (1994) Positioning the western feminist agenda: A comment, *Indian Journal of Gender Studies*, 1, 2, 248–255.

Aird, E (1985) *From a Different Perspective: Change in Women's Education* in Breaking Our Silence Series, London, Workers' Educational Association.

Alcoff, L (1988) Cultural feminism versus poststructuralism: The identity crisis in feminist theory, *Signs*, 13, 3, 405–43.

Alcoff, L (1995) Dialogue with Hilary Putnam, in M Nussbaum and J Glover (eds) *Women, Culture and Development: A Study of Human Capabilities*, Oxford, Clarendon Press.

Alcoff, L and Potter, E (eds) (1993) *Feminist Epistemologies*, New York and London, Routledge.

Alexander, D (1994) The education of adults in Scotland: Democracy and curriculum, *Studies in the Education of Adults*, 26, 1, 31–49.

Alexander, D and Martin, I (1995) Competence, curriculum and democracy in M Mayo and J Thompson (eds).

Alexander, D, Leach, T and Steward, T (1984) *Community Education, Leisure and Recreation in Three Scottish Regions*, Edinburgh, Scottish Community Education Council.

Alexander, K (1975) *The Challenge of Change*, HMSO (The Alexander Report).

Allman, P (1987) Paulo Freire's educational approach, in G. Bastiani *et al.* (eds) *Community Education*, Milton Keynes, Open University Press.

Allman, P and Wallis, J (1994) 1992 and new times: A critical reading, *1994 SCUTREA Conference Papers*, 234–45.

Apple, M W (1993) *Official Knowledge: Democratic Education in a Conservative Age*, New York, Routledge.

Arendt, H (1969) Introduction, in W. Benjamin, *Illuminations*, trans. Harry Zohn, New York, Schocken Books.

Ashmore, M (1989) *The Reflexive Thesis: Wrighting Sociology of Scientific Knowledge*, Chicago, University of Chicago Press.

Assiter, A (1996) *Enlightened Women: Modernist Feminism in a Postmodern Age*, London and New York, Routledge.

Ball, W (1992) Critical social research, adult education and anti-racist feminist praxis, *Studies in the Education of Adults*, 24, 1, 1–25.

Barad, K (1995) A feminist approach to teaching quantum physics, in Rosser (ed) *Teaching the Majority*, New York, Teachers' College Press.

Barnett, R (1994) *The Limits of Competence*, Buckingham, SRHE and Open University Press.

Barr, A, Hamilton R and Purcell, R (1996) *Learning for Change: Community Education and Community Development*, Glasgow, SOEID, Community Development Foundation Publications.

Barr, J (1984) Women's education: The ways forward, in *The Future of Women's Education, Conference Report*, Durham University.

Barr, J (1987) Keeping a low profile: Adult education in Scotland, *Adult Education*, 59, 4, 329–34.

Barr, J (1991) Women, education and counselling, *Reportback*, 1, 20–21.

Barr, J (1996) The SHEFC Review of Continuing Education, *International Journal of Lifelong Education*, 15, 6, 471–79.

Barr, J and Birke, L (1994) Women, science and adult education: Towards a feminist curriculum? *Women's Studies International Forum*, 17, 473–83.

Barr, J and Birke, L (1995) Cultures and contexts of adult education: The case of women and science, *Studies in the Education of Adults*, 27, 2, 119–32.

Barr, J and Birke, L (1998) *Common Science? Women, Science and Knowledge*, Bloomington, Indiana University Press.

Barrett, M (1987) The concept of 'difference', *Feminist Review*, 26, 29–41.

Barrett, M and Phillips, A (eds) (1992) *Destabilising Theory: Contemporary Feminist Debates*, Cambridge, Polity.

Battersby, C (1998) *The Phenomenal Woman: Feminist Metaphysics and Patterns of Identity*, Cambridge, Polity.

Beck, U (1992) *Risk Society: Towards a New Modernity*, London, Sage.

Belanger, Paul (1994) Lifelong learning: the dialectics of 'lifelong education', *International Review of Education*, 40, 35, 373–81.

Belenky, M B, Clinchy, B M, Goldberger, N R, and Tarule, J M (1986) *Women's Ways of Knowing: the Development of Self, Voice and Mind*, New York, Basic Books.

Bell, S (1994) Translating science to the people, *Women's Studies International Forum*, 17, 1, 9–18.

Benn, R and Fieldhouse, R (1995) Notions of community for university continuing education, *UACE Annual Pre-Conference Papers 1995*.

Berlak, A (1988) Teaching for outrage and empathy in the liberal arts (pre-publication draft).

Berlak, A (1989) Angles of vision on emancipatory pedagogy (pre-publication draft).

Bhaskar, R (1978) A *Realist Theory of Science*, 2nd Ed, Hassocks New Jersey, Harvester Press.

Bhaskar, R (1979) *Philosophy and the Human Sciences*, Brighton, Harvester Press.

Bhaskar, R (1989) *Reclaiming Reality*, London, Verso.

Biology and Gender Study Group (1989) The importance of feminist critique for contemporary cell biology, in N Tuana (ed.) *Feminism and Science*, Bloomington, Indiana University Press.

Birke, L (1986) *Women, Feminism and Biology: The Feminist Challenge*, Brighton, Wheatsheaf.

Birke, L (1991). Adult education and the public understanding of science, *Journal of Further and Higher Education*, 15, 15–23.

Birke, L (1992) Inside science for women: common sense or science? *Journal of Further and Higher Education* 18, 16–30.

Blundell, S (1992) Gender and the curriculum in adult education, *International Journal of Lifelong Education*, 11, 199–216

Bordo, S (1990) Feminism, postmodernism and gender scepticism, in L Nicholson (ed.) *Feminism and Postmodernism*, New York and London, Routledge.

Bordo, S (1993) *Unbearable Weight: Feminism, Western Culture and the Body*, Berkeley and Los Angeles, California University Press.

Bourdieu, P (1993) *La Misère du Monde*, Paris, Seuil.

Brah, A and Hoy, J (1989) Experiential learning: a new orthodoxy? in S W Weil and I McGill (eds) *Making Sense of Experiential Learning: Diversity in Theory and Practice*, Milton Keynes, SRHE/Open University.

Brah, A and Minhas, R (1985) Structural racism or cultural difference: schooling for Asian girls, in G Weiner (ed.) *Just a Bunch of Girls: Feminist Approaches to Schooling*, Milton Keynes, Open University Press.

Braidotti, R (1994) *Nomadic Subjects: Embodiment and Sexual Differences in Contemporary Feminist Theory*, New York, Columbia University Press.

Brighton Women and Science Group (1980) *Alice Through the Microscope: The Power of Science over Women's Lives*, London, Virago.

Brittan, A (1973) *Meanings and Situations*, London and Boston, Routledge and Kegan Paul.

Butler, S and Wintram, C (l991) *Feminist Groupwork*, London, Sage.

Cameron, D (1985) *Feminism and Linguistic Theory*, London, Macmillan.

Chalmers, A F (1982) Epidemiology and the scientific method, *International Journal of Health Studies*, 12, 4, 659–72.

Chodorow, N (1978) *The Reproduction of Mothering: Psychoanalysis and the Sociology of Gender*, Berkeley, University of California Press.

Coben, D (1998) *Radical Heroes: Gramsci, Freire and the Politics of Adult Education, Studies in the History of Education*, Volume 6, New York, Garland Publishing Inc./Taylor and Francis.

Cockburn, C (1977) *The Local State*, London, Pluto.

Code, L (1989) Experience, knowledge and responsibility, in A Garry and M Pearsall (eds) *Women, Knowledge and Reality*, London, Unwin Hyman.

Code, L (1995) *Rhetorical Spaces: Essays on Gendered Locations*, New York and London, Routledge.

Collins, H (1985) *Changing Order: Replication and Induction in Scientific Practice*, London, Sage.

Collins, P Hills (1990) *Black Feminist Thought*, Boston, Unwin Hymen Inc.

Cook, J and Fonow, M (1986) Knowledge and women's interests: issues of epistemology and methodology in feminist sociological research, *Sociological Inquiry*, 56, 2–29.

Connon, L, Higginbottom, E and Leung, M (1988) Race and class bias in qualitative research on women, *Gender and Society*, 2, 449–62.

Coward, R (1989) *The Whole Truth*, London, Faber and Faber.

Dale, R (1989) *The State and Education Policy*, Oxford, Oxford University Press.

de Lauretis, T (1994) The essence of the triangle or, taking the risk of essentialism seriously: feminist theory in Italy, the US and Britain, in N. Schor and E. Weed (eds) *The Essential Difference*, Bloomington and Indianapolis, Indiana University Press.

Edwards, R (1991a) The politics of meeting learner needs, *Studies in the Education of Adults*, 23, 1, 85–97.

Edwards, R (1991b) The inevitable future? Post-Fordism and open learning, *Open Learning*, June, 36–41.

Edwards, R (1994) 'Are you experienced?': Postmodernity and experiential learning, *International Journal of Lifelong Education*, 13, 6, 423–39.

Edwards, R (1997) *Changing Places? Flexibility, Lifelong Learning and a Learning Society*, London and New York, Routledge.

Edwards, R and Usher, R (1994a) Disciplining the subject: The power of competence, *Studies in the Education of Adults*, 26, 1, 1–14.

Edwards, R and Usher, R (1994b) Tribes and tribulations, *1994 SCUTREA Conference Papers*, 32–35.

Ehrenreich, B (1992) Life without father: reconsidering socialist feminist theory, in L McDowell and R Pringle (eds) *Defining Women: Social Institutions and Gender Divisions*, Cambridge, Polity Press in association with the Open University.

Elders, F (ed) (1974) *Reflexive Waters*, London, Souvenir Press.

Eldridge, R (1989) *On Moral Personhood: Philosophy, Literature, Criticism and Self-Understanding*, Chicago, University of Chicago Press.

Ellsworth, E (1989) Why doesn't this feel empowering? Working through the repressive myths of critical pedagogy, *Harvard Educational Review*, 59, 3, 297–324.

Evans, M (1995) Ivory towers: life in the mind, in L. Morley and V Walsh (eds) *Feminist Academics: Creative Agents for Change*, London, Taylor and Francis.

Fairclough, J (1989) *Language and Power*, London, Longman.

Fay, B (1975) *Social Theory and Political Practice*, London, Allen and Unwin.

Fay, B (1987) *Critical Social Science*, Cambridge, Polity.

Felman, S (1982) Psychoanalysis and education: teaching terminable and interminable, in B Johnson (ed.) *The Pedagogical Imperative: Teaching as a Literary Genre*, New Haven, Yale University Press.

Felman, S and Laub, D (1992) *Testimony: Crises of Witnessing in Literature, Psychoanalysis and History*, London, Routledge.

Felski, R (1989) *Beyond Feminist Aesthetics*, Cambridge, Massachusetts, Harvard University Press.

Felski, R (1995) *The Gender of Modernity*, Cambridge Massachussetts, Harvard University Press.

Fenton, J (1997) Desiring a discipline: negotiating the postmodern divide, in P Armstrong, N Miller and M Zukas, (eds), *Crossing borders breaking boundaries*, Proceedings of 27th SCUTREA Conference, SCUTREA, 152–155.

Feyerabend, P (1987) *Farewell to Reason*, London, Verso.

Field, J (1987) Power and knowledge, *Workers Education*, WEA.

Firestone, S (1970) *The Dialectic of Sex*, New York, Paladin.

Foley, G (ed) (1995) *Understanding Education and Training*, St. Leonards, NSW, Australia, Allen and Unwin.

Foley, G and Morris, R (1995) The history and political economy of Australian adult education, in G Foley (ed.).

Foucault, M (1979) *Discipline and Punish*, New York, Vintage Books.

Foucault, M (1980) *Power/Knowledge: Selected Interviews and Other Writings, 1972–77*, ed. Colin Gordon, New York, Pantheon Press.

Fraser, N (1989) *Unruly Practices: Power, Discourse and Gender in Contemporary Social Theory*, Minneapolis, University of Minnesota Press.

Freire, P (1972) *Pedagogy of the Oppressed*, New York, Penguin.

Freire, P (1983) Education and conscientizacao, in M Tight (ed.) *Adult Learning and Education*, London, Croom Helm.

Gatens, M (1991) *Feminism and Philosophy: Perspectives on Difference and Equality*, Cambridge, Polity Press.

Gatens, M (1992) Power, bodies and difference, in M Barrett and A Phillips (eds).

Gellner, E (1968) *Words and Things*, Harmondsworth, Penguin.

Gibbons, M, Limoges, C, Nowotny, H, Schwartzman, S, Scott, P and Trow, M (1994) *The New Production of Knowledge: The Dynamics of Science and Research in Contemporary Societies*, London, Sage.

Giddens, A (1990) *The Consequences of Modernity*, Cambridge, Polity Press.

Gilligan, C (1982) *In a Different Voice*, Cambridge Mass, Harvard University Press.

Gilroy, P (1987) *There Ain't no Black in the Union Jack: The Cultural Politics of Race and Nation*, London, Hutchinson.

Gilroy, P (1993) *The Black Atlantic: Modernity and double consciousness*, London, Verso.

Ginzburg, C (1980) Morelli, Freud and Sherlock Holmes: clues and scientific method, *History Workshop Journal*, 9, 5–36.

Giroux, H and McLaren, P (1994) *Between Borders: Pedagogy and the Politics of Cultural Studies*, London, Routledge.

Glasgow Women's Studies Group (1983) *Uncharted Lives*, Glasgow, Pressgang.

Goldthorpe, J, Llewellyn, C and Payne, G (1987) *Social Mobility and Class Structure in Modern Britain*, 2nd edition, Oxford, Clarendon Press.

Gorris, M (1981) *A Question of Silence*, Film.

Gramsci, A (1971) *Selections from the Prison Notebooks*, Q Hoare and G Nowell-Smith (eds) London, Lawrence and Wishart.

Grant, Linda (1994) First among equals, *Guardian Weekend*, 22/10/94.

Greer, G (1970) *The Female Eunuch*, London, Paladin.

Griffin, C (1983) *Curriculum Theory in Adult and Lifelong Education*, London, Croom Helm.

Griffiths, M (1995) *Feminisms and the Self*, London and New York, Routledge.

Grimshaw, J (1986) *Philosophy and Feminist Thinking*, Brighton, Wheatsheaf.

Habermas, J (1989) *Theory of Communicative Action*, Boston, Beacon Press.

Hamilton, D et al. (1977) *Beyond the Numbers Game: A Reader in Educational Evaluation*, Basingstock, Macmillan.

Haraway, D (1989) *Primate Visions*, London: Routledge.

Haraway, D (1991a) The contest for primate nature: daughters of man-the-hunter in the field, in D Haraway, *Simians, Cyborgs and Women*, London, Free Association Books.

Haraway, D (1991b) Situated knowledges: the science question in feminism and the privilege of partial perspective, in D Haraway, *Simians, Cyborgs and Women*, London: Free Association Books.

Harding, S (1986) *The Science Question in Feminism*, Milton Keynes, Open University Press.

Harding, S (1991) *Whose Science? Whose Knowledge?*, Milton Keynes, Open University Press.

Harding, S (1992) How the Women's Movement benefits science, in G Kirkup and L Smith Keller (eds) *Inventing Women*, Polity and Open University Press.

Harding, S (1993) (ed) *The 'Racial' Economy of Science: Towards a Democratic Future*, Bloomington and Indianapolis, Indiana University Press.

Harding, S (1994) Subjectivity, experience and knowledge: an epistemology from/for rainbow coalition politics, in J Roof and R Wiegand (eds) *Who Can Speak; Questions of Authority and Cultural Identity*, Urbana, University of Illinois Press.

Hart, M (1992) *Working and Educating for Life*, London, Routledge.

Harvey, D (1989) *The Condition of Postmodernity*, Oxford: Blackwell.

Harvey, L (1990) *Critical Social Research*, London: Unwin Hyman.

Hay, L (1984) *You Can Heal Your Life*, London, Eden Grove Editions.

Hayes, E (1992) The impact of feminism on adult education publications: an analysis of British and Americal journals, *International Journal of Lifelong Education* 11, 2, 112-38.

Head, D (1977) Education at the bottom, *Studies in the Education of Adults*, 9, 2, 127–52.

Head, D (1978) *There's No Politics Here*, London, City Lit.

Heilbrun, C (1989) *Writing a Woman's Life*, London, The Women's Press.

Highet, G (1991) Gender and education: A study of the ideology and practice of community-based women's education, in S Westwood and J E Thomas (eds).

Holt, J (1969) *How Children Fail*, Harmondsworth, Pelican.

hooks, bell (1991) *Yearning: Race, Gender and Cultural Politics*, London, Turnaround.

hooks, bell (1994) *Teaching to Transgress: Education as the Practice of Freedom*, New York, Routledge.

Hubbard, R (1990) *The Politics of Women's Biology*, New Brunswick, Rutgers.

Jackson, K (1995) Popular education and the state: a new look at the community debate, in M Mayo and J Thompson (eds).

Jaggar, A M (1989) Love and knowledge: emotion in feminist epistemology, in A Garry and M Pearsall (eds) *Women, Knowledge and Reality: Explorations in Feminist Philosophy*, London, Unwin Hyman.

Jayaratne, T B and Stewart, A J (1991) Quantitative and qualitative methods in the social sciences: current feminist issues and practical strategies, in Fonow and Cook (eds) *Beyond Methodology*, Bloomington and Indianapolis, Indiana University Press.

Johnson-Riordan, L. (1994) In and against the grain of 'New Times': discourses of adult education and the challenge of contemporary cultural theory, *Australian Journal of Adult and Community Education*, 34, 1, 10–17.

Johnson, R (1988) Really useful knowledge, in T Lovett (ed.) *Radical Approaches to Adult Education*, London, Routledge, 3–34.

Johnston, R (1994) Vision to viability, marginal to mainstream, Freire to Foucault, *1994 SCUTREA Conference Papers*, 234–45.

Jones, A (1992) Writing feminist educational research: am 'I' in the text?, in A Jones and S Middleton (eds) *Women and Education in Aoteorea*, Vol. 2.

Keat, R and Urry, J (1975) *Social Theory as Science*, London, Routledge and Kegan Paul.

Keddie, N (1980) Adult aducation: an ideology of individualism, in J Thompson (ed.).

Keddie, N (1981) Adult education: a women's service, unpublished paper.

Keller, E Fox (1983) *A Feeling for the Organism*, San Francisco W H Freeman.

Keller, E Fox (1985) *Reflections on Gender and Science*, New Haven, CT, Yale University Press.

Keller, E Fox (1992) How gender matters or why it is so hard for us to count past two, in G Kirkup and L Smith Keller (eds) *Inventing Women: Science, Technology and Gender*, Cambridge, Polity/Open University.

Keller, L A (1992) Discovering and doing: science and technology, an introduction, in G Kirkup and L S Keller (eds) *Inventing Women*, Cambridge, Polity Press.

Kirkwood, G and Kirkwood, C (1989) *Living Adult Education: Freire in Scotland*, Milton Keynes: Open University Press.

Kitzinger, C and Perkins, R (1993) *Changing Our Minds*, London, Onlywomen Press.

Knights, S (1995) Women and learning, in G. Foley (ed).

Knorr-Cetina, K (1983) The ethnographic study of scientific work: towards a constructionist interpretation of science, in K. Knorr-Cetina and M Mulkay (eds) *Science Observed: Perspectives on the Social Study of Science*, London, Sage.

Knowles, M (1978) *The Adult Learner: A Neglected Species* (2nd edn), Houston, Gulf.

Kuhn, A (1990) *Cinema, Censorship and Sexuality*, London, Routledge.

Kuhn, A (1994) *Women's Pictures: Feminism and Cinema*, second ed, London, Verso.

Kuhn, A (1995) *Family Secrets: Acts of Memory and Imagination*, London, Verso.

Langer, S (1988) *Mind: An Essay on Human Feeling*, Baltimore, Johns Hopkins University Press.

Larochelles, M and Desantels, J (1991) Of course, it's just obvious: adolescents ideas of scientific knowledge, *International Journal of Science Education*, 13, 373–89.

Lather, P (1991) *Getting Smart: Feminist Pedagogy and Research With/In the Postmodern*, London, Routledge.

Lather, P (1994) Textuality as praxis. Draft paper presented to AERA meeting, New Orleans.

Latour, B (1987) *Science in Action*, Milton Keynes, Open University Press.

Layton, D (1973) *Science for the People*, George London, Allen and Unwin.

Layton, D, Davey, A and Jenkins, E (1986) Science for specific social purposes (SSSP): perspectives on adult scientific literacy, *Studies in Science education*, 13, 27–52.

Layton, D, Jenkins, E, Macgill, S, and Davey, A (1993) *Inarticulate Science? Perspectives on the Public Understanding of Science and Some Implications for Science Education*, Driffield, Studies in Education.

Le Doeuff, M (1991) *Hipparchia's Choice: An Essay Concerning Women, Philosophy etc.*, Oxford, Blackwell.

Lerner, G (1993) *The Creation of Feminist Consciousness*, Oxford, Oxford University Press.

Lessing, D (1990) A note, *British Journalism Review*, 1, 2.

Lewis, M G (1993) *Without a Word: Teaching Beyond Women's Silence*, London, Routledge.

Linden, R (1994) *Making Stories, Making Lives*, Ohio State University Press.

Lloyd, G. (1984) *The Man of Reason: 'Male' and 'Female' in Western Philosophy*, London, Methuen.

Longino, H (1993) *Science as Social Knowledge*, Princeton, New Jersey, Princeton University Press.

Lorde, A (1984) *Sister Outsider*, NY, Crossing Press.

Lovell, T (ed) (1990) *British Feminist Thought: A Reader*, Oxford, Blackwell.

Lovibond, S (1994) The end of morality?, in K Lennon and M Whitford (eds) *Knowing the Difference*, London, Routledge.

Lugones, M and Spelman, E (1983) 'Have we got a theory for you?' Feminist theory, cultural imperialism and the demand for the woman's voice, *Women's Studies International Forum*, 6, 573–81.

Lusted, D (1986) Why pedagogy? *Screen*, 27, 2–14.

Luttrell, W (1989) Working class women's ways of knowing: effects of gender, race and class, *Sociology of Education*, 62, 33–46.

Lyotard, J F (1984) *The Postmodern Condition: A Report on Knowledge*, Minneapolis, University of Minnesota Press.

MacDonald, B and Parlett, M (1973) Re-thinking evaluation. Notes from the Cambridge conference, *Cambridge Journal of Education*, 3, 74–82.

Macmillan, J (1995) Choose your gang of thugs before night descends, *Scotland on Sunday*, 29 January.

Mair, M (1989) *Beyond Psychology and Psychotherapy*, London and New York, Routledge.

Malcolm, J (1994) *The Silent Woman: Sylvia Plath and Ted Hughes*, New York and London, Crossing Press.

Marshall, M (1984) *Breaking Our Silence: An Introduction*, in *Breaking Our Silence Series*, WEA.

Martin, E (1989) *The Woman in the Body*, Milton Keynes, Open University Press.

Mayo, M (1995) Adult education for change in the nineties and beyond: towards a critical review of the changing context, in M Mayo and J Thompson (eds).

Mayo, M and Thompson, J (eds) (1995) *Adult Learning, Critical Intelligence and Social Change*, Leicester, NIACE.

McGivney, V (1993) *Women, Education and Training*, Leicester, NIACE.

McGivney, V and Murray, F (1991) *Adult Education in Development*, Leicester, NIACE.

McIntosh, M (1978) The state and the oppression of women, in A Kuhn and A M Wolpe (eds) *Feminism and Materialism*, London: Routledge and Kegan Paul.

McIlroy, J and Westwood, S (eds) (1993) *Border Country*, Leicester, NIACE.

McNeill, M (ed) (1987) *Gender and Expertise*, London, Free Association Books.

McWilliam, E (1993) 'Post' haste: plodding research and galloping theory, *British Journal of Sociology of Education*, 14, 2, 199–206.

Merchant, C (1982) *The Death of Nature*, London, Wildwood.

Michael, M (1992) Lay discourses of science: science-in-general, science-in-particular and self, *Science, Technology and Human Values*, 17, 313–33.

Middleton, S (1984) The sociology of women's education as a field of academic study, *Discourse*, 5, 1, 43–62.

Miller, A (1978) *The Need for Good Creche Facilities for Women's Education*, WEA.

Miller, A (1987) *Castlemilk WEA Interim Report*, WEA, West of Scotland.

Miller, J D (1993) Theory and measurement in the public understanding of science: a rejoinder to Bauer and Schoon, *Public Understanding of Science*, 2, 235–43.

Miller, R and Driver, R (1987) Beyond process, *Studies in Science Education* 14, 33–62.

Millett, K (1971) *Sexual Politics*, London, Hart Davies.

Mills, C W (1959) *The Sociological Imagination*, Oxford, Oxford University Press.

Minnich, E (1989) *Transforming Knowledge*, Philadelphia, Temple University Press.

Mitchell, J (1971) *Woman's Estate*, Harmondsworth, Penguin.

Modjeska, D (1990) *Poppy*, McPhea Grimble.

Moi, Toril (1989) Patriarchal thought and the drive for knowledge, in T Brennan (ed.) *Between Feminism and Psychoanalysis*, London, Routledge.

Morrison, T (1970) *The Bluest Eye*, Washington Square Press, Pocket Books.

Morrison, T (1987) *Beloved: A Novel*, London, Chatto and Windus.

Nadeau, D (1996) Embodying feminist popular education under global restructuring, in S Walters and L Manicom, (eds).

Nandy, A (1988) Science as a reason of state, in A Nandy (ed.) *Science, Hegemony and Violence: A Requiem for Modernity*, New Delhi, Oxford University Press.

Needham, J (1993) Poverties and triumphs of the Chinese scientific tradition, in S Harding (ed).

Nelson, L H (1990) *Who Knows: From Quine to Feminist Empiricism*, Philadelphia, Temple University Press.

Nelson, L H (1993) Epistemological communities, in L Alcoff and E Potter (eds).

Newson, J and Newson, E (1976) *Seven Years Old in an Urban Community*, Harmondsworth, Penguin.

Nussbaum, M (1990) *Love's Knowledge*, New York, Oxford University Press.

Nussbaum, M (1994) *The Therapy of Desire*, Princeton, Princeton University Press.

Oakley, A (1981) Interviewing women: A contradiction in terms?, in H Roberts (ed.).

O'Rourke, R (1995) All equal now?, in M Mayo and J Thompson (eds).

O'Rourke, R and Croft, A (1994) Through the wall: adult education, social change and new University subjects, *1994 SCUTREA Conference Papers,* 87–90.

Pagano, J (1991) Moral fictions: the dilemma of theory and practice, in C Witherell and N Noddings (eds) *Stories Lives Tell*, New York, Teachers College Press.

Parsons, S (1993) Feminist challenges to curriculum design, in M Thorpe *et al.* (eds) *Culture and Processes of Adult Learning*, Routledge, London and New York, in Association with Open University Press.

Patton, M (1978) *Utilization-Focused Evaluation*, Beverley Hills, CA, Sage.

Payne, J (1995) Adult learning in the context of global neo-liberal economic policies, in M Mayo and J Thompson (eds).

Phillips, K (1983) What women know, in Glasgow Women's Group, *Uncharted Lives*.

Plath, S (1989) *The Bell Jar*, London, Faber and Faber.

Pringle, R and Watson, S (1992) 'Women's interests' and the post-structuralist state, in M Barrett and A Phillips, (eds), 53–73.

Pritchard Hughes, K (1995) Feminist pedagogy and feminist epistemology: an overview, *International Journal of Lifelong Education*, 14, 3, 214–30.

Reason, P and Rowan, J (eds) (1981) *Human Inquiry: A Sourcebook of New Paradigm Research*, Chichester and New York, J Wiley.

Rich, A (1979) *On Lies, Secrets and Silences: Selected Prose 1966–78*, New York, Norton.

Richardson, L (1996) *Fields of Play (Constructing an Academic Life)*, New Jersey, Rutgers University Press.

Riley, D (1988) *Am I that Name? Feminism and the Category of 'Women' in History*, London, Macmillan.

Roberts, H (1981) *Doing Feminist Research*, London, Routledge and Kegan Paul.

Rose, H (1994) *Love, Power and Knowledge: Towards a Feminist Transformation of the Sciences*, Cambridge, Polity.

Rose, J (1983) Femininity and its discontents, *Feminist Review*, 14, 5–21.

Rosenau, P M (1992) *Postmodernism and the Social Sciences*, Princeton, Princeton University Press.

Ross, C (1995) Seizing the quality initiative, in M Mayo and J Thompson (eds).

Rowbotham, S (1973) *Hidden From History*, London, Pluto.

Rowbotham, S (1983) *Dreams and Dilemmas*, London, Virago.

Rowbotham, S (1997) Real women of the real world, *Guardian*, April 19.

Said, E (1986) Orientalism reconsidered, in F Barter *et al.* (eds) *Liberation, Politics and Theory*, New York, Methuen.

Said, E (1993) *Culture and Imperialism*, London, Vintage.

Sawicki, J (1991) *Disciplining Foucault: Feminism, Power and the Body*, New York/London, Routledge.

Sayers, J (1983) Feminism and science, reason and passion, *Women's Studies International Forum*, 16, 4, 423–35.

Schama, S (1995) *Landscape and Memory*, London, HarperCollins.

Schiebinger, L (1989) *The Mind Has No Sex? Women in the Origins of Modern Science*, Cambridge, Mass, Harvard University Press.

Scott, J (1992) Experience, in J Butler and J Scott (eds) *Feminists Theorize the Political*, London, Routledge.

Scott, P (1995) *The Meanings of Mass Higher Education*, SRHE and Open University Press.

Segal, L (1987) *Is the Future Female?*, London, Virago.

Segal, L (1997) Generations of feminism, *Radical Philosophy*, 83, 6–16.

Seller, A (1994) Should the feminist philosopher stay at home?, in K Lennon and M Whitford, *Knowing the Difference: Feminist Perspectives in Epistemology*, London, Routledge.

Sennet, R (1977) *The Fall of Public Man*, New York: Knopf.

Shaw, M and Crowther, J (1995) Beyond subversion, in M Mayo and J Thompson (eds).

SHEFC (1995) Women in science, engineering and technology initiative, *Circular Letter 33/95*.

Shepherd, L (1993) *Lifting the Veil: The Feminine Face of Science*, London, Shambhala.

Shiva, V (1989) *Staying Alive: Women, Ecology and Development*, London, Zed Press.

Skeggs, B (1997) *Formations of Class and Gender*, London, Sage.

Smith, D (1979) A sociology for women, in J A Sherman and E T Beck (eds) *The Prison of Sex: Essays in the Sociology of Knowledge*, Madison, University of Wisconsin Press.

Smith, D (1987) *The Everyday World as Problematic: A Feminist Sociology*, Milton Keynes, Open University Press.

Smithson, M (1989) *Ignorance and Uncertainty: Emerging Paradigms*, New York, SpringerVerlag.

Sontag, S (1978) *Illness as Metaphor*, Harmondsworth, Penguin.

Sontag, S (1990) *Aids and Its Metaphors*, Harmondsworth, Penguin.

Spark, M (1959) *Memento Mori*, London, Macmillan.

Spelman, E (1988) *Inessential Woman: Problems of Exclusion in Feminist Thought*, Boston, Beacon.

Spivak, G (1988) *In Other Worlds: Essays in Cultural Politics*, New York/London, Routledge.

Spivak, G (1993) *Outside the Teaching Machine*, London, Routledge.

Stabile, C (1997) Feminism and the ends of postmodernism, in R Hennessy and C Ingraham (eds) *Materialist Feminism: A Reader in Class, Difference and Women's Lives,* New York and London, Routledge.

Stanley, L (1990) Feminist praxis and the academic mode of production, Introduction to L Stanley and S Wise (eds).

Stanley, L and Wise, S (1983) *Breaking Out: Feminist Consciousness and Feminist Research*, London, Routledge and Kegan Paul.

Stanley, L and Wise, S (1990) *Feminist Praxis: Research, Theory and Epistemology in Feminist Sociology*, London, Routledge.

Stanley, L and Wise, S (1990) Method, methodology and epistemology in feminist research processes, in L Stanley (ed.).

Steedman, C (1980) The tidy house, *Feminist Review*, 6, 1–24.

Steedman, C (1986) *Landscape for a Good Woman*, London, Virago.

Steele, T (1995) Cultural struggle or identity politics? Can there still be a 'popular' education?, in M Mayo and J Thompson (eds).

Steele, T and Taylor, R (1995) *Learning Independence: A political outline of Indian adult education, Leicester, NIACE.*

Stepan, N L and Gilman, S L (1993) Appropriating the idioms of science: the rejection of scientific racism, in S Harding (ed.).

Stewart, J (1988) Science shops in France: a personal view, *Science as Culture*, 2, 52–74.

Strickland, S (1994) Feminism, postmodernism and difference, in K Lennon and M Whitford (eds), *Knowing the Difference*, London, Routledge.

Stronach, I (1989) Transition learning: a reflexive study of education in a new age, PhD Thesis, University of East Anglia.

Taking Liberties Collective (1989) *Learning the Hard Way: Women's Oppression in Men's Education*, Basingstoke, Macmillan.

Tallantyre, F (1985) *Women at the Crossroads*, in *Breaking Our Silence Series*, WEA.

Taylor, C (1995) Explanation and practical reason, in C Taylor, *Philosophical Arguments*.

Tett, L (1994) Where have all the men gone? Adult participation in community education, *Scottish Journal of Adult and Continuing Education*, 1, 2, 41–48.

Tett, L (1995) Community education and the 'underclass', *Concept*, 6, 1, 8–10.

Thomas, K (1990) *Gender and Subject in Higher Education*, Milton Keynes, Open University Press.

Thompson, J (ed) (1980a) *Adult Education for a Change*, London, Hutchinson.

Thompson, J (1980b) Adult education and the disadvantaged, in J Thompson (ed).

Thompson, J (1983) *Learning Liberation: Women's Responses to Men's Education*, London, Croom Helm.

Thompson, J (1993) Learning liberation, an open letter to whoever's left, *Adults Learning*, 4, 9, 244.

Tuana, N (1992) The radical future of feminist empiricism, *Hypatia*, Winter, 100–14.

Usher, R and Bryant, I (1989) *Adult Education as Theory, Practice and Research*, London, Routledge.

Usher, R, Bryant, I and Johnston, R (1997) *Adult education and the Postmodernism Challenge*, London and New York, Routledge.

Usher, R and Edwards, R (1995) Confessing all? A 'postmodern' guide to the guidance and counselling of adult learners, *Studies in the Education of Adults*, 27, 1, 9–23.

Walby, S (1992) Post-post-modernism? Theorising social complexity, in M Barrett and A Phillips (eds).

Walkerdine, V (1990) *Schoolgirl Fictions*, London, Verso.

Walkerdine, V and the Girls and Mathematics Unit (1989) *Counting Girls Out*, London, Virago.

Walkerdine, V and Lucey, H (1989) *Democracy in the Kitchen: Regulating Mothers and Socialising Daughters*, London, Virago.

Walters, S and Manicom, L (eds) (1996) *Gender in Popular Education*, London and New Jersey, CACE and Zed Books.

Weil, S W (1988) From the language of observation to a language of experience: studying the perspectives of diverse adults in higher education, *Journal of Access Studies*, 3, 1, 17–43.

Weiler, K (1991) Freire and a Feminist Pedagogy of Difference, *Harvard Educational Review*, 61, 4, 449–74.

Weiner, G (1994) *Feminisms in Education*, Milton Keynes, Open University Press.

Westwood, S (1980) Adult education and the sociology of adult education: an exploration, in J Thompson (ed).

Westwood, S (1989) Enterprise culture and the re-structuring of British adult education: an Exploration, *Adults Learning*, 1, 1, 8–9.

Westwood, S (1992) Constructing the future: a postmodern agenda for adult education, in S Westwood and J E Thomas (eds).

Westwood, S and Thomas, J E (eds) (1992) *Radical Agendas: The Politics of Adult Education*, Leicester, NIACE.

Williams, R. (1993) Culture is Ordinary, in J. McIlroy and S. Westwood (eds).

Wilson, E (1977) *Women and the Welfare State*, London, Tavistock.

Winch, P (1958) *The Idea of a Social Science*, London, Routledge and Kegan Paul.

Wolf, C (1988) *A Model Childhood*, London, Virago.

Wootton, A (1975) *Dilemmas of Discourse*, London, Allen and Unwin.

Wynne, B E (1991) Knowledges in context, *Science, Technology and Human Values*, 16, 111–21.

Wynne, B E (1992) Public understanding of science research: new horizons or hall of mirrors?, *Public Understanding of Science*, 1, 37–43.

Young, I (1990) *Justice and the Politics of Difference*, New Jersey, Princeton University Press.

Zukas, M (1997) Disciplining gender: The impact of feminism and women's studies on the study of adult education, in P Armstrong, N Miller and M Zukas, (eds) (*op cit*).

Index